D1411036

THE HYPERTENSION HANDBOOK

Published by
Merck Sharp & Dohme
Division of Merck & Co., INC.
West Point, Pa. 19486
1974

Prepared in cooperation with the
National High Blood Pressure Education Program

*(This does not constitute an endorsement by the program
of any of the drug products mentioned in this book.)*

Library of Congress Catalog Card Number 73-85849

ISBN 0-911910-22-0

Copyright © 1974 by Merck & Co., Inc.

Printed in the United States of America.

THE HYPERTENSION HANDBOOK

Presented as a service to medicine
by Merck Sharp & Dohme

Publisher's Note

The title of this volume, "The Hypertension Handbook," was carefully chosen. Because handbook is defined as a concise and convenient ready reference, the title served both as our guideline and our goal for the project.

The impetus for the handbook came, in great measure, from Dr. Theodore Cooper, Director of the National Heart and Lung Institute, and from the efforts of the National High Blood Pressure Education Program and the Task Forces created by it. They recognized the need and sounded the call to action. However, it was physicians—those in research, education, and private practice —who provided the direction, established the hypothesis, undertook the studies, and confirmed the findings which provide the basis for this handbook. It was their efforts which brought this volume from "idea" to "handbook" status.

The handbook offers practical guidelines for the practicing physician confronted with the detection and treatment of hypertension. It is not intended to be the definitive work on the subject. Rather, it is designed to meet the criteria of a concise reference book. In addition to the valuable information contained in the six chapters, the appendix contains office forms that may be useful for practicing physicians, facsimile reproductions of the landmark studies in hypertension, and a comprehensive listing of resource materials available.

We are grateful to the authors who worked under demanding deadlines to make the handbook available at this critical time. Each of the experts has brought to the effort special knowledge and insights to help the reader with the management of hypertension. A special note of thanks must go to Dr. George M. Naimark and his staff for consolidating the efforts of the individual authors, compiling the material in the appendix, and for the design of the handbook.

Merck Sharp & Dohme provided the resources for printing and distributing this handbook, but the information contained between the covers is the independent opinion of the individual authors. To them must go the credit for the value of this handbook.

Foreword

Irrespective of our specific fields of medical practice, hypertension and its sequelae represent professional challenges for each of us. I hope you will find time to gain what may prove to be new and valuable insights into these problems through attention to this concise and authoritative volume.

The Hypertension Handbook represents more than a simple compilation of current expertise on a complex subject. In the past our academicians, research workers, and communicators in medicine have focused in large part on a pursuit of excellence in scientific endeavors. We have now developed a parallel need for efforts to diffuse and disseminate that store of excellence which had been achieved.

This volume is predicated upon the conviction that we have indeed learned much about the perils of hypertension, about the ways which are at hand to avert a substantial share of them, and about the relative ease of putting this knowledge to the service of the patient-public. It is a volume for the practicing physician— that one member of the health-care team who plays the key role in transmuting technical knowledge into service. The AMA is pleased to join with the authors and the publisher in dedicating this work to him.

Russell B. Roth, M.D.
President
American Medical Association

Contributing Authors

Chapter 1   **Jeremiah Stamler, M.D.**
Professor and Chairman
Department of Community Health and Preventive
    Medicine
Northwestern University Medical School
Chicago, Illinois

James A. Schoenberger, M.D.
Professor and Acting Department Chairman
Department of Preventive Medicine
Rush-Presbyterian-St. Luke's Medical Center
Chicago, Illinois

Richard B. Shekelle, Ph.D.
Associate Professor
Department of Community Health and Preventive
    Medicine
University of Illinois
Chicago, Illinois

Rose Stamler, M.A.
Assistant Professor
Department of Community Health and Preventive
    Medicine
Northwestern University Medical School
Chicago, Illinois

Chapter 2   **Theodore Cooper, M.D., Ph.D.**
Director, National Heart and Lung Institute
National Institutes of Health
Bethesda, Maryland

Chapter 3   **Morton H. Maxwell, M.D.**
             Director, Nephrology and Hypertension Service
             Cedars-Sinai Medical Center; and
             Clinical Professor of Medicine
             UCLA School of Medicine
             Los Angeles, California

Chapter 4   **Ray W. Gifford, Jr., M.D.**
   and   Head, Department of Hypertension and Nephrology
Chapter 5   Cleveland Clinic Foundation
             Cleveland, Ohio

Chapter 6   **Frank A. Finnerty, Jr., M.D.**
             Professor of Medicine
             Georgetown University Medical Division
             District of Columbia General Hospital
             Washington, D.C.

Table of Contents

Chapter 2

Chapter 3

Chapter 4

Current Views on Diagnostic Evaluation 67
Ray W. Gifford, Jr., M.D.

Chapter 5

A Practical Guide to Medical Management 83
Ray W. Gifford, Jr., M.D.

Chapter 5 (continued)

Chapter 6

THE
HYPERTENSION
HANDBOOK

Chapter 1

The Problem and the Challenge

Jeremiah Stamler, M.D.; James A. Schoenberger, M.D.;
Richard B. Shekelle, Ph.D.; and Rose Stamler, M.A.

Hypertension 1

The Problem and the Challenge

Jeremiah Stamler, M.D.
Professor and Chairman
Department of Community Health and Preventive Medicine
Northwestern University Medical School
Chicago, Illinois

James A. Schoenberger, M.D.
Professor and Acting Department Chairman
Department of Preventive Medicine
Rush-Presbyterian-St. Luke's Medical Center
Chicago, Illinois

Richard B. Shekelle, Ph. D.
Associate Professor
Department of Community Health and Preventive Medicine
University of Illinois
Chicago, Illinois

Rose Stamler, M.A.
Assistant Professor
Department of Community Health and Preventive Medicine
Northwestern University Medical School
Chicago, Illinois

Prevalence in the United States by Age, Sex, and Race

Hypertensive disease is a mass public health problem in the United States—one of the most important, if not *the* most important affliction producing premature sickness, disability, and death in our adult population. Because of this, it is worth examining the available epidemiological data and the attendant implications in some detail.

We begin with this: a sound current estimate is that 20 to 25 million Americans have hypertension. The prevalence rates rise steadily with advancing age and, in every age group, the prevalence is higher for blacks than for whites.

The data collected a decade ago by the National Health Examination Survey of the Public Health Service—data on a random sample of the U.S. adult population age 18 to 79—indicated that about 9 percent of white adults and 22 percent of black adults had hypertensive disease based on the World Health Organization criterion of diastolic pressure ≥95 mm Hg.[1-3] With the lower cut-off point of diastolic 90 mm Hg, the prevalence rates are almost 16 percent for white adults and about 30 percent for black adults. The disease is widespread in every stratum of the adult population.

Data consistent with these National Health Examination Survey estimates have been repeatedly reported by local surveys. For example, the recent findings of the Chicago Heart Association Detection Project in Industry—collected from 1967 to 1972 on employees of almost 100 companies—are typical (see Figure 1).[4,5]

High blood pressure afflicts not only the elderly, but also young and middle-aged adults, people in the prime of life and in

FIGURE 1

Prevalence of high blood pressure by age-sex-race, Chicago Heart Association Detection Project in Industry, November 1967—May 1972.[5]

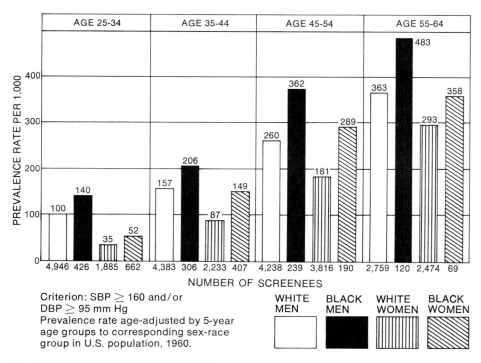

Criterion: SBP ≥ 160 and/or DBP ≥ 95 mm Hg
Prevalence rate age-adjusted by 5-year age groups to corresponding sex-race group in U.S. population, 1960.

WHITE MEN   BLACK MEN   WHITE WOMEN   BLACK WOMEN

the most productive years. The National Health Examination Survey data yield estimates that at age 25 to 34, 3.6 percent of white men and 12.5 percent of black men, and 2.3 percent of white women and 8.6 percent of black women are hypertensive. *The prevalence rates rise steadily with age.*[3]

At all ages up to 80, they are conspicuously higher for blacks than for whites. Overall, the ratio is about 2 to 1, i.e., the prevalence rates are twice as high for blacks as for whites. And hypertension, when present, tends to be more severe in blacks than in whites. For example, for severe hypertension (diastolic levels of 115 mm Hg and above) the relative rate is 3.3 times as high for black men as compared to white men (2.3 percent vs 0.7 percent), and 5.6 times as high for black women as compared to white women (5.0 percent vs 0.9 percent). For young, middle-aged, and elderly adults, men and women, white and black, a high proportion with hypertension also have ECG and/or x-ray evidence of heart involvement: hypertensive heart disease.[1-5]

In keeping with the tendency for hypertension to be not only more prevalent but also more severe among blacks than whites, hypertensive heart disease is present at rates three, four, seven, even nine times greater for blacks of a given age-sex group when compared to whites of the same age-sex group. When the disease has gone this far, risks of serious sickness, disability, and death are even greater than when elevated blood pressure is present by itself.

Morbidity, Disability, and Mortality due to Hypertensive Disease

Hypertensive disease is a serious mass public health problem despite the fact that, at any given time, a majority of persons with it are symptom-free. Hypertension—even slight elevation—markedly increases the risk of major cardiovascular "complications." Note that we deliberately avoid use of the terms "mild" and "benign" hypertension because they are disarmingly misleading and have blocked proper understanding of the seriousness of the problem. For decades, the insurance industry has been emphasizing that even slight elevation of blood pressure correlates with increased risk of premature death. For example, the Society of Actuaries' most recent (1959) study shows that for men age 35 with a blood pressure reading of 142/90 mm Hg and without any concomitant impairments, the mortality rate over the next 20 years was 19.4 percent, compared to 11.0 percent for normotensive standard risks.[6] That is to say, this "modest" elevation of blood pressure (which is all too frequently treated as insignificant and ignored by clinicians) was associated with a 76.4 percent higher death rate in middle age. Hence, our unhappiness with a word like "benign."

Similar findings have been recorded by the prospective epidemiological research studies carried out in various parts of the United States over the last 20 years. Figure 2 presents the combined findings of five of these investigations working together in the national cooperative Pooling Project: the Albany civil servant, Chicago Peoples Gas Company, Chicago Western Electric Company, Framingham community, and Minneapolis-St. Paul business and professional men studies.[7] These data deal with 7,581 white men age 30 to 59 at first examination. After exclusion of men with definite coronary heart disease, they were classified based on their diastolic blood pressure levels at that time. Mortality over the next ten years from heart attack, including sudden death, was twice as high in the group with so-called mild hypertension (diastolic levels of 95-104 mm Hg) compared to those with normal diastolic pressures. And the increase in risk of coronary death, including sudden death, was more than threefold for the group of 493 men with pressures of 105 mm Hg and greater.

For the most straightforward and crucial index available, i.e., death from all causes, the 10-year rate was 60 percent higher for men with diastolic pressures 95-105 mm Hg, compared to normotensives, and 200 percent higher for those with hypertension in the range of 105 mm Hg and greater. Note also the 60 percent greater mortality rate from all causes even for the men with diastolic pressures of 85-94 mm Hg.

The data from the Pooling Project also demonstrate one other very important point: when hypertension coexists with other major risk factors (e.g., cigarette smoking, hypercholesterolemia), the risks are additive. Thus, the men originally age 30 to 59 with hypertension as the only risk factor experienced twice as high a death rate over the next ten years as men with no risk factors. But when hypertension coexisted with cigarette smoking or hypercholesterolemia (either one of these two), the risk of dying was more than trebled. And when hypertension was present along with both these other factors, the death rate was five times higher. In terms of their implications for public health and medical practice, these data speak for themselves.

FIGURE 2

Diastolic blood pressure level at entry and 10-year age-adjusted rates per 1,000 men for: first major coronary event and sudden death (upper graph), any coronary death, stroke death, death from all causes (lower graph); first major coronary event includes nonfatal MI, fatal MI, sudden death due to CHD; U.S. white males age 30-59 at entry, national cooperative Pooling Project; all rates age-adjusted by 10-year age groups to the U.S. white male population, 1960.[7]

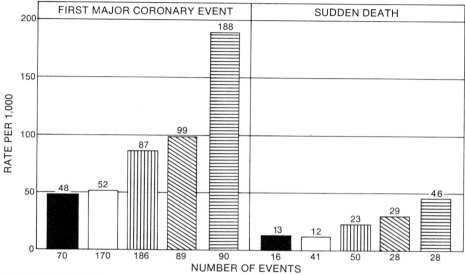

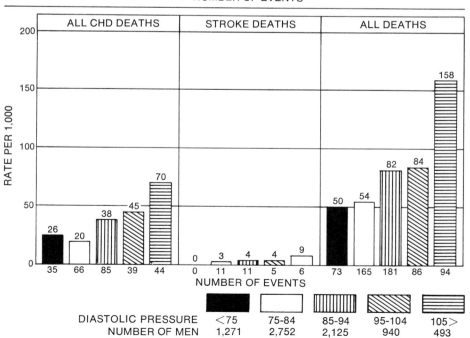

Similar data are available demonstrating that a single blood pressure recorded in a routine school examination of college entrants (young men in their late teens) is prognostically very meaningful.[8] Even that early in life, slight blood pressure elevation identified people at greater risk. Teen-age young men with systolic levels of 130 mm Hg and above had a 1.6 times higher mortality from coronary disease over the next decades compared to those who were under 130 mm Hg. College entrants with a systolic blood pressure of 130 mm Hg or above, and smoking ten or more cigarettes a day, experienced a 110 percent increase in risk of coronary death. The effects of the two risk factors are additive. The hypertensive who smokes cigarettes is at greater risk than the hypertensive who does not.

When the person with elevated blood pressure also has signs of hypertensive heart disease, the risks of morbidity and mortality are especially high. The findings in the Peoples Gas Company Study are typical in this regard (see Table 1).[9,10] For the men with

TABLE 1

HYPERTENSION, HYPERTENSIVE HEART DISEASE, AND RISK OF DEATH
COHORT OF 1,465 MEN AGE 40-59 IN 1958
Peoples Gas Company Study, 1958-70

1958 Findings	No. of Men	12-Year Age-Adjusted Mortality Rate per 1,000				
		All Causes	All CVR	Sudden Death	Myocardial Infarction	Stroke
No Organ System Abnormalities, None of 3 Risk Factors	208	70	8	0	8	0
No Organ System Abnormalities, Hypertensive	147	156	53	22	30	12
Suspect Hypertensive Heart Disease	53	268	159	57	117	21
Definite Hypertensive Heart Disease	75	385	309	142	158	99

hypertensive heart disease, definite or suspect, mortality from all causes for a 12-year period of follow-up was almost five times as high as for the group of men at lowest risk, with most of the excess deaths due to cardiovascular causes. In the cohort of middle-aged employed men, over 90 percent white and at entry free of evidence of definite coronary disease, 128 of 275 hypertensives (46.5 percent) had evidence of hypertensive heart disease. This proportion is even higher in the general population—white and black, and especially the latter. National Health Examination Survey data indicate that in 1960-62 there were about 12,000,000 white American adults age 18 to 79 with hypertensive heart disease, definite or suspect, and 3,000,000 black American adults in the same age category, totaling 15,000,000.[1-3] These numbers which are clearly substantially greater today represent a huge pool of people (many of them undiagnosed) with markedly increased risk of premature mortality.[11]

Increased premature mortality is by no means the only problem. Data from the Social Security Administration clearly show a sizeable amount of disability in the labor force attributable to hypertensive disease.[12] The economic losses to the individuals involved are great, as are the costs to government and society at large. Overall, of the 330,783 worker disability allowances in 1968 (the year of latest record) 24 percent were due to diseases of the circulatory system, with arteriosclerotic heart disease at the top of the list for each of the four major sex-race groups. At least one-third of the coronary cases have hypertension as the major contributing cause of their disabling illness. An even higher proportion of the persons disabled by stroke have the same major contributing cause.

These data conclusively rank hypertensive disease and its complications at the top of the list as producers of disability for all of the major sex-race groups in the labor force. As expected from the review of other data, this disease and its complications take a disproportionate toll among black Americans, in view of their high prevalence rates for hypertensive disease in general and hypertensive heart disease in particular.

Finally, to present a full perspective of the profound impact hypertensive disease has on health, the overall vital statistics data on mortality due to hypertensive disease merit citation (see Figure 3).[11,13]

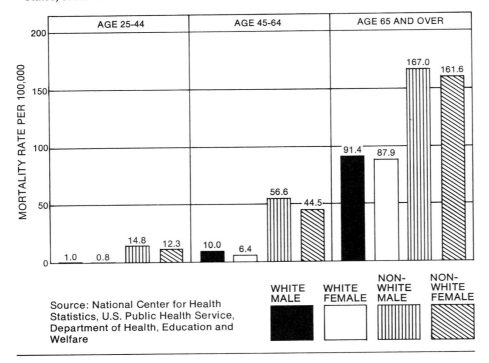

FIGURE 3

Hypertensive disease mortality rates by age, sex, and race per 100,000 population, United States, 1969.[13]

Source: National Center for Health Statistics, U.S. Public Health Service, Department of Health, Education and Welfare

In brief:
1. The patterns of mortality parallel those for prevalence, as shown in the National Health Examination Survey data.
2. For all four major sex-race groups, mortality rates rise with age.
3. At all ages up to age 85, the mortality rates for nonwhites are much higher than for whites: for males age 25 to 44, 14.8 percent vs 1.0 and for females of this age, 12.3 percent vs 0.8 —rates 15 times as high.
4. At ages 45 to 64, the rates for nonwhites are six and seven times as high as for whites, for men and women respectively.
5. Mortality rates for cerebrovascular disease show very similar patterns, reflecting the fact that hypertension is the single most important risk factor for strokes, both atherothrombotic (occlusive) and hemorrhagic.

Mortality Statistics Tell Only Part of the Story

While the foregoing statistics certainly provide a qualitatively valid insight into the impact of hypertensive disease on mortality, they are quantitatively misleading. Because of the manner in which causes of deaths are categorized and recorded, the statistics seldom reflect hypertensive diseases as the cause of death. That is, a vast number of the people who die from cardiovascular causes as a result of their hypertensive disease (at least in part) are listed under an "arteriosclerotic heart disease" or a "cerebrovascular disease" category—*not* under a *hypertensive* disease category. The coronary patient who dies of a myocardial infarct, even if "previous hypertension" is written on the death certificate, is coded as a coronary death. The same is true for a person who dies of cerebral hemorrhage or cerebral thrombosis, even though the person is known to be a hypertensive. The doctor may write "hypertension" as a second cause on the death certificate; however, the coding is to the first specified entity. Consequently, the death rate data markedly underestimate the hypertensive component although, as noted previously, hypertension is present as a key contributing cause for at least a third of premature heart attack deaths and an even higher proportion of premature stroke deaths.

Correlates of Hypertensive Disease

Even though most persons with elevated blood pressure have hypertension of unknown cause, some information is available on factors related to its occurrence in addition to the age-sex-race patterns. It should be useful to cite those which are significant in terms of the national effort to enhance public understanding and to control the disease.

1. *Family history*

The risk of developing hypertension is related to *family history*. Those who have a family history of this disease are more likely to be hypertensive than those who do not. This has been shown repeatedly.[9] And if both parents are involved, the risks are especially great.[14]

This fact is not only potentially meaningful in terms of the unsolved problem of possible mechanisms, it can also help to find hypertensive persons (or hypertension-prone persons) early in life. If family history is associated with increase in risk, obviously we should identify such people in our mass public health work, in practicing physicians' offices, in efforts by health departments, schools, factories, insurance companies, and the military. Once these persons are located, they can be given appropriate advice and followed up periodically.

2. *"Spiking" in youth*

In addition to the relevance of family history in determining the risk of developing hypertension, there is also evidence that *"spikes" of blood pressure* early in life are prognostically significant.'' Figure 4 presents data on 764 employees of the Peoples Gas Company in Chicago who worked for the company for a minimum

FIGURE 4

Relationship between initial blood pressure reading as a young adult and subsequent development of hypertensive disease in middle age, 20-year follow-up data on 764 men age 40-59 in 1958- 59, Peoples Gas Company Study.[9]

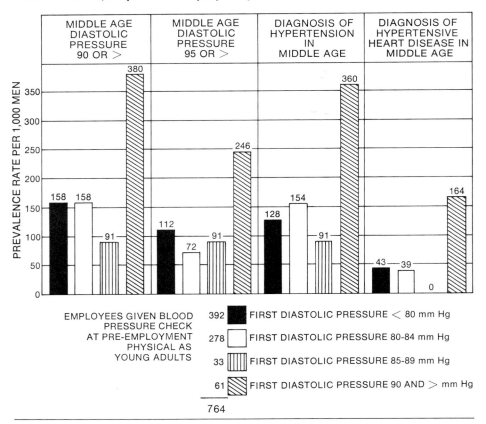

of 20 years. It correlates the single blood pressure value for each man from his pre-employment physical examination as a youth or young adult with the subsequent development of hypertensive disease. The initial reading has important predictive value. The prevalence rate of hypertension at middle age in the 61 men who had an initial blood pressure value 90 mm Hg or more was substantially higher than the men whose initial blood pressure value was below 90 mm Hg. Similar data are available from other sources.[9] These data suggest that teen-agers and young adults who "spike" in high school or college, pre-employment, or Armed Forces physical examinations should not be ignored.

Obviously, since not every "spiker" becomes a frank hypertensive, one should evaluate judiciously. The essential point is that since the risk is significantly increased, these people must be kept under surveillance and counseled to minimize risk insofar as possible. And, obviously, should the need arise, they should be placed on a therapeutic regimen promptly.

3. *Obesity/Salt*

Figure 5 illustrates another intriguingly simple fact about hypertension. Obesity and hypertension are interrelated.[9] Although we have much corroborative data on this point, we don't yet understand the mechanism. The data illustrate two aspects of the weight-blood pressure relationship: a) relative weight in young adulthood and weight gain over the next 20-plus years and b) their relationship to the risk of developing hypertension by age 50. The higher the relative weight initially, the greater the tendency to elevated blood pressure in middle age. And, both for those lean in youth and slightly overweight in youth, the greater the gain in weight from young adulthood to middle age, the greater the tendency to high blood pressure. Every analysis of this relationship has yielded similar data.[14]

There are also data that show a direct relationship between sodium balance and hypertension in obese patients. Data in a recent issue of the *American Journal of Clinical Nutrition* demonstrate that weight reduction, without dietary salt reductions in the diet, does not necessarily mean an automatic blood pressure reduction. In fact, some obese patients were kept on a diet which maintained their weight but reduced their dietary salt intake, and in these obese hypertensive patients the blood pressures were successfully lowered.[15] Although these data also suggest that

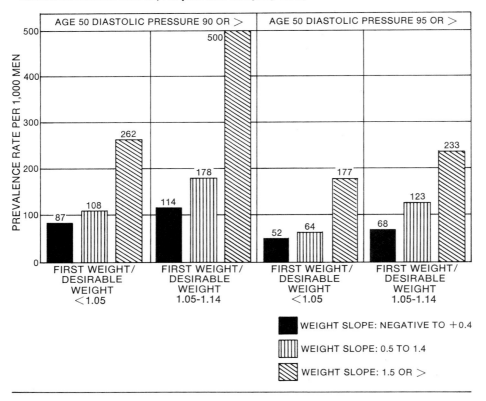

FIGURE 5

Relationship between initial weight ratio as a young adult, slope of weight curve over the next 20 years, and development of hypertensive disease in middle age, 20-year follow-up data on 764 men in 1958-59, Peoples Gas Company Study.[9]

when fat people reduce, their salt balance changes (i.e., they lose body salt), more data are required to explain fully all the reasons and answer all the questions such as "why" and "how."

This much *is* clear from all available evidence: there is a definite relationship between obesity and hypertension and it seems reasonable to suggest—particularly for such high-risk people as those with a positive family history or those "spiking" in youth—that one possibly helpful hygienic measure is the avoidance of obesity, or its correction if already present. In addition, it seems desirable to suggest corrective measures be taken not only by using diuretics to reduce the sodium levels in the body, but also stressing moderation in the use of salt.

4. *Cigarette smoking*

Another hygienic measure, of course, relates to cigarette smoking. Simply, the hypertensive who smokes is at much greater risk than one who does not. Therefore, those with a positive family history and/or "spiking" in youth, as well as those with established hypertension, would be better off not smoking cigarettes.

5. *Hypercholesterolemia/Hyperglycemia*

Similarly, such people should be advised of the added risks associated with hypercholesterolemia and told about the importance of minimizing intake of saturated fat, cholesterol, and high-calorie meals. In all likelihood, hyperglycemia also adds to the risk and provides yet another reason for stressing the prevention and correction of obesity, since fat people are more prone to carbohydrate intolerance.

Effectiveness of Antihypertensive Medication

Among the major achievements of the past 20 years are the development of drugs for the treatment of hypertension and the demonstration of their optimal usage (often in combination) and their efficacy in preventing morbidity.

Many of us remember the situation before 1950 painfully when, in desperation, we gave hypertensive people doses of barbiturates that made them somnolent throughout the day without lowering their blood pressures.

Now we have seen the development of several types of antihypertensive drugs and the painstaking research under the leadership of people like Dr. Edward Freis that elucidated the maximum benefit-to-risk ratios with combinations of these drugs. We have learned that judicious combinations minimize the problems of individual drugs given singly in large amounts—problems that can be troublesome in terms of side and toxic effects. Thanks to such research, it is now possible to prescribe proper combinations of antihypertensive drugs with lower dosages of each, and thereby achieve an acceptable ratio of benefit-to-risk.

The results of appropriate therapy are illustrated in Table 2 derived from the Veterans Administration Cooperative Study.*[16-18] As is evident, no reduction in pressure occurred with placebos. (Some patients in the placebo group were withdrawn because of excessive pressure rise.)

The effect of combination therapy (thiazide, reserpine, hy-

---

*See Appendix for complete study.

TABLE 2
**EFFECTIVENESS OF ANTIHYPERTENSIVE TREATMENT
IN LOWERING DIASTOLIC PRESSURE**
VETERANS ADMINISTRATION COOPERATIVE STUDY

Diastolic Pressures of Men Originally Averaging in the 115-129 mm Hg Range

	Control (Placebo)	Treated
Start of Study	121.0 mm Hg	121.2 mm Hg
At 4 Months	118.5	93.1
At 12 Months	118.8	91.6
At 24 Months	119.7	91.5

dralazine) was clear-cut—an average reduction of about 27 mm Hg systolic and about 17 mm Hg diastolic in men with average diastolic pressures at time of entry in the range of 90 to 114 mm Hg. Even greater average declines were observed for men with very severe hypertension (average diastolic pressures of 115-129 mm Hg at entry).

This desirable effect on blood pressure deserves special emphasis, particularly since there is ample evidence that a significant number of hypertensives under treatment are not well controlled.

Tables 3 and 4 provide a dramatic indication of the influence of adequate therapy on morbidity and mortality.[16-18] Two sets of end points are included: cardiovascular deaths and major nonfatal events. The data demonstrate the efficacy of successful therapy for men with severe hypertension: two vs twenty-seven total events, i.e., a 93 percent effectiveness. With this highly significant positive result, it was ethically necessary to transfer placebo patients to active medication, hence the trial was stopped long before

TABLE 3
**DEATH AND MAJOR NONFATAL EVENTS IN
UNTREATED AND TREATED HYPERTENSIVES**
VETERANS ADMINISTRATION COOPERATIVE STUDY

	INITIAL DIASTOLICS			
	115-129 mm Hg		90-114 mm Hg	
	70 Untreated Men	73 Actively Treated Men	194 Untreated Men	186 Actively Treated Men
Cardiovascular Deaths	4	0	19	8
Major Nonfatal Events*	23	2	57**	14

*Includes congestive heart failure, CV thrombosis, cerebral hemorrhage, M.I., grade 3 or 4 retinopathy, azotemia.
**Includes 20 patients whose diastolic blood pressure exceeded 124 mm Hg at 3 separate clinic visits.

Average period of observation: Men with diastolics 115-129 —— 18 months
Men with diastolics 90-114 —— 40 months

the originally planned five years. For men with the most common range of hypertension (diastolic pressures averaging 90-114 mm Hg at time of entry), a significantly positive result was also observed (see Tables 3 and 4). Of the 186 men randomly assigned to active treatment with a drug combination, only 22 developed major cardiovascular events, compared with the 76 of the 194 men randomly allocated to placebo.[17] The risk of developing such events over five years was reduced 70 percent by treatment. Terminating morbid events occurred in only 9 patients in the treated group, 35 in the control group. Eight deaths related to hypertension or atherosclerosis occurred in the actively treated group, 19 in the control group. In addition to the morbid events, 20 patients (all in the control group) developed persistent elevation of diastolic blood pressure to 125 mm Hg or greater. Evidence of efficacy of treatment was noted for patients with either lower (90-104 mm

TABLE 4

**EFFECTIVENESS OF ANTIHYPERTENSIVE TREATMENT
IN REDUCING DEATH AND MAJOR NONFATAL EVENTS**
VETERANS ADMINISTRATION COOPERATIVE STUDY

Initial Diastolic Blood Pressure	Percent with Events		Effectiveness* of Treatment
	Control	Treated	
90-114 mm Hg	39.3%	11.8%	70%
115-129 mm Hg	38.6%	2.7%	93%

*Effectiveness of treatment is the *difference* between percents of incidence of events in control and treated groups, *divided* by percent incidence in control group.

Hg) or higher (105-114 mm Hg) initial blood pressures, but more so in the latter.[17]

Apparently treatment was most effective in the prevention of congestive heart failure and stroke, but less effective in preventing clinical manifestations of severe coronary atherosclerosis. The limited size of the study precluded a definitive assessment of the value of drug treatment of hypertension in preventing premature coronary heart disease.[17,18]

As a result of this landmark research, the value of drug treatment of hypertension is now in a very different position than it was a few years ago. Now it is possible to be definitive about the value of therapy, at least for a much broader spectrum of hypertensives than heretofore. More data are needed, nonetheless, on the effect of treatment for the "mildest" cases, and for women, and on the ability to generalize this experience to mass public health and medical practice.

Diagnostic and Therapeutic Status of Hypertensive Persons in the United States

A vast problem exists in this country in regard to inadequacy

TABLE 5
HYPERTENSION—UNDIAGNOSED, DIAGNOSED BUT UNTREATED, DIAGNOSED AND TREATED BUT NOT NORMALIZED
35,000 EMPLOYED CHICAGOANS
CHICAGO HEART ASSOCIATION DETECTION PROJECT IN INDUSTRY
NOVEMBER 1967-MAY 1972

GROUP	White Men		Black Men		White Women		Black Women	
All	18,142 *	100.0 **	1,333	100.0	12,985	100.0	2,078	100.0
No previous history of hypertension, BP elevated	2,422	13.4	202	15.2	1,093	8.4	99	4.8
History of hypertension, not on treatment, BP elevated	697	3.8	58	4.4	397	3.1	47	2.3
History of hypertension, not on treatment, BP not elevated	891	4.9	61	4.6	604	4.7	150	7.2
History of hypertension, on treatment, BP elevated	454	2.5	33	2.5	372	2.9	38	1.8
History of hypertension, on treatment, BP not elevated	319	1.8	22	1.7	392	3.0	47	2.3
All with BP elevation	3,573	19.7	293	22.0	1,862	14.3	184	8.9
All with BP elevation and/or history of hypertension	4,783	26.4	376	28.2	2,858	22.0	381	18.3

*Number of persons
**Percent, i.e., prevalence rate per 100 persons
Elevated blood pressure (BP): systolic ≥ 160 mm Hg and/or diastolic ≥ 95 mm Hg.
Percent calculations are not age-adjusted. Since the age composition of the four sex-race groups varied considerably, these rates are not comparable across the sex-race groups.

of care for hypertensives. A recent report of the Inter-Society Commission for Heart Disease Resources, "Guidelines for the Detection, Diagnosis, and Management of Hypertensive Populations"* gives data from three studies in the 1960s, including the National Health Examination Survey.[19] Of all persons with hypertension in these community surveys, about 40 percent were unaware of their condition, about a third were under treatment, and about half of the latter (i.e., about 20 percent of all hypertensives) were under control.

More recent data (some of it previously unpublished) collected on 35,000 employed Chicagoans from November 1967 through May 1972 are available from the Chicago Heart Detection Project in Industry.[4,5] Table 5 presents data on the percentage of previously undetected hypertensives in this screened population. Hypertension in this instance is defined using the World Health Organization criteria: ≥ 160 systolic and/or ≥ 95 mm Hg diastolic. The situation is no better, to put it conservatively, than

*See Appendix for complete report.

19

in the early and mid-1960s. A majority of the hypertensives are unaware of their condition. And, please note, these are gainfully employed persons—not the unemployed, not the victims of ghetto deprivation.

This is one cardinal problem. Instances of *undetected hypertension* are vast and widespread.

The second problem is *treatment*, as is clearly demonstrated in Table 5. Of the screenees who already knew that they were hypertensive, a sizeable percent were not on treatment.

More detailed analysis revealed that this was true for both the more and less educated persons.[5] And it was true throughout the time period 1967-72. Apparently publication of the two Veterans Administration studies on efficacy of treatment (in the Journal of the American Medical Association in 1967 and 1970 and reprinted extensively for physicians) has had little impact on increasing the percentage of hypertensive persons under treatment.

FIGURE 6

Persons previously diagnosed and on current treatment for hypertension, percentage with systolic blood pressure less than 160 mm Hg and diastolic blood pressure less than 95 mm Hg, Chicago Heart Association Detection Project in Industry, November 1967—May 1972.[5]

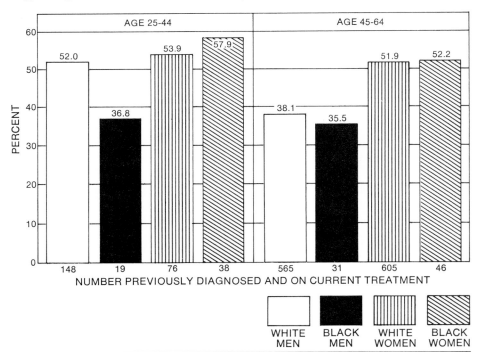

If anything, that percentage has declined from 1967 to 1972.

With respect to the effectiveness of therapy, the findings again should cause concern. Half of the hypertensives *on treatment* had blood pressures below the World Health Organization criteria for definitely abnormal levels (Table 5, rows 4 and 5, and Figure 6). Again, this is true for men and women, white and black, more and less educated persons, younger and older, and throughout these years. There is little evidence of improvement in the 1970s as compared to the late 1960s.[5]

A few studies have gone still further into the question of consistency of therapy. It seems reasonable to assume that to be useful in preventing "complications," effective therapy should be continued without interruption for years. Unfortunately, this is often not the case, as exemplified by the data from the Peoples Gas Company study in Chicago. These men had been followed by yearly physical examinations, told that they had hypertension, and then referred to their private physicians. After about a decade, they were interviewed about their treatment status and examined briefly. Amazingly enough, 6.1 percent professed not to know they were hypertensive. (Hard to believe, since they were repeatedly informed. This again illustrates the communication problem.) Only two-thirds of the group gave a history of any treatment whatever. Thirty percent were never treated, despite continuous referrals by the company medical department to the employees' own doctors. Of those who had any history of treatment, less than half received regular treatment. For those on treatment at the time of the survey, only 30 percent had a reduction of blood pressure of 6 mm Hg or more (based on the accumulated records of past years in the medical department charts), and only 11 percent had a reduction of 16 mm Hg or more. (It is important to recall that a fall of 17 mm Hg was the average reduction in the Veterans Administration Cooperative Study for hypertensives in the range 90-114 mm Hg at baseline.)

Similar data are available from the study in Baldwin County (Atlanta).[20,21]

A simple "formula" is useful for remembering the somber, harsh realities of the problem and pinpointing the challenge to our health education and medical care delivery system: "½ x ½ x ½."

— One-half of the hypertensives are undetected.
— One-half of the known hypertensives are untreated.
— One-half of the treated hypertensives are inadequately treated.

QED: only one-eighth of the 20 to 25 million hypertensives are detected and adequately treated, based on the modest criterion of a current lowering of blood pressure to a systolic level of less than 160 and/or diastolic level of less than 95 mm Hg. For an optimal blood pressure response, lower values sustained long-term are clearly appropriate. To maximize the prevention of "complications," comprehensive care (not just drugs to lower blood pressure) is necessary, i.e., correction of cigarette smoking, hypercholesterolemia, hyperglycemia-diabetes, obesity. With only one-eighth of the 20 to 25 million hypertensives being detected and adequately treated, there are the other seven-eighths being inadequately served. We are talking about finding and treating well over 20 million people—quite a challenge indeed!

Why is this situation so unsatisfactory? One thing is suggested by the data from the Peoples Gas Company. The majority of these hypertensive men were going to their doctors at least quarterly, so that frequent visits to physicians don't necessarily provide the whole answer.

Patients often stop taking medication. In Baldwin County, patients were asked: "Why did you stop taking medication?" Cost of drug was a reason but not the main one. They just didn't realize that they should continue on medication. They felt better. They took the drug "when needed." Obviously, successful doctor-patient communication on the importance of regular, sustained, long-term therapy for hypertension, though vital, has not yet been achieved.[21]

And when the nature of therapy is evaluated, it is clear that the medical profession is not sufficiently aware of the value of combining antihypertensive medications, and particularly the use of three drugs as were employed so effectively in the Veterans Administration Cooperative Study. For example, a minority of the patients on treatment in the Peoples Gas Company were taking effective combination therapy at the time of the survey in 1969. Obviously, there is still an immense challenge in the area of physician education.

Are these problems rectifiable? Figure 7 illustrates one of the few experiences on this. These are data collected in the Baldwin County study.[20] At the time of the first mass survey in 1964 the treatment situation was deplorable. Accordingly, a special program was begun. A home visiting program by nurses was instituted. Good control was defined as diastolic pressure under 95 mm Hg. The rates went up to 86 percent on prescription, and 80 per-

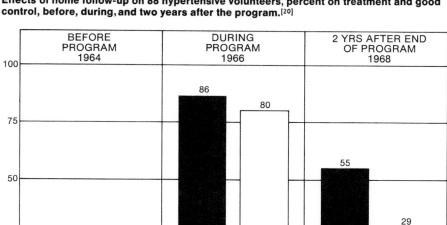

FIGURE 7

Effects of home follow-up on 88 hypertensive volunteers, percent on treatment and good control, before, during, and two years after the program.[20]

cent under good control. The pilot program was discontinued, having proved its efficacy! Not unexpectedly, when the firm, steady persuasion and education of such a program ceased, matters slipped markedly. Two years after the end of the program, both treatment status and effectiveness of control had regressed.

The lesson is clear: in any successful medical care program for chronic disease, good long-term sustained therapy must be systematically assured, whether for hypertension or other problems.

Programmatic Proposals for the Control of Hypertension

The entire history of modern public health teaches a fundamental lesson about the control of mass disease problems, a lesson highly relevant for this one: mass public health problems require mass public health approaches to their solution (i.e., community, in addition to individual, methods). The simple doctor-patient relationship, as important and essential as it is, can't do the whole job.

This fundamental point was made almost a decade ago in 1964, at the Second National Conference on Cardiovascular Diseases, jointly and appropriately cosponsored by the national voluntary and official agencies, the American Heart Association, the Heart Disease Control Program of the Public Health Service, and the National Heart Institute.

Here are the recommendations in its Community Service Summary Report:

> *Hypertension as defined by the World Health Organization is a problem which is amenable to community efforts in detection, diagnosis and management.*
>
> *Casefinding is essential but of little value unless it is followed by referral to sources of medical care and systematic follow-up.*
>
> *Physicians should be shown the importance of early and adequate treatment of mild benign hypertension. All those identified as hypertensive should have further diagnostic work-up to find curable forms of hypertension.*[22]

In the 1970s, the Inter-Society Commission for Heart Disease Resources, in its reports "The Primary Prevention of the Atherosclerotic Diseases" and "Guidelines for the Detection, Diagnosis, and Management of Hypertensive Populations," reaffirmed this basic concept and elaborated specific approaches for its implementation and fulfillment.[7,19] These reports merit complete reading and detailed study by every physician as well as full support to achieve their early and vigorous implementation.

Short quotations of particularly salient portions are relevant here. From the first of these two reports:

Recommendations For Primary Prevention

> *The Commission recommends the immediate and concurrent implementation of the following recommendations for the primary prevention of the atherosclerotic diseases:*
>
> *National Policy Commitment to Strategy of Primary Prevention*
>
> *A. The Commission recommends that a strategy of primary prevention of premature atherosclerotic diseases be*

adopted as long-term national policy for the United States and to implement this strategy that adequate resources of money and manpower be committed to accomplish:

> *...Changes in diet to prevent or control hyperlipidemia, obesity, hypertension and diabetes*
> *...Elimination of cigarette smoking*
> *...Pharmacologic control of elevated blood pressure*

Detection and Control of Hypertension

E. The Commission recommends a major national effort to detect and control hypertension. Recent studies have shown that the prevalence of elevated blood pressure is generally high in the United States, especially in the black population. Many hypertensives have not been identified; many others known to have the disease are not receiving adequate therapy. Programs are urgently needed to identify hypertensives in the community and assure their subsequent treatment. The recent published positive results from the Veterans Administration field trial of drug therapy for so-called "mild" hypertension underscore the potential significance of such programs.

Community Programs

F. The Commission recommends that community programs be developed and expanded for the detection and treatment of persons of all ages who are very susceptible to premature atherosclerotic diseases due to combinations of the major risk factors.

This recommendation is premised on extensive experience demonstrating that effective community programs for prevention of disease generally combine measures addressed to the entire population with concerted efforts for the detection and care of high risk individuals. All available evidence indicates that this well-established principle applies to the prevention of the atherosclerotic diseases.

Of the basis of recent experience, detection programs are likely to identify a very large proportion of the population— e.g., about 20 or 30 percent of middle-aged adults—as being at unusually high risk. For such individuals, community services should be provided to assist their physicians in long-term management. Such programs will require the training and use of large numbers of allied health personnel, as well as physicians.[7]

And from the second of these two reports, this latter one presenting comprehensive 10-page-long concrete and detailed "Guidelines for the Detection, Diagnosis, and Management of Hypertensive Populations":

> *Community control of hypertension represents a great challenge to American medicine. The large numbers affected and the relatively small percentage of hypertensive patients under adequate control suggest the magnitude of the opportunity. The scope of the problem is reflected by the lack of adequate diagnostic and therapeutic facilities to manage the case load and the relatively high prevalence of hypertension in economically underprivileged areas including overcrowded urban centers. Solutions to the problems of detection and maintenance of effective treatment for populations of hypertensives will require long-term planning and the allocation of sufficient funds for the training of needed manpower, facilities and other related costs. In the long run it should be less expensive to control hypertension than to care for those who become disabled and economically unproductive as a consequence of the disease.*[19]

These two Inter-Society Commission Reports were published in 1970 and 1971 respectively. Viewed optimistically, only the barest beginning has been made in the implementation of their recommendations, whether or not the basis of judgment is the matter of an overall commitment to a strategic policy of prevention and control, or the commitment of money, manpower, and resources.

Essentially, it is still unclear whether these reports and their recommendations will become effective guidelines for a determined national effort or, as with some similar previous efforts, merely esoteric tomes doomed to gather dust in the archives and libraries.

Although humanistic considerations must continue to be regarded as the overriding determinant of public policy and national priority, it is obviously necessary to go beyond the focus of our commentary thus far—the biomedical and health aspects of the hypertension problem—and briefly discuss the social, medical, and financial aspects.

The Financial and Social Soundness of the
Effort to Control Hypertension

The Inter-Society Commission for Heart Disease Resources stated: "In the long run it should be less expensive to control hypertension than to care for those who become disabled and economically unproductive as a consequence of the disease."[19] If we use this statement as a guideline, the effort to control hypertension (like other preventive medicine undertakings to control mass disease) should more than pay for itself financially.

Although only limited facts are available, there are data that permit a specific assessment of this relevant question:

1. The President's Commission on Heart Disease, Cancer and Stroke in its 1964 Report made estimates of the economic costs of heart disease and stroke in 1962.[23]

TABLE 6

ESTIMATED ECONOMIC COSTS TO THE NATION DUE TO MORBIDITY AND MORTALITY FROM ARTERIOSCLEROTIC AND HYPERTENSIVE DISEASES, UNITED STATES.

Diagnosis	Amount (in millions)			
	Total	Morbidity		Mortality Costs**
		Direct Costs*	Indirect Costs	
Total (Arteriosclerotic or hypertensive)	$23,887	$4,291	$1,133	$18,463
Arteriosclerotic Heart Disease	15,545	2,072	370	13,103
Stroke***	4,605	971	235	3,399
Diseases of Arteries	1,082	354	31	697
Hypertensive Diseases****	2,655	894	497	1,264

*Includes physicians' services, drugs, hospital and nursing home care, other medical and professional services.
**Present value of lifetime earnings (discounted at 6%) of persons who died of arteriosclerotic and hypertensive diseases.
***Includes 20% not due to arteriosclerosis.
****Does not include all arteriosclerotic disease in which hypertension was involved.

2. The American Heart Association has recently published projections of costs of cardiovascular diseases for 1973.[13]

3. The 1971 Report of the National Heart and Lung Institute Task Force on Arteriosclerosis (Vol. II) gives the most detailed estimates for 1967 including specific estimates for the costs of hypertension per se.[24]

Table 6 summarizes these data.

Morbidity, disability, and mortality from hypertensive disease per se is costing the nation over 1.7 billion dollars annually in indirect costs.[24] If we assume that hypertension is a contributing factor in about a third of premature heart attacks and strokes, roughly another 5.9 billion dollars in indirect costs of hypertensive disease could be concealed in these categories, totaling about 7.6 billion dollars in indirect costs alone. A similar calculation gives a direct cost estimate of almost two billion dollars. Therefore, the total costs of hypertensive disease add up to over 9 billion dollars for 1967.

The data of the Veterans Administration field trials indicate that effective comprehensive control programs can cut morbidity, disability, and mortality from hypertensive disease by over 50 percent. It therefore seems reasonable to project a program for the next years—a well-planned, well-organized, well-controlled, steadily mounting effort—that would bring this benefit to at least one-half of the 20 to 25 million hypertensives in the United States by 1978, in increments of 10 percent per year. It seems reasonable to budget for this purpose in amounts that can really begin to accomplish something, especially since this preventive effort (like all others) will in the long run save money, not to mention the savings of human misery and premature death.

Where is the money to come from right now? That is part of the big question of our national priorities and their re-ordering, especially now that the war in Vietnam has been ended.

It may be useful to close by citing one more table—of vital statistics data, on life expectancy for white males in this country[25] (table 7). Note that for white men who have reached age 30 or beyond, life expectancy in the 1970s is just about what it was in 1900. No progress has been made. Gains in one area (e.g., against tuberculosis and lobar pneumonia) have been offset by setbacks in others (e.g., the major adult cardiovascular diseases considered overall). (The three other major sex-race groups have fared only slightly better in terms of life expectancy as adults.)

An effective long-term national effort to control hypertension

TABLE 7

EXPECTATION OF LIFE (YEARS)
WHITE MALES, UNITED STATES, BY YEAR AND AGE,
1900 TO 1970

AGE	YEAR				
	1900	1920	1940	1960	1970
0	52.8	60.3	65.4	67.4	67.7
5	59.9	62.4	64.3	64.4	64.4
20	47.9	49.1	50.1	50.1	50.1
30	39.6	40.8	40.9	40.9	40.9
40	31.2	31.7	31.7	31.7	31.7
50	23.1	23.2	23.2	23.2	23.2

Prepared by Lew, E. A. and Seltzer, F. from basic data presented by Jacobson, P. A., *Cohort Survival of Generations Since 1840,* Milbank Memorial Fund Quarterly, July, 1964, and publications of The National Center for Health Statistics, Department of Health, Education and Welfare.

could get us dramatically off dead center in that regard. It is undoubtedly a national goal—and a goal for practicing physicians—that deserves to be second to none.

References

1. U.S. Department of Health, Education and Welfare: Blood pressure of adults by race and area, United States, 1960-1962. National Health Survey, National Center for Health Statistics Series 11: Number 5, 1964.

2. U.S. Department of Health, Education and Welfare: Blood pressure of adults by age and sex, United States, 1960-1962. National Health Survey, National Center for Health Statistics Series 11: Number 4, 1964.

3. U.S. Department of Health, Education and Welfare: Hypertension and hypertensive heart disease in adults, United States, 1960-1962. National Health Survey, National Center for Health Statistics Series 11: Number 13, 1966.

4. Schoenberger JA, Stamler J, Shekelle RB, and Shekelle S: Current status of hypertension control in an industrial population. JAMA 222:559, 1972.

5. Stamler J: High blood pressure in the United States—an overview of the problem and the challenge. In: Proceedings of the National Conference on High Blood Pressure Education. National Heart and Lung Institute. U.S. Department of Health, Education and Welfare publication number (NIH) 73-486, 1973, p. 11.

6. Lew EA: Blood pressure and mortality—life insurance experience. In: The Epidemiology of Hypertension. J Stamler, R Stamler, and TN Pullman, Editors. New York, Grune and Stratton, 1967, p. 392.

7. Inter-Society Commission for Heart Disease Resources. Atherosclerosis Study Group and Epidemiology Study Group: Primary prevention of the atherosclerotic diseases. Circulation 42:A55, 1970.

8. Paffenbarger RS, Notkin J, Krueger DE, Wolf PA, Thorne MC, LeBauer EJ, and Williams JL: Chronic disease in former college students. II. Methods of study and observations on mortality from coronary heart disease. Amer J Pub Health *56*:962, 1966.

9. Stamler J: Lectures on Preventive Cardiology. New York, Grune and Stratton, 1967.

10. Stamler J, Berkson DM, and Lindberg HA: Risk factors: their role in the etiology and pathogenesis of the atherosclerotic diseases. In: Pathogenesis of Atherosclerosis. RW Wissler and JC Geer, Editors. Baltimore, Williams and Wilkins, 1972, p. 41.

11. Moriyama IM, Krueger DE, and Stamler J: Cardiovascular Diseases in the United States. Cambridge, Mass., Harvard University Press, 1971, p. 119.

12. U.S. Department of Health, Education and Welfare, Social Security Administration, Office of Research and Statistics: Social Security disability applicant statistics 1968. DHEW Publication No. (SSA) 73-1911, June 1972.

13. American Heart Association: 1973 Heart Facts. New York, American Heart Association, 1972.

14. The Epidemiology of Hypertension. J Stamler, R Stamler, and TN Pullman, Editors. New York, Grune and Stratton, 1967.

15. Dahl LK: Salt and hypertension. Amer J Clin Nutr *25*:231, 1972.

*16. Veterans Administration Cooperative Study Group on Antihypertensive Agents: Effects of treatment on morbidity in hypertension: I. Results in patients with diastolic blood pressures averaging 115 through 129 mm Hg. JAMA *202*:1028, 1967.

*17. Veterans Administration Cooperative Study Group on Antihypertensive Agents: Effects of treatment on morbidity in hypertension: II. Results in patients with diastolic blood pressure averaging 90 through 114 mm Hg. JAMA *213*:1143, 1970.

*18. Veterans Administration Cooperative Study Group on Antihypertensive Agents: Effects of treatment on morbidity in hypertension: III. Influence of age, diastolic pressure, and prior cardiovascular disease; further analysis of side effects. Circulation *45*:991, 1972.

*19. Report of Inter-Society Commission for Heart Disease Resources: Guidelines for the detection, diagnosis, and management of hypertensive populations. Circulation *44*:A263, 1971. (Revised August 1972.)

20. Wilber JA and Barrow JG: Reducing elevated blood pressure—experience found in a community. Minnesota Med *52*:1303, 1969.

21. Wilber JA: Detection and control of hypertensive disease in Georgia, U.S.A. In: The Epidemiology of Hypertension. J Stamler, R Stamler, and TN Pullman, Editors. New York, Grune and Stratton, 1967, p. 439.

22. Barrow G: Community Service—Summary. In: The Heart and Circulation, Second National Conference on Cardiovascular Disease, Vol. II. Washington, D.C., Community Services and Education, 1965, p. 689.

23. The President's Commission on Heart Disease, Cancer and Stroke: Report to the President. A National Program to Conquer Heart Disease, Cancer and Stroke. Vol. II, February 1965.

24. National Heart and Lung Institute Task Force on Arteriosclerosis: Arteriosclerosis Vol. II. U.S. Department of Health, Education and Welfare, Public Health Service, DHEW Publication No. (NIH) 72-219, June 1971 (1972).

*See Appendix for complete study.

25. Lew EA and Seltzer F: Use of the life table in public health. Milbank Mem Fund Q *48*:15, Suppl., 1970.

Acknowledgments

It is a pleasure to acknowledge the cooperation of the authors' senior colleagues in the long-term investigations presented here: especially David M. Berkson, M.D., and Howard A. Lindberg, M.D.

It is also a pleasure to express appreciation to the many Chicago organizations giving invaluable cooperation in the cited research efforts, particularly the Peoples Gas Light and Coke Company, its Chairman, Remick McDowell, and its Medical Director, Howard A. Lindberg, M.D. Acknowledgment is also gratefully extended to all those involved in the Chicago Heart Association Detection Project in Industry: Louis deBoer, Executive Director, and Kay Westfall, Program Director; the Chicago Heart Association Detection Project in Industry Staff: Pamela Desmond, Thelma Black, Clarice Blanton, Joan Carothers, Arlene Dungca, Mary Ann Foelker, Susan Forkos, Carol Fulgenzi, Harold Gram, Jean Graver, Inger Hansen, Cherry Latimer, Audrona Misiunis, Susan Shekelle, Karen Strentz, R.N., Steven Simons, Michael Thompson, and Suzann Ward, R.N.; Volunteer Members of the Heart Disease Detection Committee of the Chicago Heart Association and its subcommittees: Howard Adler, Ph.D., Rene Arcilla, M.D., Robert Arzaecher, Ph.D., Richard A. Carleton, M.D., Angelo Cottini, Edwin Duffin, Ph.D., Morton B. Epstein, Ph.D., Robert E. Fitzgerald, M.D., Philip Freedman, M.D., Burton J. Grossman, M.D., Mark H. Lepper, M.D., Robert R. J. Hilker, M.D., Robert S. Kassriel, M.D., Howard A. Lindberg, M.D., Clinton L. Lindo, M.D., Gerald Masek, Ph.D., Richard McNamara, Robert A. Miller, M.D., Robert D. Moseley, Jr., M.D., Milton H. Paul, M.D., Willie Reedus, R.N., Raymond Restivo, Wallace Salzman, M.D., Robert Sessions, Howard H. Sky-Peck, Ph.D., Donald Singer, M.D., Sachahida N. Sinha, M.D., Grace Smedstad, Ralph Springer, J. Martin Stoker, M.D., Carl Vogel, Ira T. Whipple, M.S., Quentin D. Young, M.D.

The authors are most grateful to the principal investigators of the prospective studies of Albany civil servants, Chicago Western Electric Company employees, Framingham community residents, Los Angeles civil servants, and Minneapolis-St. Paul business and professional men, and to the coordinators of the national cooperative Pooling Project. It is a pleasure to acknowledge the cooperation and aid of our colleagues in this endeavor: Drs. Henry Blackburn, John M. Chapman, Thomas R. Dawber, Joseph T. Doyle, Frederick H. Epstein, William B. Kannell, Ancel Keys, Felix J. Moore, Oglesby Paul, and Henry L. Taylor.

Appreciation is also expressed to the following colleagues and publishers for permission to cite from published works: Edward D. Freis, M.D., Joseph A. Wilber, M.D.; the American Heart Association, Journal of the American Medical Association, Minnesota Medicine.

The authors' research has been supported by the American Heart Association; Chicago Heart Association; Illinois Regional Medical Program; and the National Heart and Lung Institute, National Institutes of Health, United States Public Health Service.

Chapter 2

A Time for Action

Theodore Cooper, M.D., Ph.D.

Hypertension

2

A Time for Action

Theodore Cooper, M.D., Ph.D.

Director, National Heart and Lung Institute
National Institutes of Health
Bethesda, Maryland

In the preceding chapter, Dr. Stamler presented abundant evidence that we are facing a medical problem of staggering proportions. His and other studies indicate that high blood pressure directly contributes to about 60,000 deaths a year. I call these true hypertension deaths because they are related to the basic wear and tear which high blood pressure puts on the cardiovascular system, on the heart, very often on the kidneys, and sometimes on the brain.

High blood pressure is frequently an underlying factor in stroke, contributing greatly to the 200,000 deaths from stroke each year. And it can be blamed for disabling hundreds of thousands of stroke victims each year.

We are not sure that the actual prevalence of hypertension is increasing, but we are sure that the number of people who require treatment for hypertension is increasing. We now know that moderate elevations of blood pressure should not be ignored. Many asymptomatic hypertensive patients who were formerly considered normal must now receive medical attention.

We learned in medical school that mild to moderate hypertension is usually benign. That concept is out of date. Persistent hypertension is not benign. It is dangerous because it threatens life, and often shortens life.

The degree of danger an individual faces increases in a very close relationship to his blood pressure. This brings many millions of people into a risk situation. Fortunately, the new treatments, particularly a wide range of drugs for different levels of blood pressure and types of patient, have made it possible to control hypertension and prevent disability and death on a massive scale.

Critical Mass of Knowledge

Interestingly enough, there has been no single spectacular discovery in hypertension to compare with the polio vaccine breakthrough. However, within the last five years, we have accumulated a critical mass of knowledge which, for the first time, has given us sound and adequate information for taking positive action to control high blood pressure.

Carefully done studies, particularly the Veterans Administration Cooperative Studies* by Dr. Edward D. Freis, have shown that drugs can control high blood pressure and greatly reduce the amount of damage which might otherwise be done over a period of years.

So, to review briefly, we do not have startling new information about the prevalence of hypertension, there is no major breakthrough in methods of measurement, and we do not have a miracle drug to treat it.

The new element we have is an awareness that millions of Americans who we thought had benign elevations of blood pressure actually face a risk of premature disability or death. In practical terms, even mild to moderate elevations of blood pressure now loom as a new threat.

Relating this to day-to-day practice, I believe it calls for the same kind of commitment physicians would give to any other epidemic which affects a significant part of their practice.

Mobilizing Resources

At the National Institutes of Health, we are keenly aware that we have responsibilities beyond the mere acquisition of new knowledge. Like many others in medicine, research investigators realize that we have let a gap develop between the accomplishments of research and the practice of medicine.

With others, we share the obligation to see that new knowledge reaches the field and the patient where it can do some good. Society is asking, even demanding, that physicians improve the mechanism by which new findings get into actual practice, and the

---

*See Appendix for complete studies.

physicians in research know that we have a part to play in that process.

It was against this background that the National High Blood Pressure Education Program was organized. The effort involves virtually every public, private, and professional agency with an interest in hypertension.

The basic purpose of the program is to foster a public and professional awareness that hypertension is a real threat, its detection is important, and its treatment can reduce morbidity and mortality.

In the past few months, many people from many different segments of society have come to meetings at the Institute on matters related to hypertension. We have talked with people from business, from the black community, from unions, from insurance companies, and even from professional football. A few years ago, this activity would have been regarded as an interruption of business. Today, these visits are very much a part of our business.

Public Awareness Efforts

Every physician, and I am no exception, has had occasion to wish that the layman would not ask medical questions based on an article he read, and very often misinterpreted, in a newspaper or magazine. The layman could be a Congressman or a barber but, in either case, he wants to be sure that his doctor is keeping up with the latest medical advances.

We have started asking the American people to find out what their blood pressure is. As mentioned earlier, our main purpose is to create a public awareness that hypertension is a real threat, that detection is important, and that those who have it should follow medical advice.

Our early efforts have already resulted in major articles on high blood pressure in national magazines, including *Reader's Digest* and *The New York Times Sunday Magazine*. Various kinds of public service advertising have been prepared for television and radio, and educational films are being readied that can be used for television, for schools, or for other organized groups.

There is no doubt that some old patients and some new patients will be asking about blood pressure. They will want assurance that they do not have "it." And if they have "it," they will want treatment.

There is also no doubt that this public awareness campaign

will cause some unnecessary alarm. We have sought the aid of responsible professional associations in trying to design material that we feel will do a great deal more good than harm. However, in mass media campaigns, one must assume that misinterpretations are bound to occur in some instances.

Physicians can be expected to receive many requests for information about high blood pressure. To help physicians respond to these inquiries, the local chapters of the American Heart Association and many other health educational groups are producing and distributing leaflets and other material that contain the latest information in an interesting and authoritative form.*

Major private firms have sponsored booklets, films, and audio cassettes that have already reached tens of thousands of key health professionals, and more are on the way.

Screening Efforts

The National High Blood Pressure Education Program is not planning a large-scale detection and screening program. However, federal agencies charged with direct patient care are providing expanded detection and treatment services. These would include the armed services and the Veterans Administration.

Many federal offices are willing to cooperate with private groups planning to set up temporary or continuing programs for screening, detection, referral, and follow-up.

The Community Role

The American Medical Association last year scheduled an excellent program on hypertension, and it was perfectly clear from the panelists' reports that while the management of hypertension is basically the physicians' job, there are opportunities for the community to assist with that job.

Awareness, education, and motivation are important to get the patient to a physician for evaluation and treatment. Various community agencies can help in these areas. Health education is most convincing when it goes from one person to another, from a doctor to a patient, from a nurse to a patient, from a mother to a child, from a teacher to a child.

I have long hoped for the day when children would be taught to take care of their hearts as automatically as they are taught to take care of their teeth. That day is probably coming closer with the current interest in high blood pressure. My hope is that this

*See page 223 in the Appendix for a listing of this information.

will have lasting effects on how people and society view both preventive care and preventive medicine.

The Need for Innovation

This major chronic health problem presents us with important challenges. We need to build bridges between researchers and practitioners. We need to find innovative approaches to patient motivation and management. We need to overcome resistance to change. And we need to extend our reach by using paramedical personnel so that our valuable time is reserved for the work that only physicians can perform.

As Dr. Finnerty discusses in Chapter 6, much of the routine recording of blood pressure and monitoring of patients can be done by paramedical personnel. Some physicians have found that teaching a patient to take his own blood pressure is very worthwhile. Nothing is so educational to the patient as seeing the results when he takes his medication and seeing the results when he misses his medication.

An interesting innovation is developing in the insurance realm. Some alert insurance officials are reducing life insurance premiums for hypertensive patients who follow treatment. In some cases, the savings can be significant, and may provide special motivation for some patients. To enlarge on this innovation, organizations like the American Medical Association and the American Heart Association are working with physicians and insurance companies in local communities to encourage premium reductions for hypertensive patients who are under effective medical control.

Conclusion

The facts of the situation present a direct challenge to the physician. The numbers are great. Detection is simple. Methods of control are simple, though not inexpensive.

Science cannot do this job. Research to date has only been able to find a partial answer, i.e., providing the means of control while still looking for the causes and a real cure.

No government agency and, in fact, no professional association can do this job, although many are helping in a public awareness campaign.

This is a job for the physician, and it offers the opportunity and satisfaction of providing the kind of medical care that can literally help millions of people enjoy extra years of living.

Chapter 3

A Functional Approach to Screening

Morton H. Maxwell, M.D.

Hypertension

3

A Functional Approach to Screening

Morton H. Maxwell, M.D.

Director, Nephrology and Hypertension Service
Cedars-Sinai Medical Center
Los Angeles, California

Clinical Professor of Medicine
UCLA School of Medicine
Los Angeles, California

The foregoing chapters make three things obvious:

1. Hypertension is a major public health problem.
2. It can be readily detected.
3. Antihypertensive drug therapy may be expected to prolong life and to reduce the incidence of certain cardiovascular morbid events in a large proportion of the hypertensive population.

But since people with high blood pressure usually have few or no symptoms[1] and hypertension can be neither detected nor treated unless the blood pressure is actually measured, how do we go about finding our missing hypertensives? Should we put sphygmomanometers around the upper arms of every American to find the 20 to 25 million with elevated blood pressure? And if so, how can this be done?

How to Find the Hypertensives

Hypertension must be taken more seriously

At the present time, most subjects with hypertension are detected through incidental screening procedures, i.e., insurance examinations, pre-employment examinations, Armed Forces examinations, blood donor screening, and in physicians' offices, emergency rooms, or clinics. However, it has been found that even in university hospitals, hypertension is often considered an "incidental" finding and ignored, so that even "detected" hypertensives are often not taken seriously. One report points out that in one-quarter of the patients no arterial pressures were recorded by the admitting physicians.[2]

Is widespread community screening the answer?

Because the majority of the hypertensive population is presently undetected, untreated, or inadequately treated, community control of hypertension is being widely recommended[3] and a centrally organized national screening program is being studied (see Figure 1). The word "community" refers to any group which either lives or works in a defined area. A number of pilot community screening programs have been or are being conducted in the United States. They may involve entire communities, civil servants, company employees, selected census tracts, mixed or stratified populations. Blood pressures have been obtained in supermarkets, churches, schools, clinics, homes, and mobile vans, and have been measured by physicians, nurses, paramedical personnel, and volunteers. The majority of these projects have been publicly funded epidemiological studies, and have confirmed the high incidence, poor prognosis, and inadequate treatment of high blood pressure.

They have also been extremely expensive in terms of cost versus the actual numbers of individuals with hypertension detected and/or treated. For example, a national cooperative effort involving large, publicly funded, long-term prospective studies of adult cardiovascular disease is concerned with a total of only 1433 hypertensive subjects.[4] The widely publicized cooperative Veterans Administration study*of therapy in mild and moderate hypertension encompassed a total of 380 subjects.[5] Furthermore, no generally applicable model for hypertension screening or therapy has been developed. In Atlanta, mass media publicity and individual letters to households were ineffective, whereas in Los Angeles they were very useful. It is generally agreed that very few of the adult population can be induced to come to an outside facility for free blood pressure measurements.[6] The detection teams, therefore, must go to the target population, either with mobile vans set up in places where people naturally congregate or with door-to-door screening. There is also agreement that premature mass screening without prior provisions for adequate di-

---

*See Appendix for complete study.

FIGURE 1

A STRATIFIED ORGANIZATION OF MEDICAL RESOURCES
FOR HYPERTENSION CONTROL

Adapted from Report of Inter-Society Commission for Heart Disease Resources: Guidelines for the detection, diagnosis, and management of hypertensive populations. Circulation *44:* A269 (Figure 2), 1971. (Revised August 1972.)*

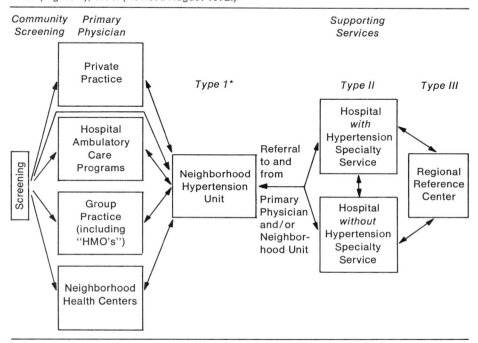

*The Neighborhood Hypertension Unit *is a community service which assists the primary physician with long term follow-up and management of his hypertensive patients. Since many patients with hypertension have combinations of cardiovascular risk factors, it is preferable that this service be incorporated as part of a comprehensive risk factor intervention program, e.g., diet and cigarette smoking control, exercise programs, diabetes control. Depending on local needs, these services can stand alone in their own facility or, what is more likely, they can be incorporated into other facilities and programs such as comprehensive neighborhood health centers, hospital ambulatory care programs, group practices (including HMO's), health department programs, community health educations centers, etc.*

agnostic, therapeutic, and follow-up facilities and services would be unwise.[7]

Because of the diversity of the American population ethnically and socio-economically, the lack of available massive funding for an alternative system of medical care with regard to hypertension, and the unsound medical and economic aspects of stratified screening by disease, I am skeptical regarding a centralized,

*See Appendix for complete report.

standardized national hypertension screening program. High blood pressure screening and control can be integrated into our present system of health care, which is largely the private practice of medicine.

How can the present system cope with the problem?

It is estimated that the supply of physicians will catch up with the demand prior to 1980. Thus, except for possible maldistribution of physicians in some regions, if hypertension detection is conducted in presently available medical facilities—private offices, hospitals, prepaid health groups, clinics, industrial health facilities, Armed Forces and Veterans Administration facilities—prompt and adequate medical follow-up of screened hypertensives can be assured with no dislocation of personnel and at a minimum cost.

In order to accomplish this widespread screening practice, it is:

assumed that blood pressures will be measured on *all* patients at every visit and by *all* subspecialties, including dermatologists, otolaryngologists, ophthalmologists, gynecologists, surgeons, etc. (Many do not now routinely do so.)

suggested that blood pressures be routinely measured in dentists' offices

urged that the recording of blood pressure be also added to all multiphasic screening schedules

recommended that the actual blood pressure measurements be performed by physicians, nurses, medical aides, laboratory technicians, secretaries, or even bookkeepers* (The continuous presence of paramedical personnel in a medical facility simplifies adequate training in the techniques of blood pressure measurement and permits periodic rechecking by qualified medical personnel.)

suggested by some experts that blood pressure also be measured in pharmacies, with prompt referral to a panel of local physicians

thought that perhaps in addition to the patients themselves, additional screening could be performed on all accompanying patient family members and visitors.

Such a comprehensive approach, combined with more careful follow-up during the usual type of incidental hypertension

---

*See page 55 for a discussion on the training of medical and paramedical personnel. See also Chapter 6 and the Appendix for forms and instructions.

screening now taking place in schools, industry, and the Armed Forces, would greatly reduce the proportion of undetected and untreated hypertensive subjects. A small number of specially funded community screening projects could then be established regionally in response to specific needs where adequate medical care is now unavailable or the local population is at a particularly high risk, i.e., inner city and black populations.*

In brief, current enthusiastic but as yet inchoate plans for a centralized, immediate, massive hypertension detection screening of the entire American population to be conducted largely by newly trained paramedical personnel in shopping centers, churches, and other public areas are ill-founded, premature, costly, unscientific, and inappropriate for our cultural patterns. It has not been demonstrated that government or industry can provide better health care at a lesser cost, no generally acceptable community model has been developed, and the requisite money and resources are not available for an alternative system. Therefore, high blood pressure control must be integrated into our present health care system. A workable manner to achieve this is described above.

The Technique of Blood Pressure Measurement

The value of any screening test such as blood pressure measurement may be evaluated by the following criteria:[8]

1. *Simplicity*—easy to administer and capable of use by paramedical and other personnel.
2. *Acceptability*—acceptable to the subjects to be screened.
3. *Accuracy*
4. *Cost*—expense of screening versus benefits to be obtained from the early detection of the disease.
5. *Precision* (repeatability)—consistent results in repeated trials.
6. *Sensitivity*—test is positive when the individual screened has the disease or abnormality under investigation.
7. *Specificity*—test is negative when the individual does not have the disease or abnormality under investigation.

Applying these standards to some of the newer techniques for blood pressure measurement (e.g., ultrasound kinearteriography) uncovers problems which tend to mitigate against their widespread use at this time.

It is likely, therefore, that hypertension screening will con-

---

*See Chapter 6 for information on the formation and operation of such hypertension clinics.

tinue to utilize the usual indirect auscultatory method. The auscultatory determination of blood pressure fulfills the criteria of simplicity and patient acceptability. And although it suffers from lack of accuracy, precision, sensitivity, and specificity, these drawbacks can be minimized by careful attention to the details of proper blood pressure measurements as well as to the common variations and pitfalls. It is particularly pertinent to review these techniques at this time since the ultimate responsibility for the training of medical and paramedical personnel must fall upon the physician.

The Korotkoff Sounds[9]

When the blood pressure cuff is rapidly increased to pressures greater than systolic pressure, distal arterial inflow and venous outflow cease. The pressure in the distal arterial segment decreases to approximately 50 mm Hg, and the venous pressure rises slightly. As the cuff pressure is slowly decreased, a series of sounds can be heard through the stethoscope applied over the brachial artery in the antecubital fossa:

> *Phase 1*—the first sounds heard consist of clear tapping sounds which gradually increase in intensity. Systolic pressure is read as the first regular tapping sound which appears during deflation of the cuff.
> *Phase 2*—during further deflation, a softer muffled sound or murmur replaces the clear tapping tones of phase 1.
> *Phase 3*—the reappearance of a sharper tone resembling the first phase but less well marked.
> *Phase 4*—a sudden change when the tapping sounds of phase 3 become muffled and have a soft blowing quality.
> *Phase 5*—the disappearance of all sounds.

Despite numerous investigations on the origin of the Korotkoff sounds, there is still no unanimity of opinion as to their source.[9] Some investigators favor vibration of the arterial wall. Others attribute the sounds to flow phenomena. The presence of both factors has been clearly demonstrated. It is probable that the tapping sound of phase 1 is secondary to oscillation of the arterial wall and is produced by sudden distention of the collapsed artery as a jet of blood surges under the cuff. The intensity is related to the forcefulness of the jet stream of blood. The murmur of phase 2 is probably caused by the turbulent flow of blood from the still narrowed artery beneath the cuff into the wider distal artery. The intensity of the murmur will depend upon the difference of pressure between the blood under the cuff and the arterial pressure distal to the cuff. Venous congestion in the forearm distal to the cuff may reduce the amplitude of the auscultatory sounds and result in an auscultatory gap (see below). Venous congestion can be minimized and the intensity of the sounds increased by (a) rapid inflation of the blood pressure cuff and (b) raising the arm and forearm for several seconds and inflating the cuff while the arm is elevated.

Criteria for systolic and diastolic blood pressures

As indicated, the first tap of phase 1 is read as systolic blood pressure, and has been shown to correspond very closely to direct intra-arterial measurements. There is still disagreement, however, with regard to indirect diastolic pressure. In 1967, a committee of the American Heart Association recommended using the onset of muffling (phase 4) as the diastolic pressure, and if there is a difference in cuff pressure between the point of muffling and cessation of sound (phase 5), both pressures should be reported.[10] One of the reasons for this decision is that phase 4 is less variable than phase 5 following exercise and in certain diseased states when an increased cardiac output is present, such as in aortic regurgitation, severe anemia, and thyrotoxicosis. In these conditions and in some individuals, presumably with a hyperkinetic circulation, there may be no fifth phase or disappearance of sound, i.e., Korotkoff sounds can be heard all the way down to zero on the sphygmomanometer.

Nevertheless, phase 5 (the disappearance of sound) is usually closer to the true diastolic pressure than is the beginning of phase 4.[9] Moreover, in our experience as well as that of others, there is far greater reproducibility in recording phase 5 within and between observers than with phase 4. Training of paramedical personnel is also facilitated by considering the complete disappearance of sound as the criterion for diastolic blood pressure. Since phase 5 depends on the presence or absence of sound, its determination is dependent only on the hearing acuity of the examiner, on the level of room noise, and on technique. The problem is further compounded by the fact that some persons lack a phase 4. Lastly, the great majority of physicians have traditionally considered diastolic pressure as the disappearance of sound. *For these reasons, we feel that phase 5 is the correct criterion for diastolic blood pressure.*

Measuring the blood pressure

 —The patient should be lying supine for several minutes, or comfortably seated and relaxed with forearm on a table at heart level.

 —The meniscus of the mercury manometer should be at zero when the cuff is deflated and the air vent at the top of the tube must be clean so that air easily enters and leaves the tube.

 —An aneroid manometer should be checked periodically against the mercury manometer by connecting both instruments to the same pressure source.

 —Prior to taking blood pressure, the location of the brachial artery should be determined by palpation for proper placement of the cuff and the stethoscope.

 —The deflated cuff should be applied snugly around the upper arm with its lower edge about one inch above the antecubital space; the bladder of the cuff should be over the brachial artery.

 —While the radial artery at the wrist is palpated with one hand, the cuff is rapidly inflated with the other hand to a pressure approximately 30 mm Hg higher than the disappearance of the radial pulse.

 —The stethoscope is placed without undue pressure over the brachial artery and the cuff is deflated at a rate of about 2 to 3 mm per second.

For accurate blood pressure recording, the cuff pressure must be evenly transmitted to the underlying artery, and this is determined by the width of the occluding cuff in relation to arm girth.[9] The usual commercially available cuff is approximately 12 cm wide and 22 cm long. In very obese or muscular arms the pressure in the standard cuff may not be adequately transmitted to the brachial artery, yielding falsely high readings; conversely, the use of the standard cuff may underestimate true blood pressure in children or in women with very slender arms. It is possible that applying the cuff to the forearm and auscultating over the radial artery may be more accurate in very obese subjects, but this is not proved. These errors may be reduced by careful placement of the cuff bladder directly over the brachial artery.

Errors in techniques and variations of blood pressure

At times during deflation of the cuff the sounds appear (phase 1), disappear (phase 2), and then reappear again. This phenomenon of disappearance of audible beats (called the *auscultatory gap*) is caused by congestion of the blood vessels distal to the cuff. If the cuff has not been initially inflated to above the true systolic pressure and an auscultatory gap is present, then the start of phase 3 may be improperly read as the systolic pressure. These inaccuracies can be prevented by palpation of the radial artery during *rapid* inflation of the cuff to 30 mm higher than the disappearance of the radial pulse *with the patient's arm held at least at heart level or higher* (see above). In this regard, if a recheck of the systolic pressure is desired while the cuff pressure is being lowered, the pressure must not be pumped up again above the systolic level. The cuff must be completely deflated between successive blood pressure readings for at least fifteen seconds to permit venous return to take place.

—Blood pressure varies from moment to moment and has a diurnal pattern, being lowest in the morning upon awakening and increasing until the early evening hours.
—Anxiety, apprehension, sudden loud noises, pain, cigarette smoking, exercise, and other factors may acutely alter the blood pressure.

For these reasons, blood pressure screening should be conducted, whenever possible, in quiet surroundings with the subject at ease and in the seated position. The time of day that the blood pressure is measured should be noted during initial screening.

In atrial fibrillation, the strength of each beat varies considerably. During deflation, only a few strong beats are heard, becoming more numerous as the cuff is further deflated. An estimate of systolic and diastolic pressure can be made by repeated determinations, with systole considered the average pressure at which most beats come through.

Pulsus alternans consists of regular, alternating strong and weak pulses, with the variation in systolic pressure between the alternate beats as much as 10 mm Hg. At the beginning of systole only the strong beats are heard. It is diagnostic of left ventricular failure. It must be distinguished from *pulsus bigeminus* resulting from extrasystoles after each regular beat; in this disorder the rhythm is not regular but consists of alternating beats of longer and shorter duration.

Some Factors That Influence Blood Pressure

As discussed in prior chapters, numerous studies have demonstrated a quantitative relationship between arterial pressure and mortality as well as cardiovascular risk over the entire range of arterial pressure, even within the range considered to be normal. (Nevertheless, it should be noted that prospective antihypertensive drug therapy studies have not yet established a clear-cut benefit for those with mild hypertension or for women with moderate hypertension.) Furthermore, epidemiological data indicate that this relationship between blood pressure and risk holds for both systolic and diastolic blood pressure in both men and women. Accordingly, finding the hypertensive is important, but complicating the search is the fact that blood pressure is a continuum; there is no precise dividing line between normal and elevated.

There are other complicating factors:

—Blood pressure is related to age and sex.[11,12]
—Blood pressure tends to be lower in females than in males early in life, with the reverse being true after age 55.
—In both sexes, diastolic pressure increases until about age 50 and then levels off, whereas systolic pressure is log-normally distributed, tending to rise more abruptly in later life; these phenomena are generally held to reflect increasing rigidity and decreased elasticity of the aorta and large arteries with the aging process.
—In addition to the increased prevalence of elevated arterial pressure in Blacks, any given level of hypertension for Blacks has a worse prognosis with regard to target organ damage and death.
—Recorded blood pressures tend to be successively lower when repeated during one session or during repeated examinations.

Comment has already been made regarding the moment-to-moment variation of blood pressure and the effects of emotional and sensory stimuli, such as apprehension or the surrounding environment. As noted by Pickering:[13] "One of the most tantalizing aspects of the study of arterial pressure is that the methods used for measurement affect the value we seek to measure.... Moreover, all the circumstances of measurement, the office, clinic, hospital ward or home, the doctor, nurse or technician, each provokes the orienting reflex or the defense reaction, part of which is cardiovascular and includes a rise of blood pressure." Clearly, then, many factors are involved in an individual's blood pressure.

Blood Pressure: When Should It Be Labeled "High"?

Several questions must be answered before we can begin to screen a population:

1. What should be the dividing line that delineates when blood pressure is "high"?
2. Is it systolic or diastolic, or the mean blood pressure?
3. Should the blood pressure be age and sex corrected?
4. Should we use different norms for Blacks and Caucasians?
5. Is a single blood pressure measurement sufficient for stratification, or are repeated measurements necessary?
6. How many individuals will be needlessly frightened and how many subjects with hypertension will be falsely reassured?

And there are related questions. For example:

1. Should only well-defined, high-risk populations be screened?
2. Do the risks, side effects, and inconvenience of a lifetime of drug therapy justify screening for mild hypertension in women?

These are thorny problems and there are no precise answers. The approach has to depend to a large extent upon the purpose of the individual screening program and the characteristics of the populations being screened. Two tentative proposals that address themselves to some of these questions have been made.

The Report of Inter-Society Commission for Heart Disease Resources[3] suggests the criteria for rescreening and referral of different population segments based on age and blood pressure levels as outlined in Figure 2. Mobile screening units are used primarily for initial case findings, whereas secondary screening and diagnostic evaluation are conducted in a fixed unit.

The preliminary Report of Task Force I of the Hypertension Information and Education Advisory Committee (1973), on the other hand, recommends a coarser screen "designed to identify the large majority of those with higher levels of blood pressure who... are at the greatest risk and are known to benefit by treatment." Their basic criteria of 160/95 mm Hg for younger subjects are those recommended by the World Health Organization.[14] It is recommended that each subject who has been identified as "possibly hypertensive" by the initial screen be further evaluated during a secondary screen on the basis of the average of three resting

FIGURE 2

BLOOD PRESSURE CRITERIA FOR RESCREENING AND REFERRAL

Adapted from Report of Inter-Society Commission for Heart Disease Resources: Guidelines for the detection, diagnosis, and management of hypertensive populations. Circulation *44*: A266 (Figure 1), 1971. (Revised August 1972.)

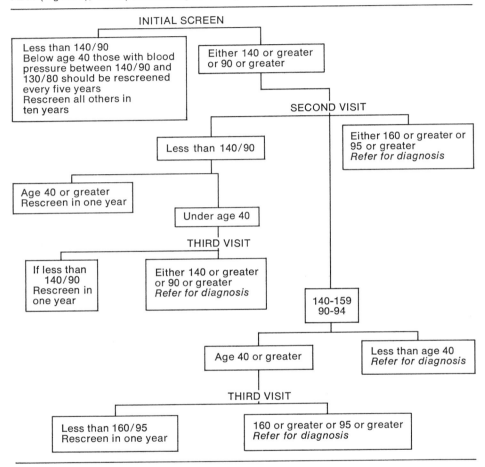

blood pressures and a brief, self-administered history designed to elicit a past or family history of hypertension, its complications, and risk factors. The critical blood pressures are shown in Figure 3.

If, as suggested in the first part of this chapter, most of the screening is conducted in presently available medical facilities, then the lower figure of 140/90 mm Hg might well be utilized since secondary screening and adequate follow-up could be conducted incrementally with no undue burden on our health care facilities.

As stressed previously, the planned community screening projects, with additional personnel and facilities, could then be reserved for specific longitudinal studies of scientific importance and for specific high-risk populations and regions.

FIGURE 3

BLOOD PRESSURE SCREENING AND REFERRAL

Adapted from Preliminary Report of Task Force I of the Hypertension Information and Education Advisory Committee and Inter-Agency Working Group, February 17, 1973 (draft).

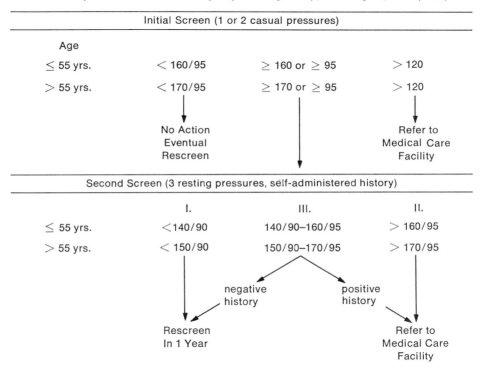

Initial Screen (1 or 2 casual pressures)			
Age			
≤ 55 yrs.	< 160/95	≥ 160 or ≥ 95	> 120
> 55 yrs.	< 170/95	≥ 170 or ≥ 95	> 120
	No Action Eventual Rescreen		Refer to Medical Care Facility

Second Screen (3 resting pressures, self-administered history)			
	I.	III.	II.
≤ 55 yrs.	<140/90	140/90–160/95	> 160/95
> 55 yrs.	< 150/90	150/90–170/95	> 170/95
		negative history positive history	
	Rescreen In 1 Year		Refer to Medical Care Facility

The Training of Medical and Paramedical Personnel*

Improving the conditions of blood pressure measurement

There is a serious question as to the comparability of blood pressure recordings by multiple observers in various surroundings. As discussed above, there is also a considerable within-patient variability in individual blood pressures from moment to moment.

*See also Chapter 6.

Some of the factors that influence blood pressure are:
- The time of the day
- Fear
- Physical discomfort
- Apprehension
- A full bladder
- Body position
- Surroundings
- Appearance, position, and attitude of person recording the measurement.

How can these problems be minimized? Some of these variables may be partially overcome by a reasonable attempt at standardization of the environment and circumstances. Thus, minimum criteria would suggest that the subject be seated comfortably in a quiet, pleasant environment for five minutes prior to the measurement of the blood pressure. These circumstances presumably could be satisfied in the home environment, in the physician's office, in a large mobile van, or in a segregated area of a waiting room—but *not* in a parking lot, a shopping center, a factory corridor, or a busy out-patient clinic.

Ideally, multiple blood pressure recordings should be obtained, even at the primary screen.[15] One epidemiological study showed differences between blood pressure readings at the beginning and at the end of the patient's visit to exceed 5 mm Hg diastolic in 33 percent and 10 mm Hg diastolic in 11 percent, and 10 mm Hg systolic in 27 percent of the population.[16] Interestingly enough, re-examination revealed that 27 percent of those patients whose *initial* diastolic pressures were greater than 95 mm Hg were lower than 90 mm Hg one year later. On the other hand, re-examination seldom reveals hypertension in subjects in whom even a single casual blood pressure reading is clearly within normal limits.[6,16] With all the operative variables, how do we proceed to improve the accuracy of screening?

Improving the accuracy of blood pressure measurement

The greatest single problem in hypertension screening is the competence of the observer in measuring blood pressure accurately. In specific tests, graduate nurses demonstrated standard deviations of up to 16 mm Hg systolic and 45 mm Hg diastolic in rereading the same prerecorded and filmed blood pressures.[17] Physicians performed no more reliably.[18] In an early phase of a current epidemiological survey in Los Angeles, three of our intensively trained interviewers were recording diastolic blood pressures in the home which were consistently up to 25 mm Hg higher than those measured a few days later in the clinic.

The following sources of observer error and variability are now well recognized (see Figure 4).[18]

a) *Hearing acuity.* Partial loss of hearing, hereditary or acquired, is often unknown until tested for. The Korotkoff sounds are low-energy acoustic phenomena, often just above the normal hearing threshold when monitored with a stethoscope. Thus, environmental noises may cause difficulties. The responsibility of telling a subject that he is hypertensive and the inexorable series of events set in motion by that decision suggests that tests of auditory acuity should be part of training programs for blood pressure observers.

b) *Observer bias.* There is often unconscious observer bias toward over- or under-reading the screening blood pressures. This is most evident when an arbitrary dividing line is established between normal and high blood pressure, e.g., 140/90 or 160/95 mm Hg, especially when too few observations are recorded. Thus, if an observer is participating in a screening program which has publicized the fact that "a large proportion of the population has undetected hypertension," this observer may exhibit a bias toward proving this hypothesis and over-read the screening pressures. Observer bias may be partially overcome by adequate prescreening discussion, and by follow-up of consistent differences between primary and secondary screening pressures. In this follow-up procedure, identification of individual observers by name or code on the initial screening form is required.

c) *Terminal digit preference.* Strong preference for certain terminal digits—particularly "0" and "5"—has been consistently demonstrated. Test films and tapes are available for group training, and there is evidence that analysis of the terminal digits in these test recordings with the individual observers and intensive training may be of help. Screening blood pressures are usually read to the closest even number, i.e., accuracy of 2 mm Hg.

d) *Differences in mental concentration and reaction time.* These are the most difficult differences to detect or to overcome. A training tape of the Korotkoff sounds, during which the observer blindly records the first, fourth, and fifth phases by depressing keys which control stopwatches has been developed by the London School of Hygiene.[19] This is said to improve reaction time and interpretation of the blood pressure sounds, and to reduce observer differences.

FIGURE 4

SOURCES OF OBSERVER ERROR AND VARIABILITY

Adapted from Rose GA, Holland WW, and Crowley EA: A sphygmomanometer for epidemiologists. The Lancet 1:297, 1964.

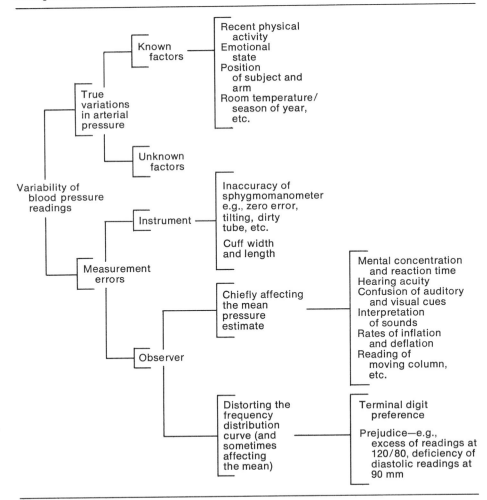

e) *Rates of inflation and deflation and proper placement of the cuff*. These points have been discussed previously. For a review, see page 47.

Unfortunately, an observer passing a test during the morning hours in a training office at a time when he or she is applying for a job, or is vitally interested in any one program, has little bearing on subsequent accuracy during the third hour of continuous blood pressure recording
—in the evening
—in a crowded supermarket
—one year later.

There are no simple devices or methods for detecting observer fatigue and error during a long-term screening program. We don't know how long it takes for ears to become painful because of stethoscopes continuously in place, or for hands to hurt from repeated cuff inflation. And whatever films, tapes, and other training devices are available depend solely upon comparing an untrained to a trained observer, and the human eye and ear rather than upon intra-arterial pressure measurements.

For all these reasons, we feel that an intensive period of training in proper techniques is mandatory to reduce technical and observer errors.

The training program

Following auditory testing, our observer training encompasses six two-hour sessions in groups of six to eight, conducted immediately prior to the actual field screening. The training units are as follows:

a) An introductory session is conducted by a physician explaining the importance of blood pressure, its public health implications, the Korotkoff sounds, and the sources of error. (The remainder of those training sessions are supervised by specially trained hypertension nurses.)

b) A training film[17] is viewed two times by the entire group, followed by a comparison of individual "results" emphasizing digit preference, observer variation, and possible sources of error, e.g., breath sounds, extraneous sounds, ausculatory gap, observer reaction time, etc. This training film is viewed again several sessions later, with comparison to initial readings, to demonstrate greater proficiency.

c) A training audio cassette* is played, explained, and demonstrated. The training cassette and a cassette recorder are both borrowed for additional practice at home.

d) Training with audio cassette and stopwatches[19] is carried out (see above) to improve reaction time and minimize observer differences. A second audio cassette is used for final testing prior to approval as a qualified participant in the screening program.

e) Starting with the second training session, and at all sessions thereafter, the students record blood pressures on each other with a standard sphygmomanometer and a stethoscope with double sets of earpieces so that two individuals are simultaneously measuring the blood pressure on a third subject. Trained hypertension nurses and aides circulate and act as the "second" observer. This two-observer stethoscope is easily made with a single end-piece (bell-diaphragm), a rubber "Y" tube of appropriate thickness, and two standard head pieces. In our opinion, this is the most valuable training. It serves to detect consistent over- or under-reading rapidly. It is also possible to detect repetitive individual errors in technique such as misapplication of the cuff or improper rate of deflation. It is useful for answering specific questions and for reinforcing important technical details.

In the final analyses, then, the best training is on a one-to-one basis by a highly trained and motivated individual. And with such training, one's confidence in hypertension screening activities improves.

Conclusions

Various epidemiological and a smaller number of prospective antihypertensive drug therapy studies have converged to demonstrate that hypertension is a major public health problem susceptible to amelioration. This has resulted in unprecedented publicity to the medical and nonmedical public and a good deal of enthusiastic activity with the goal of an immediate, massive, national program to detect subjects with hypertension and to treat them with a standard therapeutic regimen. For all the reasons cited, I believe that the suggested approach is unfeasible, premature, costly, unscientific, and inappropriate for our cultural and ethnic patterns. Instead, it is best achieved by the present system of health care, supplemented with a small number of specially funded

---

*"The Clinical Significance of the Sounds of Korotkoff," by Abe Ravin, M.D., University of Colorado School of Medicine (distributed by Merck Sharp & Dohme).

regional community screening projects established in response to specific community needs or for scientific purposes.

Whatever the screening approach, the number of variables involved in blood pressure determination should be minimized by careful and persistent training and assessment of both the personnel and techniques used in such programs. By such means, we can find the hypertensives. Without this essential first step, nothing else can happen.

References

1. Bechgaard P: The natural history of benign hypertension—one thousand hypertensive patients followed from 26 to 32 years. In: The Epidemiology of Hypertension. J Stamler, R Stamler, and TN Pullman, Editors. New York, Grune and Stratton, 1967, p. 357.

2. Frohlich ED, Emmott C, Hammarsten JE, Linehan WM, Pollack D, and Horsley AW: Evaluation of the initial care of hypertensive patients. JAMA *218*:1036, 1971.

*3. Report of Inter-Society Commission for Heart Disease Resources: Guidelines for the detection, diagnosis, and management of hypertensive populations. Circulation *44*:A263, 1971. (Revised August 1972.)

4. Stamler J: The national cooperative pooling project in the United States. In: Preventive Cardiology. G Tibblin, G Keys, and L Werko, Editors. New York, John Wiley and Sons, 1972, p. 43.

*5. Veterans Administration Cooperative Study Group on Antihypertensive Agents: Effects of treatment on morbidity in hypertension: II. Results in patients with diastolic blood pressure averaging 90 through 114 mm Hg. JAMA *213*:1143, 1970.

6. Wilber JA and Barrow JG: Hypertension—a community problem. Amer J Med *52*:653, 1972.

7. American Heart Association: Report of joint council/community program task force on hypertension. September 1971.

8. Cochrane AL and Holland WW: Validation of screening procedures. Brit Med Bull *27*:3, 1971.

9. Geddes LA: The Direct and Indirect Measurement of Blood Pressure. Chicago, Year Book Medical Publishers, 1970.

10. Kirkendall WM, Burton AC, Epstein FH, and Freis ED: Recommendations for human blood pressure determination by sphygmomanometers. Circulation *36*:980, 1967.

11. Miall WE and Oldham PD: The hereditary factor in arterial pressure in the general population. Clin Sci *17*:409, 1963.

12. Master AM, Dublin LT, and Marks HH: The normal blood pressure range and its clinical implications. JAMA *143*:1464, 1950.

13. Pickering J: High Blood Pressure. New York, Grune and Stratton, 2nd edition, 1968.

*See Appendix for complete study.

14. WHO Expert Committee on Arterial Hypertension and Ischaemic Heart Disease Report. WHO Tech Rep Ser *231*:1, 1962.
15. Varady PD and Maxwell MH: Cooperative study of renovascular hypertension. Assessment of statistically significant changes in blood pressure. JAMA *221*:365, 1972.
16. Aleksandrow D: Studies on the epidemiology of hypertension in Poland. In: The Epidemiology of Hypertension. J Stamler, R Stamler, and TN Pullman, Editors. New York, Grune and Stratton, 1967, p. 82.
17. Wilcox J: Observer factors in the measurement of blood pressure. Nurs Res *10*:4, 1961.
18. Rose GA, Holland WW, and Crowley EA: A sphygmomanometer for epidemiologists. The Lancet *1*:296, 1964.
19. Rose GA: Standardisation of observers in blood-pressure measurement. The Lancet *1*:673, 1965.

Chapter 4

Current Views on Diagnostic Evaluation

Ray W. Gifford, Jr., M.D.

Hypertension 4

Current Views on Diagnostic Evaluation

Ray W. Gifford, Jr., M.D.

Head, Department of Hypertension and Nephrology
Cleveland Clinic Foundation
Cleveland, Ohio

It is unfortunate but true that the diagnostic aspects of hypertension often receive more emphasis than the therapeutic aspects in medical schools, specialty training, and continuing education programs.

Evaluation of the patient should be looked upon as a prelude to rational therapy. Information gleaned from the diagnostic evaluation should determine the need for treatment, the type of treatment (e.g., dietary, drug, surgical), the urgency of initiating therapy, and should influence the selection of drugs when medical treatment is indicated.

Except in emergency situations when hypertension is severe or complications are impending or present, treatment should be withheld until the diagnostic work-up is complete. If the patient is already on therapy it is best to proceed with the history and physical examination before deciding about the advisability or even the necessity of stopping it.

For patients with mild and labile hypertension it is reasonable to defer evaluation until a series of measurements confirms that the average blood pressure is consistently and significantly elevated. The Hypertension Study Group of the Inter-Society Commission for Heart Disease Resources[1]* has proposed as a guideline that evaluation be carried out for persons less than 40 years of age who have blood pressures in excess of 140 mm Hg systolic

*See Appendix for complete report.

and/or 90 mm diastolic on at least two of three successive determinations on different days. For patients older than this, the limits were 160 mm Hg systolic and/or 95 mm diastolic on two of three successive readings. For children less than 15 years of age, limits should be reduced.

The evaluation as proposed in this chapter is not so formidable as to be impractical or objectionable for patients with borderline blood pressure that does not exceed the limits stated above. As a matter of fact, it is little more than a good routine history and physical examination with pertinent laboratory procedures that are advocated by many physicians for health maintenance for the general population.

The purposes of the diagnostic evaluation of the hypertensive patient are:

1. to determine the severity of hypertension and the presence or absence of damage to target organs (brain, heart, eye, kidney);
2. to identify any coexisting disease which might affect prognosis or alter the therapeutic approach to the patient;
3. to identify other risk factors for stroke or coronary disease that might also require appropriate treatment; and
4. to search for curable causes of hypertension which, if corrected, would obviate the need for lifelong medical therapy.

Because a nationwide screening program may deluge our health care delivery system with 15 million hypertensive patients who have never had their hypertension adequately evaluated or treated, it is obvious that the diagnostic work-up must be relevant, feasible, practical, and as brief and inexpensive as possible, consistent with accomplishing the objectives listed above. Consideration must be given to delegating to well-trained allied health professionals certain of the routine aspects of evaluation, always under close supervision of a physician.

History and Physical Examination

The most important part of evaluation is the history and physical examination. They can provide clues to the severity of hypertension, the presence of target organ involvement, and the presence of curable causes that cannot be obtained in any other way. Similarly, the absence of certain historical features or physical findings may make unnecessary an exhaustive search for some of the esoteric curable causes for hypertension. Moreover, a thorough history and physical examination may reveal unsuspected and unrelated disease which may alter the prognosis and the approach to therapy.

History

Most patients with essential hypertension have a family history of hypertension but the presence or absence of a family history alone does not clearly discriminate between primary and secondary hypertension. Many patients do not know for certain what their relatives' blood pressures are, or they have the mistaken impression that stroke or heart attack is prima facie evidence that their relative had hypertension and therefore, innocently, give a falsely positive response to this question. It is best to use the term "high blood pressure" when interrogating a patient about family members because many lay persons believe that hypertension is synonymous with nervousness and excitability.

A family history of premature death or disability from stroke or heart attack is particularly ominous, and the more family members so affected and the younger the age at which they were affected, the greater the concern for the patient.

A history of acute glomerulonephritis, proteinuria, hematuria, recurrent urinary tract infections, renal colic, or renal trauma should make the physician suspect that the hypertension may be due to chronic renal disease, especially when it can be established that the urinary tract symptoms or abnormalities (especially proteinuria) preceded the onset of hypertension.

It is important to ascertain as closely as possible the duration of hypertension. Abrupt onset of hypertension with rapid progression suggests renovascular disease. On the other hand, a long history of unusual lability of blood pressure that gradually progressed to sustained hypertension is characteristic of essential hypertension. Onset of sustained hypertension before the age of 25 years or after the age of 50 years should prompt the physician to suspect renovascular hypertension.

Women should be asked about the ingestion of estrogen preparations, especially oral contraceptive agents which can precipitate or aggravate hypertension. The relationship between the onset of hypertension and the initiation of estrogen therapy should be sought. It is entirely possible that oral contraceptive therapy is the most frequent cause of curable hypertension in women.

The smoking habits of the patient should be ascertained because cigarette smoking is one of the most potent risk factors in sudden death from coronary disease. The more cigarettes smoked per day, the greater the risk.

A history of headache, excessive perspiration, palpitations and/or tachycardia, tremor, unusual anxiety, and episodic pallor of the face, suggests pheochromocytoma especially when symptoms occur paroxysmally in combination and are accompanied by recent weight loss. Other historical clues to pheochromocytoma include paradoxical response to antihypertensive agents, hypertension during induction of anesthesia, and diabetes.

The patient should be questioned carefully for evidence of atherosclerotic complications including transient ischemic attacks, stroke, angina pectoris, myocardial infarction, or intermittent claudication—all of which compromise prognosis and often influence the choice of drugs.

Unusual exertional dyspnea, orthopnea, paroxysmal nocturnal dyspnea, and pedal edema provide evidence of heart failure which demands prompt reduction of blood pressure in most instances.

The patient should be queried about previous antihypertensive therapy, its effectiveness and side effects. Particularly discouraging is a history of intolerance to all antihypertensive drugs, especially when the alleged side effects are vague and much the same for each and every drug, bearing no relationship to their pharmacologic action. Patients who relate this type of history usually experience similar adverse effects from placebo and it is unlikely that an acceptable regimen can be established.

Physical examination

The physical examination of the hypertensive patient should be complete, with special attention to certain details that are particularly relevant to hypertensive cardiovascular disease.

Blood pressure measurement. It is unnecessary and impractical to take basal blood pressures for most patients. The blood pressure should be measured in both arms after the patient has been supine for at least five minutes. Most authorities use 5th Korotkoff phase (disappearance of sounds) as the diastolic pressure, although both the 4th (muffling of sounds) and 5th phase should be recorded if there is more than a 5 mm Hg disparity between the two. Blood pressure should also be measured after the patient has been standing for at least 60 seconds. If there is no significant disparity in blood pressure between the two arms in the supine position, it is unnecessary to measure it in both arms while the patient is standing. Any disparity of 10 mm Hg or more in systolic or diastolic blood pressure between the two arms should be confirmed by repeated measurements. If it is consistent, it most often signifies an occlusive atherosclerotic plaque in the subclavian artery, usually on the left. For follow-up purposes and evaluation of treatment, the blood pressure should always be taken in the arm that gives the highest reading. In order to minimize falsely high readings in patients with obese arms, a cuff that is longer and wider (thigh cuff) than the standard cuff should be used.

Blood pressure measurements in the thigh are cumbersome and difficult to make and are grossly inaccurate because of the large muscle mass in the thigh. They are not necessary if pulsations in the femoral arteries are unimpaired. Even a large cuff grossly overestimates blood pressure in the thigh, so that any reading equal to or less than the blood pressure recorded in the arm is abnormal and indicates obstructive disease in the aorta, iliac, or femoral or popliteal arteries proximally.

Optic fundus. The appearance of the retina is a more important and more reliable index to the severity and prognosis of hypertension than are casual blood pressure readings. Because it is important to visualize the retinal arterioles and veins peripherally, pupils should be dilated unless there is a contraindication to the use of a mydriatic agent. The severity of arteriolar constriction, either generalized or focal, correlates well with the level of diastolic blood pressure. Arteriolar sclerosis (increased light reflex manifested by silver or copper wire changes, A-V nicking, and compression) relates more to chronicity than to severity of hypertension. Retinal hemorrhages, "cotton-wool" exudates, and papilledema signify accelerated or "malignant" hypertension, which demands prompt and vigorous therapy and more extensive diagnostic studies. These retinal changes usually reflect the presence of necrotizing arteriolitis in the kidney and elsewhere. Angiospastic retinopathy is characterized by minimal sclerosis with severe focal and generalized constriction of arterioles with or without hemorrhages, exudates, or papilledema, and connotes recent onset or recent exacerbation of hypertension. On the other hand, minimal constriction with high grade sclerosis usually indicates mild hypertension of long standing. Minimal or no constriction and sclerosis of the retinal arterioles is reassuring because this usually means that hypertension is labile even though one or more casual readings may have been alarmingly high.

Microemboli in the retinal arterioles are easily visible and usually indicate that there is an ulcerated plaque in the internal carotid artery on the side of the microemboli. Usually, but by no means always, patients who have retinal microemboli also have symptoms of transient ischemic attacks.

Cardiac examination. The heart is frequently a target organ of hypertension. Left ventricular hypertrophy with ultimate dilatation and failure (hypertensive heart disease) and angina pectoris, coronary insufficiency, and myocardial infarction (atherosclerotic heart disease) are frequent cardiac complications of untreated hypertension. One of the earliest physical signs of cardiac involvement is the presence of a 4th heart sound (atrial gallop). This may be audible before there is any detectable cardiac enlargement. Physical signs of left ventricular hypertrophy include an exaggeration of the normal left ventricular thrust against the precordium, both in amplitude and duration. A 3rd heart sound (ventricular gallop) is usually a late manifestation of hypertensive heart disease and heralds the onset of left ventricular failure with moist rales in both lung bases. When the right heart also fails there is hepatomegaly, jugular venus distention, and pedal edema. When hypertension is severe a decrescendo diastolic murmur may appear in the second right interspace and along the left sternal border indicative of relative aortic insufficiency. If this murmur does not disappear when hypertension is successfully treated, the physician should suspect that it is due to intrinsic disease of the aortic valve or its ring.

The syndrome of the hyperdynamic circulation usually occurs in adolescents and young adults and is characterized by labile, predominantly systolic hypertension, resting tachycardia, a hyperactive precordium due to increase in left ventricular contractility, prominent pulsations in the carotid arteries, and a systolic "flow" murmur heard best along the left sternal border.

Examination of the peripheral arteries. Special attention should be given to examination of the peripheral vascular system, looking for evidence of occlusive disease, bruits, and aneurysms. The incidence of atherosclerotic occlusive arterial disease of the carotid-subclavian-vertebral systems and of the aorta-iliac-femoral systems is increased in hypertensives. Aneurysms, especially of the abdominal aorta, are more frequently found in hypertensive than in normotensive individuals and the prognosis is worse in hypertensives. Occlusive disease of the renal artery is sometimes the cause of hypertension. In addition to careful palpation of the peripheral arteries, the physician should listen for bruits over the carotid arteries in the neck, the subclavian arteries in the supraclavicular spaces, the abdominal aorta and renal arteries, and the femoral arteries in the groins. A diastolic component to an arterial bruit is usually indicative of a significant gradient, whereas systolic bruits may be present when there is intimal disease with little or no stenosis. Sometimes a thrill can be palpated at the bifurcation of the carotid artery or in the supraclavicular space. The presence of a thrill also indicates a high grade stenosis. Bruits arising from stenotic renal arteries are usually heard in the epigastrium and over the upper quadrant on the side of the lesion. It is sometimes difficult, if not impossible, to distinguish clinically between bruits that arise in the renal artery and those that arise from a stenotic celiac or superior mesenteric artery. A systolic bruit over the femoral artery in the groin signifies atherosclerotic disease of the aorta and/or the ipsilateral iliac artery but it does not necessarily indicate that is it occlusive.

Neurologic examination. While gross neurologic deficits from previous cerebral infarcts will be immediately apparent, it is surprising how often a slight hemiparesis with some incoordination and hyperreflexia will escape the notice of both the patient and physician unless it is carefully looked for.

Abdominal examination. Palpable enlargement of one or both kidneys should make the examiner suspect polycystic renal disease, hydronephrosis, or renal tumor.

General observations. Tremor, tachycardia, restlessness, and excessive perspiration can be manifestations of pheochromocytoma, the syndrome of hyperdynamic circulation, and renovascular hypertension as well as anxiety, hyperthyroidism, and chronic alcoholism. Truncal obesity, frontal baldness, prominent striae, and atrophy of the skin with spontaneous ecchymoses are clues to the diagnosis of Cushing's syndrome.

Laboratory and Roentgenographic Examination

The "routine" laboratory examinations which are desirable for nearly every hypertensive patient are listed in Table 1. These examinations are readily available, easy to perform, relatively inexpensive, and conform in general to the recommendations of the Hypertension Study Group of the Inter-Society Commission for Heart Disease Resources.[1] Determinations of serum cholesterol and triglycerides are important because hyperlipidemia is an additional risk factor for coronary disease. There is no evidence that treatment of hyperlipidemia is helpful for patients older than 65 years of age. The hemogram is an aid in evaluating the patient's general health status. Urinalysis and determinations of serum creatinine and/or BUN are included to assess the kidney as a target or inciting organ in hypertension. Roentgenogram of the chest and electrocardiogram are included to evaluate the heart as a target organ. Determination of blood sugar is included because of the relatively high frequency of diabetes among hypertensives and because diabetes is an additional risk factor for stroke and coronary disease, although admittedly there is no good evidence that control of diabetes will lessen this risk. The serum potassium is a good screening test for primary aldosteronism and, in addition, serves as a base line for subsequent diuretic therapy.

It is noted that peripheral vein renin assay (PVRA) is not included in the routine examinations suggested in Table 1. The PVRA is not a reliable screening test for renal artery disease and most patients with suppressed PVRA do not have primary aldosteronism. PVRA must always be related to sodium balance which is difficult in the ambulatory patient. Moreover, until there is confirmation of the prognostic and therapeutic implications of PVRA, it is premature to recommend this procedure for routine evaluation of the hypertensive patient.

The Search for Curable Causes

Procedures such as the intravenous urogram and tests for pheochromocytoma and primary aldosteronism, which are designed primarily to discover curable causes, have been intentionally omitted from the routine procedures listed in Table 1 because curable causes are so rare that it seems unreasonable to subject every patient to these examinations. Less than 6 percent of 5000 consecutive hypertensive patients first seen at the Cleveland Clinic in 1966-67 were found to have a curable cause for their hypertension.[2] This hardly warrants an exhaustive search in every patient. It seems more reasonable to limit the laboratory and x-ray procedures to those listed in Table 1 during the initial examination unless there are definite indications to proceed further (Table 2). More often than not there are clues in the history or physical examination that will prompt a more detailed investigation for one or more curable causes of hypertension. In the absence of these clues, the search is likely to be fruitless. If the hypertension does not respond satisfactorily to treatment, or if the patient cannot or will not tolerate effective doses of antihypertensive drugs, a more thorough and exhaustive "second diagnostic look" is then justified.

TABLE 1

**ROUTINE LABORATORY AND ROENTGENOGRAPHIC EXAMINATIONS
RECOMMENDED FOR EVALUATION OF HYPERTENSION**

Hemogram	Blood glucose (preferably 2 hr postprandial)
Routine urinalysis	BUN and/or serum creatinine
Serum potassium	Roentgenogram of chest
Serum cholesterol and triglycerides (for patients < 65 yrs of age)	Electrocardiogram

Pheochromocytoma

This rare chromaffin tumor almost always produces symptoms which should alert the physician to this diagnostic possibility. The indications for performing tests to rule out pheochromocytoma are listed in Table 2. Retrospective analyses indicate that the diagnosis of pheochromocytoma would seldom be missed if these criteria were observed.[3] When hypertension is sustained, the most reliable screening procedure for pheochromocytoma is determination of metanephrines and/or VMA (by paper chromotography) in a 24-hour urine collection. When hypertension is intermittent, indicating that the tumor may not be functioning continuously, a provocative test using either histamine or glucagon intravenously should be performed immediately before starting a 24-hour collection of urine for metanephrines and VMA to be certain that the tumor has been stimulated to secrete catecholamine.

Renovascular hypertension

This is probably the most frequent cause for potentially cura-

TABLE 2

**INDICATIONS FOR SPECIAL PROCEDURES FOR DIAGNOSIS
OF SOME CURABLE FORMS OF HYPERTENSION**

PHEOCHROMOCYTOMA

Symptomatic paroxysms of hypertension

Headache, tachycardia, palpitations, tremor

Excessive sweating, paroxysmal or continuous

Hypertensive retinopathy (Group 3 or 4 Keith-Wagener-Barker)

Unusual lability of blood pressure

Substandard weight or recent weight loss

Hypermetabolism without hyperthyroidism

Abnormal carbohydrate metabolism

Short history of hypertension ($<$ 2 years)

Pressor response to antipressor drugs or during induction of anesthesia

RENOVASCULAR HYPERTENSION

Indications for rapid sequence intravenous pyelogram

$<$ 30 yrs of age with diastolic $>$ 110 mm Hg

Diastolic $>$ 130 mm Hg at any age

Systolic and diastolic bruit in epigastrium or either upper quadrant

Accelerated hypertension (Group 3 or 4 Keith-Wagener-Barker)

History of hematuria, renal trauma, acute flank pain, or abrupt onset of hypertension

Hypertension resistant to medical treatment

Indications for renal angiography

Abnormal IVP with or without any of the above indications

PRIMARY ALDOSTERONISM

Serum $K^+ <$ 3.5 mEq/L with urinary $K^+ >$ 40 mEq/24 hrs
in the absence of diuretic therapy (at least 72 hrs)

COARCTATION OF AORTA

Absence or diminution in amplitude of femoral, popliteal,
and posterior tibial pulsations

Absence or decreased prominence of aortic knob and presence
of rib notching on roentgenogram of chest

CUSHING'S SYNDROME

Characteristic body habitus
(truncal obesity, moon facies, cervicodorsal hump, striae,
cutaneous atrophy with ecchymoses)

ble hypertension with the possible exception of oral contraceptive therapy in women. The most reliable examination to screen for renovascular hypertension is the rapid sequence urogram and the indications for this are listed in Table 2. Differences in renal size and/or appearance time of rapidly injected contrast medium are urographic clues that renovascular disease may be present. A significant disparity in size of kidneys as measured from pole to pole is at least .5 cm when the right is larger and at least 1.5 cm when the left is larger, because the left kidney is normally .5 cm longer than the right. When indications for renal angiography are definite, there is no objection to proceeding with this examination without a prior intravenous urogram or in spite of a normal intravenous urogram.

Once the diagnosis of renovascular disease is made by angiography, the pathophysiologic significance of the lesion must be determined by comparing renin activity in renal venous blood from the two kidneys after the patient has been salt deprived (500-mg sodium diet) and has received an oral diuretic for 48 hours. To be prognostically significant, the renal vein renin activity must be at least 1.5 times greater on the side of the lesion than on the opposite, uninvolved side. When renal artery lesions are bilateral, renal vein renin activity ratio is less reliable in predicting the outcome of operation but may indicate the more ischemic kidney.

Primary aldosteronism

This diagnosis can be ruled out by finding a normal serum potassium concentration (greater than 3.9 mEq/L) when the patient is consuming a diet unrestricted in sodium (at least 100 mEq daily). Diuretic-induced hypokalemia may persist for as long as 6 weeks after stopping therapy but diuretic-induced kaluresis rarely lasts longer than 48 hours after stopping therapy. Consequently, further investigation is indicated whenever inappropriate kaluresis (greater than 40 mEq/24 hours) accompanies hypokalemia (less than 3.5 mEq/L) provided that a diuretic has not been administered within the previous 72 hours. When serum potassium concentration is between 3.5 and 4 mEq/L or when urinary potassium excretion is less than 40 mEq/24 hours when the serum potassium is less than 3.5 mEq/L, extensive investigation for primary aldosteronism can be deferred in favor of repeating determinations of serum and urinary potassium concentrations at monthly intervals until a trend is established. During this period of observation it is preferable not to administer diuretic agents in order to avoid confusion in interpretation of the results.

The detailed investigation for primary aldosteronism requires hospitalization for at least 10 days, during which an attempt is made to demonstrate: (a) suppressed renin activity in peripheral venous blood before and during sodium deprivation and administration of a diuretic, and (b) elevated levels of urinary aldosterone which are not suppressed by high sodium intake and/or the administration of desoxycorticosterone.

Coarctation of the aorta

This congenital anomaly should be detected on physical examination and confirmed by roentgenogram of the chest (Table 2). Most surgeons do not require preoperative thoracic aortograms if findings are classical and the patient is less than 30 years of age. In older patients it is sometimes necessary to rule out atherosclerotic occlusive disease of the aortoiliac area as a cause for bilateral absence or diminution of the femoral pulses.

Cushing's syndrome

This syndrome should be suspected from characteristic appearance of the patient and the finding of striae, atrophy of the skin, and ecchymoses on physical examination. Determinations of urinary 17-ketosteroids and 17-hydroxycorticoids are only necessary for patients who have typical body habitus, skin changes, and facies (Table 2).

Hypertension and Renal Parenchymal Disease

When significant proteinuria, microhematuria, or azotemia occurs singly or in various combinations in the hypertensive patient, more detailed diagnostic studies are usually indicated to determine, if possible, whether the renal disease is the cause or the result of hypertension, whether it is potentially reversible, the severity of renal failure, and whether specific treatment for the renal disease is indicated. Estimation of creatinine clearance and quantitative urinary protein and appropriate roentgenographic visualization of the upper urinary tract are almost always indicated. If creatinine clearance is greater than 50 ml/min, the standard intravenous urogram will usually suffice to visualize the upper urinary tract; if creatinine clearance is between 15 and 50 ml/min, an infusion urogram will be necessary; if it is less than 15 ml/min, retrograde pyelography will probably be required. Other examinations which may be helpful include urine culture,

Addis count, cystoscopy, serum and urinary electrolytes, serum calcium, phosphorous and uric acid concentrations, and, in selected cases, renal biopsy.

Summary

The evaluation of the hypertensive patient should be considered a prelude to rational treatment and should be practical and economical yet relevant to stated objectives. More extensive diagnostic examinations should be reserved for patients who present special indications for these procedures or whose blood pressure cannot be controlled readily with medication.

References

*1. Report of Inter-Society Commission for Heart Disease Resources: Guidelines for the detection, diagnosis, and management of hypertensive populations. Circulation *44*:A263, 1971. (Revised August 1972.)

2. Gifford RW Jr: Evaluation of the hypertensive patient with emphasis on detecting curable causes. Milbank Mem Fund Q *47*:170, 1969.

3. Gifford RW Jr, Kvale WF, Maher FT, Roth GM, and Priestley J T: Clinical features, diagnosis and treatment of pheochromocytoma: A review of 76 cases. Mayo Clin Proc *39*:281, 1964.

*See Appendix for complete report.

Chapter 5

A Practical Guide to Medical Management

Ray W. Gifford, Jr., M.D.

Hypertension

5

A Practical Guide to Medical Management

Ray W. Gifford, Jr., M.D.

Head, Department of Hypertension and Nephrology
Cleveland Clinic Foundation
Cleveland, Ohio

I. Essential Hypertension

The treatment of essential hypertension is necessarily empiric and palliative because its cause and cure are unknown. Nevertheless, it has now been conclusively demonstrated that effective treatment will prevent or forestall cardiovascular complications and will prolong life for men with diastolic blood pressures greater than 104 mm Hg.[1-3]

It is reasonable to assume that women will derive similar benefit from antihypertensive therapy, and this was true in the small group of women in Hamilton's well-designed prospective study.[4]

It is a sad commentary, then, that less than 20 percent of the estimated 23 million hypertensive patients in this country are receiving adequate antihypertensive therapy,[5] especially when we have at our disposal a large number of antihypertensive agents which can control hypertension effectively for most patients.

For too long the medical profession and the public have regarded hypertension with unwarranted indifference. It is admittedly difficult to change attitudes and correct misconceptions that have existed for years, yet this is a necessary initial step in preventing premature death and disability from hypertensive cardiovascular disease.

Whom to Treat

With few exceptions, antihypertensive treatment is indicated for all patients whose average diastolic blood pressure (at least three measurements on separate days) is in excess of 104 mm Hg. The higher the blood pressure and the younger the patient, the more urgently treatment is indicated.

Many authorities would advocate treatment for patients with diastolic blood pressures between 90 and 105 mm Hg even though statistical proof of its efficacy in this range is lacking. In making the decision as to whether to treat patients with diastolic blood pressures between 90 and 105 mm Hg, the physician must consider other factors.

Caucasians tolerate hypertension better than Blacks do; women tolerate hypertension better than men do. The younger the patient and the higher the diastolic blood pressure within this range, the greater the indication for treatment. A family history of premature death from hypertension and/or atherosclerotic cardiovascular disease, and the presence of target organ involvement should weigh heavily in favor of treatment. The presence of diabetes and/or hyperlipoproteinemia should favor treatment of hypertension in this borderline range.

The emphasis on diastolic pressure as a determinant for therapy does not imply that systolic hypertension is unimportant. In fact, systolic blood pressure is as reliable as the diastolic in predicting cardiovascular morbidity and mortality.[6,7] However, it has not been established that treatment of systolic hypertension reduces morbidity and mortality if the diastolic blood pressure is normal. Similarly, the value of treating labile hypertension when the elevations of blood pressure are intermittent has not been adequately investigated.

In these borderline situations, the physician must weigh the potential risks of long-term drug therapy against the estimated risk of untreated hypertension. If drug treatment does not seem advisable, patients with borderline hypertension should be warned that their blood pressure may well increase and should be advised accordingly to have their blood pressure measured at regular intervals.

It is particularly important to emphasize to these patients that they cannot rely on symptoms to alert them to higher blood pressure since hypertension is notoriously an asymptomatic disease until complications occur.

Before the long-term effects of antihypertensive drugs and the sinister implications of untreated hypertension were known, there was a dictum that said "when in doubt, do not treat."

All of the evidence that has emerged in the last ten years regarding the safety and efficacy of long-term treatment and the ominous prognosis for even mild hypertension would favor a change in this dictum to: "when in doubt, treat."

While this chapter is primarily concerned with the treatment of essential (primary) hypertension, it should be understood that medical treatment of renovascular hypertension is usually effective and is sometimes preferable to surgical treatment.[8]

Hypertension associated with primary aldosteronism can also be managed with appropriate antihypertensive drugs. It is imprudent (and usually impossible) to manage hypertension secondary to pheochromocytoma with the usual antihypertensive agents.

Alpha and beta receptor blockade can control hypertension secondary to pheochromocytoma while the patient is being prepared for an operation or when an operation is not possible due to metastases. Coarctation of the aorta should be treated surgically.

Hypertension secondary to chronic renal parenchymal disease must be controlled with appropriate drugs (see section "Complicated Hypertension" on page 100).

When to Treat

In general, for the patient with mild or moderate uncomplicated hypertension I prefer to defer treatment until the patient has had an appropriate diagnostic evaluation* and has had his blood pressure recorded on at least three separate office visits.

It is unwise to defer the initiation of drug treatment when hypertension is severe (diastolic $>$125 mm Hg) and/or complications are present or impending. If the patient has retinal hemorrhages and/or exudates with or without papilledema (Keith-Wagener-Barker, Groups 3 and 4) it is sometimes advisable to initiate treatment with parenteral agents (see section "Hypertensive Crises" on page 104).

Usually it is advisable to draw blood for a serum potassium and a renin assay, when indicated, before starting emergency therapy because these are the two determinations which are most likely to be affected acutely by antihypertensive drugs.

Ancillary Measures

Antihypertensive drugs should be regarded as the most important facet of therapy and all other measures should be considered ancillary. For reasons that are not apparent, many physicians

*See Chapter 4 for techniques of diagnostic evaluation.

place undue emphasis on diet, smoking, and a change in "life-style" for the hypertensive to the exclusion of drug treatment.

It is preferable to emphasize and rely on antihypertensive drugs, and to interfere as little as possible with the patient's life-style.

Sedation. Sedation, once the keystone of antihypertensive therapy, is neither an integral nor desirable part of modern programs of treatment. Sedatives or tranquilizers are sometimes helpful in alleviating the side effects of specific antihypertensive drugs, especially during the initiation of treatment, but the objective is to construct a regimen with minimal or no side effects so that sedation will not be required for this purpose. Other indications for sedation are the same for hypertensive as for normotensive patients.

Diet. Because a diuretic should be incorporated in almost every antihypertensive regimen, it is no longer necessary to impose severe dietary sodium restriction for every hypertensive patient.

Even patients with congestive heart failure or oliguric renal failure can usually tolerate 2 grams of sodium in the daily diet if a diuretic is used. For patients who have normal cardiac and renal function, it is usually unnecessary to recommend any change in salt intake.

Dietary sodium restriction is annoying to many people and difficult to follow unless all meals are prepared at home. Admittedly some patients consume such large quantities of salt (>10 grams daily) that average doses of diuretics cannot prevent sodium retention and consequently their hypertension may not respond readily to the usual regimens. When this occurs, moderate curtailment of sodium in the diet will suffice.

Obesity should be corrected by appropriate reduction in calories. Contrary to a widespread misconception, weight reduction is not usually accompanied by a significant decrease in blood pressure, and is not a substitute for drug therapy. There are, however, other good medical reasons for control of obesity.

Limitation of dietary protein to 40 or 50 grams daily is indicated for hypertensive patients with advanced azotemia (serum creatinine>3 mg/100 ml). Appropriate dietary limitations in saturated fat, cholesterol, and sometimes carbohydrate are indicated for hypertensive patients less than 65 years of age who have abnormally high concentrations of serum cholesterol and/or triglycerides. Hyperlipidemia, like hypertension, is a potent risk factor for coronary diseases, and both should be treated.

Rest. Unless the hypertensive patient also has severe cardiac or renal disease, extra daily rest, more than that dictated by common sense, is not necessary in this era of effective antihypertensive therapy. It serves no useful purpose, and is objectionable to some patients for whom the daily rest period and the early-to-bed injunctions are constant reminders that they are ill, and often produces more mental turmoil, not less. Regular vacations and fostering of hobbies and avocations are especially recommended for the hypertensive patient.

Exercise. Exercise should not be restricted for the hypertensive patient so long as cardiac and renal functions are not impaired. For those who are accustomed to strenuous physical exercise such as tennis, handball, and swimming, these pursuits should be permitted as long as the patient engages in them often enough to maintain good physical condition. For other patients, milder forms of exercise such as golf, bowling, and walking should be encouraged.

Tobacco. Cigarette smoking should be prohibited because it is an important risk factor in sudden death from coronary disease. It makes little sense to treat one risk factor for coronary disease (hypertension) and ignore others (i.e., cigarette smoking, hyperlipidemia, physical inactivity) which are almost equally important. Except in a few susceptible individuals, smoking has only a temporary, if any, effect on blood pressure and hence prohibition of smoking is not a substitute for antihypertensive therapy. I permit cigar and pipe smoking, provided that the patient does not inhale.

Objectives of Therapy

The ultimate goal of antihypertensive therapy is prolongation of useful life by preventing cardiovascular complications. To accomplish this, the blood pressure must be reduced to normal levels or as nearly normal as possible. There is little, if any, virtue in prescribing medication that does not reduce blood pressure.

Antihypertensive Drugs

A knowledge of the pharmacology, potential side effects, and relative potency of the antihypertensive agents is essential if the physician is to design a regimen that is both effective and well tolerated.

In spite of the bewildering array of antihypertensive agents available, there are only three classes of drugs:

1. diuretics
2. direct vasodilators
3. sympathetic inhibitors

Oral diuretics

The diuretics, described in a convenient tabular form in Table 1, probably reduce blood pressure by decreasing plasma and extracellular volumes and by reducing sympathetic nervous activity which should ordinarily compensate for small decrements in plasma volume.[9]

The diuretics also prevent sodium and water retention often induced by the peripheral vasodilators and by the sympathetic inhibiting drugs, a phenomenon which explains the frequency with which apparent "resistance" (pseudoresistance) develops to the antihypertensive effect of nondiuretic agents when administered without a diuretic. When plasma volume is controlled by a diuretic, resistance to the antihypertensive effect of other agents seldom develops.

An oral diuretic alone satisfactorily controls blood pressure for at least a third of patients with mild hypertension. When more potent antihypertensive agents are needed, the concomitant administration of a diuretic often permits control of blood pressure with smaller doses of the nondiuretic agent. For these reasons, an oral diuretic should be included in almost every antihypertensive regimen. For patients with mild or moderate hypertension, treatment should be started with an oral diuretic alone.

The choice of diuretic is of little importance if renal function is normal and if adequate doses are given. If renal function is impaired, furosemide is preferred because it does not reduce glomerular filtration rate as do the other diuretics.

The sulfonamide diuretics (e.g., chlorothiazide) seem to be more potent as antihypertensive agents than the distal tubular diuretics (e.g., spironolactone) and they are less expensive. Unlike the distal tubular diuretics, the sulfonamides tend to cause hypokalemia, hyperuricemia, and hyperglycemia. These abnormalities do not ordinarily require cessation of therapy and, in many cases, do not require corrective measures.

TABLE 1
ORAL DIURETIC AGENTS USEFUL IN MANAGEMENT OF HYPERTENSION

DRUGS	TRADE NAME	TABLET SIZE (mg)	DAILY DOSE* (mg) USUAL	DAILY DOSE* (mg) MAXIMAL	CHARACTERISTIC SIDE EFFECTS (1)
Sulfonamide Derivatives Benzothiadiazines: Chlorothiazide	Diuril®	250-500	1000**	1500**	Serum electrolyte disturbances (usually asymptomatic): 1. BUN ⋏ 2. uric acid ⋏ 3. potassium ⋎ (supplement not usually necessary) 4. calcium ⋏ 5. glucose ⋏ Gastrointestinal irritation, weakness, dry mouth, bad taste, leukopenia, anemia, thrombocytopenia, purpura without thrombocytopenia, pancreatitis, skin rash, photosensitivity, temporary deafness in azotemia (furosemide, especially if given rapidly intravenously)
Hydrochlorothiazide	Hydrodiuril® Esidrix® Oretic®	25-50 25-50 25-50	100**	150**	
Hydroflumethiazide	Saluron®	50	100**	150**	
Bendroflumethiazide	Naturetin®	2.5-5	10	15	
Trichlormethiazide	Naqua® Metahydrin®	2-4 2-4	4	8	
Methyclothiazide	Enduron®	2.5-5	10	15	
Benzthiazide	Exna®	50	100**	150**	
Polythiazide	Renese®	1-2-4	2	8	
Cyclothiazide	Anhydron®	2	2	6	
Anthranilic Acid Derivative: Furosemide	Lasix®	40	80**	160***	
Phthalimidine Derivative: Chlorthalidone	Hygroton®	50-100	50	100	
Quinazoline Derivative: Quinethazone	Hydromox®	50	100-150**	150**	
Distal Tubular Diuretics Spironolactone	Aldactone®	25	100***	400***	Hyperkalemia, gynecomastia, drowsiness, mental confusion, hirsutism, irregular menses, rash, headache, diarrhea, ataxia
Triamterene	Dyrenium®	100	100	300**	Hyperkalemia, diarrhea, nausea, vomiting, weakness, dry mouth, headache, photosensitivity, rash

* Given once daily unless otherwise indicated
** Usually divided and given twice daily
*** Usually divided and given four times daily
(1) For a complete review of contraindications, side effects, and adverse reactions, consult the prescribing information provided by manufacturers.
NOTE: The usual and maximal doses listed above are those in use at the Cleveland Clinic and do not necessarily reflect the exact recommendations of the manufacturers.

We have found that furosemide must be given three or four times daily to achieve the same hypotensive effect as one or two tablets of a thiazide derivative, and this is a disadvantage because it decreases compliance with the regimen.

The usual dose of spironolactone to manage hypertension is 100-200 mg daily, making this drug significantly more expensive and less convenient than one or two tablets of a sulfonamide derivative.

We have found that the hypokalemia induced by sulfonamide derivatives is usually asymptomatic and of such a degree that it does not require special treatment for most patients. Unless the patient is also receiving a digitalis preparation, and/or has a severely diseased myocardium which would predispose to serious arrhythmias in the presence of hypokalemia, it is our practice to monitor serum potassium levels on a periodic basis.

If the serum potassium concentration falls below 2.5 mEq/L, we usually take specific steps to correct the hypokalemia. Profound hypokalemia frequently occurs in the immediate postoperative period or during acute illnesses characterized by anorexia, vomiting, or diarrhea in patients who are receiving a sulfonamide diuretic daily.

Since our approach to potassium supplementation is to provide amounts in excess of 80 mEq daily, we do not rely on diet alone. Nor do we rely on oral preparations of potassium chloride because we have found that patients do not tolerate them well and often refuse to take enough. In view of these problems, we have found that the most reliable method to correct significant hypokalemia is to add spironolactone to the regimen, usually in doses of 25 mg, four times daily.

Spironolactone or triamterene should be used cautiously and for only one or two days at a time in azotemic patients because of the very real possibility of inducing serious or even fatal hyperkalemia.

Asymptomatic, diuretic-induced hyperuricemia requires no treatment and should not constitute an indication for stopping the diuretic. If there is a history of gout or if gout develops, probenecid or allopurinol should be added to the regimen in doses large enough to keep the serum uric acid concentration below 8 mg/100 ml, and therapy with the antiuricemic agent should be continued indefinitely. The acute attack should be treated with appropriate medication.

Diabetes is not a contraindication to the use of a sulfonamide diuretic to manage hypertension. Usually the diuretic has no perceptible effect on the diabetes. If it does, appropriate changes should be made in the diet and/or the dosage of hypoglycemic agents. Very rarely, a sulfonamide diuretic will cause severe hyperglycemia ($>$400 mg/100 ml) within a few days after therapy has been started. Under these circumstances, it is best to substitute spironolactone for the sulfonamide preparation.

Diuretic-induced hypercalcemia has been observed by us in a few patients. Until more is known about this, it is our practice to substitute spironolactone for the sulfonamide derivative. We have found that some patients who exhibit hypercalcemia during diuretic therapy have parathyroid adenomas, including a few whose serum calcium returns to normal, at least temporarily, after treatment is discontinued.

Spironolactone, sometimes in large doses (i.e., 200-400 mg daily) and often with a sulfonamide diuretic and/or a sympathetic inhibiting drug, is especially indicated in hypertension associated with primary aldosteronism because it is a specific aldosterone antagonist.

Determinations of serum potassium, uric acid, two-hour postprandial glucose, and calcium should be made within six weeks after initiating therapy and should be repeated at least twice yearly for patients on chronic therapy with one of the sulfonamide diuretics.

Vasodilators

Hydralazine is the only agent presently available for oral use which reduces blood pressure by dilating arterioles, thereby decreasing peripheral resistance without interrupting sympathetic pathways. (See Table 2.) Drugs with similar action are under investigation. Diazoxide and sodium nitroprusside which are used intravenously for managing acute hypertensive crises are also direct vasodilators (see section "Hypertensive Crises" on page 104).

The administration of hydralazine causes an increase in sympathetic nervous activity when the carotid sinus reflex is activated by a decrease in blood pressure. This results in tachycardia, heart consciousness, and a rise in cardiac output and work which is annoying and can be potentially dangerous for patients with coronary disease or compromised myocardial reserve.

These cardiac effects can be prevented if the sympathetic nervous system is blocked by prior treatment with reserpine,

TABLE 2
VASODILATING DRUG FOR ORAL ADMINISTRATION
IN MANAGING HYPERTENSION

| DRUG | TRADE NAME | TABLET SIZE (mg) | DAILY DOSE (mg) | | CHARACTERISTIC SIDE EFFECTS (1) |
			USUAL	MAXIMAL	
Hydralazine hydrochloride	Apresoline®	10, 25, 50, 100	50*	300**	Headache, tachycardia, palpitations, fever, nausea, vomiting, flushing, exacerbation of angina or congestive heart failure, toxic psychosis, mesenchymal ("lupus-like") reaction

* Usually divided and given twice daily
** Usually divided and given four times daily
(1) For a complete review of contraindications, side effects, and adverse reactions, consult the Prescribing Information provided by manufacturer.
NOTE: The usual and maximal doses listed above are those in use at the Cleveland Clinic and do not necessarily reflect the exact recommendations of the manufacturer.

methyldopa, guanethidine, or propranolol.* Even pretreatment with an oral diuretic will partially prevent hydralazine-induced tachycardia. For this reason, we do not use hydralazine as the sole agent.

When used in combination with an oral diuretic (to prevent secondary fluid retention) and a sympathetic blocking agent, we find it useful in managing mild or moderate hypertension. It is our experience that hydralazine combined with an oral diuretic and propranolol* is useful in controlling severe hypertension.

Hydralazine reduces renal vascular resistance and tends to maintain or increase renal plasma flow, making it advantageous for the patient with renal failure.

If the daily dose of hydralazine does not exceed 300 mg, the advanced manifestations of a mesenchymal reaction or lupus-like syndrome ("hydralazine disease") are unlikely to occur.

Sympathetic inhibiting agents

Except for the diuretics, the most commonly used antihypertensive agents block sympathetic nervous activity at one or more sites. These agents are described in a convenient tabular form in Table 3.

Rauwolfia compounds. The popularity of these once widely used antihypertensive agents has waned since the advent of more effective and better tolerated drugs. They interfere with sympathetic activity in the brain and in the peripheral autonomic sys-

*Publisher's note. The Food and Drug Administration has approved the use of propranolol for the management of cardiac arrhythmias, hypertrophic subaortic stenosis, and pheochromocytoma. Its use for other purposes must be considered investigational at the time of this writing.

tem by depleting the sympathetic nerve endings of norepineph-rine.

Drowsiness, lethargy, and lassitude are frequent and poorly tolerated side effects, undoubtedly related to the effect of reser-pine on the central nervous system. Depression occurs in a signifi-cant number of patients.

If reserpine is to be used at all in the management of chronic hypertension, it should be used with a diuretic in patients with mild or moderate hypertension. Its bradycrotic effect is especially helpful for patients with symptomatic tachycardia and/or pal-pitations.

Therapy with rauwolfia compounds is not a contraindication to anesthesia for elective operations, provided the anesthesiologist is forewarned so that intraoperative fluid and blood replacement will be generous and prompt. Hypotension occurs only when the patient treated with a rauwolfia compound becomes depleted of plasma volume. Blood pressure will respond promptly to volume replacement and careful administration of norepinephrine or an-giotensin II, if necessary.

Ganglion blocking agents. These drugs block both the sym-pathetic and parasympathetic systems at the autonomic ganglia. Although they are among the most potent agents available, they are seldom used any more because parasympathetic blockage causes many annoying and disabling, but unnecessary, side effects, including blurred vision, dryness of mouth, constipation, urinary retention, and impotence. They should be used only in conjunc-tion with an oral diuretic for managing severe or malignant hyper-tension when guanethidine is ineffective or cannot be tolerated because of diarrhea.

Selective sympathetic inhibitor. Guanethidine interferes with release of norepinephrine at the sympathetic neuroeffector junction. It does not inhibit parasympathetic activity. It is the most potent antihypertensive agent available for oral use, and should be reserved for severe or resistant hypertension because it frequently causes annoying side effects, including diarrhea, ortho-static hypotension, and impotence or inability to ejaculate.

It is our opinion that guanethidine should always be used in conjunction with a diuretic. Usually it is also advisable to incorpo-rate methyldopa in the same regimen to reduce the dosage re-quirements for guanethidine, and to minimize the marked diurnal

TABLE 3
SYMPATHETIC INHIBITING DRUGS FOR ORAL ADMINISTRATION
IN MANAGING HYPERTENSION

DRUGS	TRADE NAME	TABLET SIZE (mg)	DAILY DOSE *(mg)	
			USUAL	MAXIMAL
Central & Peripheral Inhibition Rauwolfia Reserpine (Single Alkaloid)	Serpasil® Sandril® Reserpoid®	0.1-0.25	0.1	0.25
Whole Root	Raudixin®	50-100	100	300
Alseroxylon Fraction	Rauwiloid®	2	2	4
Ganglionic Blockade Pentolinium	Ansolysen®	20-40-100	40**	No limit***
Mecamylamine	Inversine®	2.5-10	5	No limit**
Blockade of Neuro-effector Transmission Guanethidine sulfate	Ismelin®	10-25	10	No limit
False Neurotransmitters Methyldopa	Aldomet®	250	500**	2000***
Pargyline	Eutonyl®	10-25	10	No limit
Receptor Blockade Beta Propranolol†	Inderal®	10-40	80**	320***
Alpha Phenoxybenzamine	Dibenzyline®	10	20**	80***

* Given once daily unless otherwise indicated
** Usually divided and given twice daily
*** Usually divided and given four times daily

† Publisher's note. The Food and Drug Administration has approved the use of propranolol for the management of cardiac arrhythmias, hypertrophic subaortic stenosis, and pheochromocytoma. Its use for other purposes must be considered investigational at the time of this writing.

NOTE: The usual and maximal doses listed above are those in use at the Cleveland Clinic and do not necessarily reflect the exact recommendations of the manufacturers.

CHARACTERISTIC SIDE EFFECTS (1)
Drowsiness, sedation, lassitude, nasal congestion, myalgia, edema, laxation, bradycardia, depression, gastric hyperacidity, nightmares, Parkinsonian rigidity
Orthostatic hypotension, dry mouth, blurred vision, constipation, urinary retention, impotence
Orthostatic hypotension (esp. in A.M.), exertional weakness, bradycardia, diarrhea, nasal congestion, impotence or loss of ejaculation or both
Orthostatic hypotension (rare), drowsiness, dry mouth, fever, nasal congestion, depression, abnormal liver function tests (with or without jaundice), positive direct Coombs test, usually without hemolytic anemia
Orthostatic hypotension, nausea, vomiting, insomnia, nervousness, impotence or loss of ejaculation or both, urinary retention, hypertensive crisis after ingestion of foods containing tyramine (certain cheeses, beers, wines, pickled herring, chicken livers)
Nausea, vomiting, light-headedness, depression, constipation or diarrhea, fever, rash, thrombocytopenia, congestive heart failure, aggravation of bronchial asthma or peripheral ischemia, hallucinations, masking of symptoms of hypoglycemia
Nasal congestion, miosis, orthostatic hypotension, tachycardia, inhibition of ejaculation, and gastrointestinal irritation

(1) For a complete review of contraindications, side effects, and adverse reactions, consult the prescribing information provided by manufacturers.

variations in blood pressure (lowest in the morning and highest in the late afternoon and evening) that occur frequently when large doses of guanethidine are necessary.

When these diurnal fluctuations of blood pressure are large, it is practically impossible to adjust the dose intelligently without knowledge of the blood pressures in the supine and standing positions, as measured by the patient or his family at home in the morning and evening.

Like reserpine, guanethidine depletes the sympathetic nerve endings of norepinephrine, but this is not a contraindication to anesthesia for elective operations if the anesthesiologist is forewarned (see similar comments about rauwolfia compounds on page 92).

Concomitant therapy with amphetamines, chlorpromazine, and especially tricyclic antidepressants will interfere with the antihypertensive action of guanethidine because these compounds prevent guanethidine from getting into the sympathetic nerve ending where it exerts its effect.

False neurotransmitters. It has been postulated that methyldopa and perhaps pargyline inhibit sympathetic nervous activity by formation of a false neurotransmitter which is a weaker substitute for norepinephrine. In the case of methyldopa, the false neurotransmitter is alpha methylnorepinephrine. In the case of pargyline, it is believed to be octopamine.

Methyldopa. When used by itself, methyldopa has a moderate antihypertensive activity which can be variable, depending on dose administered (varies between 500 mg and 3 grams) and absorption (varies between 26 and 74 percent from individual to individual). Its potency is enhanced, and its effect made more predictable when used with an oral diuretic. It should be used in the management of sustained moderate hypertension, or when the diuretic alone has not reduced the blood pressure to normal. It may be used to advantage in severe hypertension in combination with an oral diuretic and guanethidine.

Disadvantages of methyldopa include the expense and patient inconvenience when it must be given at the higher dosage levels. Preliminary results of an investigation to explore the feasibility and efficacy of a single morning dose are encouraging, but, because of excessive drowsiness from a large single dose, it would appear advisable to administer it at bedtime.[10]

Although 10 to 20 percent of patients receiving methyldopa develop a positive direct Coombs test, hemolytic anemia is rare. The Coombs test may remain positive for several months after stopping treatment. A positive direct Coombs test is not, therefore, a contraindication to continuing therapy with methyldopa. It is important clinically only when it causes difficulty in cross matching. It is our procedure to perform a blood hemoglobin concentration approximately every six months for patients receiving methyldopa.

Methyldopa should be discontinued if hemolytic anemia occurs. Other reasons for discontinuing the drug include fever in the absence of infection, jaundice, or abnormal liver function. Methyldopa is contraindicated in active hepatic disease and in persons known to be sensitive to the drug. It should be used with caution in patients with a history of liver disease or dysfunction.

Like hydralazine, methyldopa decreases renal vascular resistance and tends to maintain renal plasma flow, despite significant reductions in blood pressure. Methyldopa causes fluorescence in urine and plasma similar to that of catecholamines; therefore, spuriously high values could lead to an erroneous diagnosis of pheochromocytoma when the fluorescent technique is used.[11] Methyldopa does not interfere with determinations of urinary metanephrines and vanillylmandelic acid (VMA).

Pargyline. Pargyline is a nonhydrazine monoamine oxidase inhibitor whose antipressor potency rivals that of guanethidine. Like guanethidine, it has a prolonged effect so that it need be given only once daily, and it frequently produces orthostatic hypotension. Concomitant treatment with an oral diuretic usually enhances the response to pargyline. The maximal effect on blood pressure may not be realized for 7 to 14 days after initiation of therapy with, or increase in dosage of, pargyline and its effect may persist for comparable periods after therapy is discontinued. This long latent period must be considered in adjusting the dosage, or the cumulative effect of the drug can result in profound and prolonged orthostatic hypotension.

Ingestion of foods and beverages containing large amounts of tyramine (Table 3) may precipitate dangerous hypertensive crises by releasing increased stores of norepinephrine in patients taking pargyline. Methyldopa, guanethidine, antihistaminic agents, sympathomimetic drugs, and other types of monoamine oxidase inhibitors should not be prescribed for patients who are also receiving pargyline. Because of the dangers and inconvenience of these drug and food incompatibilities, and because the antipressor effect is not superior to that of guanethidine, pargyline, though effective, is seldom used.

Sympathetic receptor blockade. Sympathetic nervous activity can be reduced by blocking the receptors in the heart or blood vessels. Beta receptors in the heart mediate the increase in heart rate and myocardial contractility that characterizes sympathetic stimulation. Stimulation of beta receptors in the small blood vessels causes vasodilation, while stimulation of the alpha receptors in the blood vessels causes vasoconstriction.

Beta blockade. Propranolol is the only agent available in the United States which blocks the beta receptors in the heart and peripheral vessels.* In this manner it reduces cardiac rate and output, but increases peripheral resistance. The net effect on blood pressure is usually negligible unless the hypertension is primarily due to high cardiac output (e.g., hyperdynamic heart syndrome, hyperdynamic circulatory state, etc.) in which case it may have dramatic hypotensive effect.

It has been used successfully in England in large doses (up to 1600 mg daily) to control essential hypertension.[12] Some patients with essential hypertension have a delayed response to therapy with propranolol* because of a downward readjustment of peripheral resistance after a few months.[13]

Propranolol has been used to prevent the reflex tachycardia and increase in cardiac output induced by therapy with hydralazine.* It is superior to reserpine, methyldopa, or guanethidine in this role. Furthermore, hydralazine prevents the rise in peripheral resistance induced by propranolol. The combination of propranolol and hydralazine, usually with a diuretic, has been effective in managing moderate and severe hypertension. [14,15]

The use of propranolol as an antihypertensive drug is considered investigational by the Food and Drug Administration at the time of this writing. We feel that its use to control or prevent hydralazine-induced tachycardia can be construed as an accepted indication.*

Alpha blockade. Phenoxybenzamine and phentolamine block the alpha receptor in the blood vessel. Phentolamine is not well tolerated when given by mouth and its absorption is unpredict-

---

*Publisher's note. The Food and Drug Administration has approved the use of propranolol for the management of cardiac arrhythmias, hypertrophic subaortic stenosis, and pheochromocytoma. Its use for other purposes must be considered investigational at the time of this writing.

able. The only indication for phenoxybenzamine in the management of hypertension is to control hypertension secondary to pheochromocytoma before surgery or when metastases preclude surgery. It should be used in conjunction with propranolol for this purpose* so that both the cardiac and peripheral effects of excess circulating catecholamines will be blocked.

Phenoxybenzamine is not effective in managing essential hypertension, nor is it specifically indicated.

Choice of Drug Regimens

Uncomplicated hypertension. Some suggestions for regimens for management of uncomplicated hypertension of differing severity are listed in Table 4. When the diastolic blood pressure is less than 120 mm Hg, it is usually preferable to start treatment with an oral diuretic. If the blood pressure does not respond optimally after three to six weeks, a second drug, usually methyldopa, should be added. A third drug may be added or substituted for the second drug (always maintaining the diuretic in the regimen) if blood pressure is not adequately controlled after another three or four weeks.

When diastolic blood pressure exceeds 120 mm Hg, it is usually preferable to start treatment with an oral diuretic and a sympathetic inhibiting drug (either methyldopa or guanethidine) simultaneously. When the diastolic blood pressure exceeds 140

TABLE 4
SUGGESTED REGIMENS FOR UNCOMPLICATED HYPERTENSION

	Pretreatment Diastolic Blood Pressure (mm Hg)		
	<120	120-140	>140**
Initial	Oral Diuretic	Oral Diuretic and Methyldopa	Oral Diuretic, Methyldopa, and Guanethidine
Supplementary #1	Methyldopa or Reserpine	Guanethidine	Hydralazine
Supplementary #2	Hydralazine	Hydralazine	Propranolol*
Supplementary #3	Guanethidine or Propranolol*	Propranolol*	

**Parenteral therapy with reserpine or diazoxide often indicated to reduce blood pressure promptly.

*Publisher's note. The Food and Drug Administration has approved the use of propranolol for the management of cardiac arrhythmias, hypertrophic subaortic stenosis, and pheochromocytoma. Its use for other purposes must be considered investigational at the time of this writing.

mm Hg, therapy should be started with an oral diuretic, methyldopa, and guanethidine simultaneously. When complications are impending and/or there are hemorrhages, exudates, and papilledema in the retina, it is usually advisable to hospitalize the patient and administer a parenteral agent such as reserpine or diazoxide to get the blood pressure down promptly, and at the same time initiate the oral regimen.

Complicated hypertension. The presence of certain complications should influence the choice of drugs for the management of hypertension. Some suggestions for regimens in complicated hypertension are listed in Table 5.

TABLE 5
SUGGESTED DRUGS FOR COMPLICATED HYPERTENSION

COMPLICATION	PREFERRED DRUGS	DRUGS TO BE USED WITH EXTRA CAUTION WHEN NECESSARY
Congestive heart failure	Oral diuretic Methyldopa Guanethidine	Hydralazine Propranolol*
Azotemia (Serum creatinine >3.0 mg/100 ml)	Furosemide Methyldopa Hydralazine Propranolol*	All other diuretics, especially distal tubular diuretics Guanethidine Ganglion blocking agents
Cerebrovascular insufficiency	Oral diuretic Methyldopa Hydralazine Propranolol*	Guanethidine Ganglion blocking agents Pargyline
Coronary insufficiency	Oral diuretic Methyldopa Propranolol*	Hydralazine (unless pretreated with propranolol*) Guanethidine Ganglion blocking agents Pargyline

*Publisher's note. The Food and Drug Administration has approved the use of propranolol for the management of cardiac arrhythmias, hypertrophic subaortic stenosis, and pheochromocytoma. Its use for other purposes must be considered investigational at the time of this writing.

Congestive heart failure. When hypertension is complicated by congestive heart failure without clinical evidence of coronary atherosclerosis, blood pressure should be reduced promptly, preferably by combination therapy with an oral diuretic and either methyldopa or guanethidine, depending upon the severity of the hypertension. Occasionally it is advantageous to use all three drugs in combination. Digitalis and a diet restricted in sodium are also indicated. Hydralazine may increase cardiac output and cardiac work, and is therefore not recommended for hypertensive patients with congestive heart failure. Propranolol, because it blocks sympathetic innervation of the heart, may aggravate or precipitate congestive heart failure in patients who have decreased myocardial reserve.*

Azotemia. When renal function is impaired, furosemide becomes the diuretic of choice because it does not depress glomerular filtration rate as do other diuretics, and it will usually induce diuresis in spite of severely impaired renal function if given in sufficiently large doses. Other diuretics are virtually ineffective when the glomerular filtration rate is less than 20 ml/min.

Methyldopa and hydralazine are particularly useful in managing hypertension in the presence of renal failure since both reduce renal plasma flow to a lesser extent than they reduce systemic blood pressure. Glomerular filtration rate is therefore preserved in spite of a falling blood pressure.

Reduction in blood pressure by guanethidine or ganglion blocking agents usually results in a proportional reduction in renal plasma flow. Nevertheless, it is sometimes necessary to use guanethidine in combination either with methyldopa or hydralazine to manage severe hypertension in azotemic patients.

Coronary and cerebral atherosclerosis. After acute myocardial or cerebral infarction, it is our practice to postpone antihypertensive treatment for four to six weeks unless hypertension is severe and is embarrassing myocardial function. Thereafter, regimens such as those already outlined are indicated. Treatment also is indicated for hypertension patients who have angina pectoris or cerebrovascular insufficiency without actual infarction of the myocardium or brain.

Hydralazine should be used with extra caution for patients with coronary disease because it sometimes aggravates coronary insufficiency, unless the beta receptors in the heart have been previously blocked by propranolol.* Similarly, ganglion-blocking drugs, guanethidine, and pargyline must be administered carefully to avoid sudden hypotension that might aggravate ischemia or precipitate infarction of the heart or brain.

The use of an oral diuretic alone or in combination with methyldopa is not likely to produce orthostatic hypotension, and is therefore indicated for patients who have myocardial or cerebral

*Publisher's note. The Food and Drug Administration has approved the use of propranolol for the management of cardiac arrhythmias, hypertrophic subaortic stenosis, and pheochromocytoma. Its use for other purposes must be considered investigational at the time of this writing.

ischemia. If hypertension cannot be adequately controlled on combination therapy with a diuretic and methyldopa, guanethidine should be added cautiously in small doses. We have found that it is sometimes helpful to initiate long-term treatment with anticoagulants before we attempt to reduce blood pressure for patients with transient ischemic attacks.

Labile hypertension. It is known that labile hypertension is often the forerunner of sustained essential hypertension, yet there is no evidence that treatment in the labile phase will favorably alter the natural history. Often patients with labile hypertension are young and have elevated cardiac output (hyperdynamic heart syndrome, hyperkinetic circulatory state, etc.). If the physician elects to treat labile hypertension, consideration should be given to the use of propranolol,* either by itself or in combination with a diuretic, because propranolol,* by reducing cardiac output, specifically corrects the hemodynamic abnormality that is present in many of these patients.[16]

Sometimes an oral diuretic alone is effective, and if it isn't, a second drug may be added to the regimen. While treatment of labile hypertension is optional, it is mandatory that patients be followed closely to detect at an early stage any progression of the hypertension (see section "Whom to Treat" on page 83).

Systolic hypertension. The value of medical treatment for the systolic hypertension that occurs frequently in elderly persons has not been established. As long as the diastolic blood pressure does not exceed 90 mm Hg, and the systolic blood pressure does not exceed 180 mm Hg, treatment is probably unnecessary, unless congestive heart failure is present. When the systolic blood pressure is consistently higher than 180 mm Hg, and especially when it exceeds 200 mm Hg, an effort to reduce the systolic levels by specific measures is probably justified if for no other reason than to reduce cardiac work.

One of the oral diuretics is frequently the only drug needed to achieve our clinical objective of a reduction of systolic pressure to levels between 150 and 170 mm Hg. Since elderly patients tolerate reserpine and guanethidine poorly, it is our approach to add methyldopa to the regimen, if necessary. We use a starting dose of 250 mg once or twice daily, gradually increasing to 250 mg four times daily as needed.

*Publisher's note. The Food and Drug Administration has approved the use of propranolol for the management of cardiac arrhythmias, hypertrophic subaortic stenosis, and pheochromocytoma. Its use for other purposes must be considered investigational at the time of this writing.

Side effects. The pharmacologic side effects of antihypertensive drugs cannot be ignored for, though not often serious, they can be so annoying that they limit the doses of drugs the patient will accept, or they lead to abandonment of an otherwise effective regimen.

Anticipation of side effects based on pre-existing symptoms or coexisting disease which may be entirely unrelated to the hypertension should influence the choice of drugs. Pertinent examples are listed in Table 6.

TABLE 6

SYMPTOMS OR CONDITIONS UNRELATED TO HYPERTENSIVE CARDIOVASCULAR DISEASE THAT MAY INFLUENCE THE CHOICE OF ANTIHYPERTENSIVE AGENTS

SYMPTOM OR CONDITION	DRUGS THAT MAY AGGRAVATE THE SYMPTOM OR CONDITION
Depression	Rauwolfia compounds
Anxiety-tension state, insomnia, or both	Pargyline
Palpitations and heart consciousness ("cardiac neurosis")	Hydralazine
Tension or migraine headache	Hydralazine
Diarrhea	Guanethidine Rauwolfia compounds
Postural dizziness	Guanethidine Ganglion-blocking agents Pargyline
Hepatic dysfunction	Methyldopa Pargyline
Gout	Sulfonamide diuretics

Some Secrets to Success in the Treatment of Hypertension

1. Know the drugs and learn to combine them to achieve maximal hypotensive potency with minimal side effects.
2. Include a diuretic in every regimen.
3. Except in severe hypertension, do not start treatment with combination therapy because many patients with mild hypertension will respond satisfactorily to a diuretic alone, making another ingredient unnecessary.
4. Keep the regimen as simple and inexpensive as possible, compatible with good control of blood pressure.

5. Use as few tablets and space doses as far apart as possible.
6. Inform the patient at the outset about the risks of untreated hypertension and the benefits of treatment. Encourage him to endure those side effects which can't be eliminated by appropriate changes in the regimen.
7. Advise and encourage most patients to take their blood pressure at home.*
8. Resist attempts of the patient to stop treatment. With rare exceptions, treatment must be lifelong, and it is best for physician and patient to understand this from the outset.
9. Establish an automatic follow-up on all hypertensive patients who cancel or fail to keep appointments for their regular office visits.
10. Do not be misled by neurotic symptoms which some patients want to attribute to antihypertensive therapy.

II. Hypertensive Crises

Most of the antihypertensive drugs that are used orally are also available for parenteral administration to manage various types of hypertensive crises. These drugs are listed in Table 7. The intravenous administration of either ethacrynic acid (50-100 mg) or furosemide (40-120 mg) is usually advisable to enhance and prolong the action of the antihypertensive agent and to prevent secondary fluid and sodium retention. This is particularly true in hypertensive crises associated with acute left ventricular failure, eclampsia, and acute or chronic renal disease.

In managing hypertensive crises, the rapidity of onset and duration of action of the drug as well as antihypertensive potency should match the urgency and severity of the crisis. For instance, prompt and rapid reduction of blood pressure is indicated for patients with hypertensive encephalopathy, eclampsia, pheochromocytoma, dissecting aneurysm, acute left ventricular failure, and hypertensive crises associated with sudden catecholamine release resulting from interaction between an indirect acting sympathomimetic amine and a monoamine oxidase inhibitor.

More gradual and less drastic reduction in blood pressure is indicated for patients whose hypertension is associated with acute coronary insufficiency or acute brain stem ischemia.

Frequently it is desirable to maintain the blood pressure at low normotensive or even modestly hypotensive levels for patients

---

*See page 147 in the Appendix for an instructional aid for the home measurement of blood pressure.

TABLE 7
**DRUGS AVAILABLE FOR PARENTERAL ADMINISTRATION IN THE
TREATMENT OF HYPERTENSIVE EMERGENCIES**

PREPARATION	METHOD OF ADMINISTRATION AND DOSE			ONSET OF ACTION
	I.M.‡ (mg)	INTERMITTENT I.V. (mg)	CONTINUOUS I.V. (mg/L)	
Direct Vasodilators Hydralazine (Apresoline®)	10-60	20-40/20 ml*	50-100	I.M.: 30 min I.V.: 10 min
Diazoxide (Hyperstat®)	—	300 (rapidly)	—	3-5 min
Sodium nitroprusside	—	—	50-150	Instantaneous
Sympathetic Inhibitors Reserpine (Serpasil®)	1-5	—	—	2-3 hrs
Ganglion blocking agents Pentolinium (Ansolysen®)	1-25	5/20 ml*	50-150	I.M.: 30 min I.V.: 5-10 min
Trimethaphan (Arfonad®)	—	—	1000	5-10 min
Methyldopa (Aldomet® Ester)	—	250-500/100 ml†	—	4-6 hrs
Phentolamine** (Regitine®)	5-20	5-20 (rapidly)	100-500	Instantaneous

‡Start with smallest dose listed.
*Inject from syringe at rate of 1 ml/min until desired effect obtained.
†Infuse over period of 30-60 minutes.
**For pheochromocytoma and for crises associated with monoamine oxidase inhibition.

with dissecting aortic aneurysms or intracranial hemorrhage.

Sodium nitroprusside, diazoxide, trimethaphan, and phentolamine produce an abrupt depressor response within one to five minutes, while it may take two or three hours for reserpine (whether administered intravenously or intramuscularly) or methyldopa to have a significant depressor effect. Consequently, reserpine and methyldopa induce a more gradual reduction in blood pressure than do the other agents. Intermediate between these two extremes are hydralazine and pentolinium which will usually produce an appreciable reduction in blood pressure within 30 minutes following an intramuscular injection and within 10 minutes when given intravenously.

Route of Parenteral Administration

Sodium nitroprusside, diazoxide, trimethaphan, and methyldopa can only be administered intravenously. The others can be administered either intravenously or intramuscularly and, as mentioned in the preceding paragraph, the choice of the route affects the rapidity with which blood pressure is reduced by either hydralazine or pentolinium, but not by reserpine. Hence, there is no advantage to give reserpine intravenously. It is preferable to give phentolamine by intravenous injection because it is more rapidly and consistently effective than when given intramuscularly.

Diazoxide must be given very rapidly intravenously in a single bolus, within 15 seconds, otherwise avid binding by serum protein will inactivate the drug.[17] Phentolamine must also be injected rapidly as a single intravenous bolus.

Methyldopa should be administered by intravenous infusion over a period of 30 to 60 minutes. Because of their evanescent duration of action, sodium nitroprusside and trimethaphan must be given by continuous intravenous infusion, the rate of administration being governed by the blood pressure response. Both of these agents have a short duration of action and hence the blood pressure can be titrated to almost any level and, if excessive hypotension results, discontinuation of the infusion will usually be followed by a rise in blood pressure within a few seconds or minutes.

This is an advantage in managing hypertension associated with brain stem ischemia or intracranial hemorrhage where rapid and excessive reduction in blood pressure might aggravate the neurologic deficit. Hydralazine or pentolinium can be given as a single dose intravenously by injecting it slowly from a 20- or 50-ml syringe, or it may be administered in a continuous infusion. More details about dosage and administration are listed in Table 7. Sometimes it is advantageous to give the first dose intravenously from a syringe to obtain a prompt antipressor response, then maintain the blood pressure at the desired level by continuous intravenous infusion or by intermittent intramuscular injections.

Usually the blood pressure can be controlled more smoothly by continuous intravenous infusions than by intermittent injections, whether intravenous or intramuscular. However, continuous intravenous infusions of potent antihypertensive agents must be so closely monitored by experienced personnel that it is almost mandatory to have the patient in an intensive care unit.

Though less desirable than intravenous infusions from the standpoint of ideal control of blood pressure, intermittent intramuscular injections are more practical than intravenous infusions when it is not possible to observe the patient closely in an intensive care unit. Furthermore, nurses can give intramuscular injections according to a schedule determined by the physician predicated on the blood pressure, whereas most hospitals require that intravenous injections from a syringe be given by physicians.

Diazoxide offers advantages which other agents do not have. Although it must be given intravenously from a syringe, it is promptly effective[18] and one injection often controls the blood pressure without wide fluctuations for periods up to 18 hours, hence close observation of the patient in an intensive care unit is not so critical as when continuous intravenous infusions are being administered.

Antihypertensive Drugs for Parenteral Administration

With the exception of diazoxide and sodium nitroprusside, all of the drugs used for parenteral administration in the management of hypertensive crises have been discussed in the previous section on management of essential hypertension. Therefore, the following remarks are brief and pertinent only to their parenteral administration. Preferred drugs and those to use with extra caution for selected hypertensive crises are listed in Table 8.

Hydralazine. For reasons that are not clear, hydralazine seems to be less effective in managing hypertensive encephalopathy complicating essential hypertension than it is in managing hypertensive encephalopathy complicating acute or chronic glomerulonephritis or eclampsia. Because of its cardiostimulatory effect, this agent should not be administered to patients with compromised myocardial reserve and/or coronary disease as it has the potential to aggravate or to precipitate congestive heart failure or coronary insufficiency. On the other hand, a decrease in blood pressure produced by hydralazine is not accompanied by a commensurate decrease in renal blood flow and, consequently, this agent is especially suited for managing hypertensive emergencies associated with renal insufficiency.

Diazoxide. Like hydralazine, diazoxide is a direct vasodilating drug which causes an increase in cardiac output and rate but does not compromise renal blood flow. Its effect on the blood pressure is so profound that the net result is usually a decrease in cardiac work; therefore it can be administered to patients with decreased myocardial reserve. It can also be given safely to patients with renal insufficiency. In spite of the fact that it is related chemically to chlorothiazide, it causes sodium retention and therefore it is usually advantageous to administer a diuretic with it, especially when patients are edematous, either from cardiac or renal failure. The abrupt decrease in blood pressure could conceivably be detrimental to patients with cerebrovascular or coronary insufficiency. A frequent adverse effect is hyperglycemia which has not been a deterrent to its use for short periods to control hypertensive emergencies, even in diabetic patients. Other side effects are uncommon and include nausea, vomiting, rash, fever, leukopenia, flushing, and sweating.

Sodium nitroprusside. Sodium nitroprusside is the most rapidly and consistently effective agent presently available for managing acute hypertensive crises.[19] It is effective in the small percentage of patients whose hypertension does not respond to diazoxide. Like hydralazine, it is a direct vasodilating agent but it does not increase cardiac output unless heart failure is present, in which case it improves cardiac function.[20] Because of the precipitous fall in blood pressure that it causes, it should be used cautiously in patients with overt cerebrovascular and/or coronary insufficiency. The nitroprusside ion is converted to thiocyanate and serum levels of thiocyanate should be determined every other day if the infusion must be continued for longer than 72 hours. The infusion should be discontinued if the serum concentration of thiocyanate exceeds 12 mg/100 ml to avoid acute toxicity manifested by psychosis and a confusional state. Other side effects include nausea, vomiting, retching, twitching, apprehension, and sweating when blood pressure is reduced too rapidly. Sodium nitroprusside is not available commercially, but solutions for intravenous injections can easily be prepared by any qualified pharmacist.

Reserpine. In parenteral doses large enough to reduce blood pressure, reserpine causes profound somnolence in most patients and this is a major deterrent to its use in hypertensive encephalopathy, intracranial hemorrhage, and head injuries, because it interferes with clinical assessment of the sensorium which is so important in evaluating the progress of these patients. The delayed onset of antihypertensive action of reserpine is not desirable when a true emergency exists. Moreover, repetition of doses at intervals of less than three hours can lead to a cumulative effect and profound hypotension.

TABLE 8

**PREFERRED DRUGS FOR PARENTERAL ADMINISTRATION
IN THE MANAGEMENT OF SELECTED HYPERTENSIVE CRISES**

HYPERTENSIVE EMERGENCY	PREFERRED DRUGS	DRUGS TO AVOID OR USE WITH EXTRA CAUTION
Hypertensive encephalopathy	Diazoxide Sodium nitroprusside Pentolinium Trimethaphan	Reserpine Methyldopate
Severe hypertension associated with acute or chronic glomerulonephritis	Diazoxide Hydralazine Methyldopate Sodium nitroprusside	Pentolinium Trimethaphan
Eclampsia and pre-eclampsia	Hydralazine Reserpine Methyldopate	Pentolinium Trimethaphan
Head injuries	Pentolinium Trimethaphan Hydralazine Sodium nitroprusside	Reserpine Methyldopate
Severe body burns	Diazoxide Reserpine Pentolinium Trimethaphan Sodium nitroprusside	
Pheochromocytoma and MAO inhibition	Phentolamine Sodium nitroprusside	All others
Acute coronary insufficiency	Reserpine Methyldopate	Hydralazine Diazoxide
Acute brain stem ischemia	Hydralazine Trimethaphan Sodium nitroprusside	Reserpine Methyldopate Diazoxide
Malignant hypertension	Diazoxide Reserpine Pentolinium Trimethaphan Sodium nitroprusside	
Acute left ventricular failure	Sodium nitroprusside Pentolinium Trimethaphan Diazoxide	Hydralazine
Intracranial hemorrhage	Sodium nitroprusside Pentolinium Trimethaphan Hydralazine	Reserpine Methyldopate
Dissecting or leaking aneurysm of aorta	Pentolinium Trimethaphan Reserpine Sodium nitroprusside	Hydralazine Diazoxide

Ganglion blocking agents. Because the antihypertensive effect of pentolinium and trimethaphan is primarily an orthostatic one, large doses must be employed to reduce blood pressure in supine patients. Elevation of the head of the bed augments their antipressor action. Inhibition of the parasympathetic system leads to atony of the bowel and bladder. Indwelling catheters are necessary for most men and many women receiving large doses of these agents for more than two or three days. The physician must be constantly vigilant for signs of paralytic ileus, and these drugs are not recommended in the immediate postoperative period for they almost always prolong the bowel and bladder paralysis that characterize this state. Neither of these drugs should be administered to pregnant women near term because of the danger of producing meconium ileus in the newborn. Inactivation of pupillary reflexes by ganglioplegic drugs can cause confusion in the neurologic evaluation of the patient with hypertensive encephalopathy or intracranial hemorrhage, but this is less of a problem than the somnolence induced by reserpine and methyldopa. When blood pressure is reduced by parenteral administration of a ganglion blocking agent, there is usually an accompanying commensurate acute decrease in glomerular filtration rate; thus, it is preferable to use another agent when renal insufficiency complicates the hypertensive crisis. The ganglion blocking drugs relax large veins and this makes them uniquely suited for managing hypertensive crises associated with congestive heart failure and elevated central venous pressure.

Methyldopa. When given intravenously, methyldopa can cause enough drowsiness to interfere with the evaluation of the patient's sensorium. Like reserpine, methyldopa has a delayed onset of action. It is not as popular as reserpine because it has to be given by intravenous infusion and is less consistently effective than reserpine.

Phentolamine. The alpha receptor blocker phentolamine is specifically indicated for managing hypertensive crises associated with increased circulating catecholamines, whether from a pheochromocytoma or from sudden release of tissue catecholamine stores by certain drugs or foods containing tyramine in patients receiving monoamine oxidase inhibitors. Phentolamine is ineffective in managing hypertensive crises from other causes. The antipressor effect of a single intravenous injection of phentolamine is short-lived, usually lasting less than 15 minutes; consequently, it is desirable to administer phentolamine by intravenous infusion (Table 7) after the blood pressure has been controlled initially by a rapid intravenous injection from a syringe. Side effects include hypotension, tachycardia, cardiac arrhythmias, weakness, dizziness, flushing, nasal congestion, nausea, vomiting, and diarrhea.

The Role of Oral Antihypertensive Drugs

In any hypertensive crisis it is desirable to initiate treatment with appropriate oral antihypertensive agents as soon as the patient can tolerate them so that the inconvenience of parenteral therapy will not be unduly prolonged.

References

*1. Veterans Administration Cooperative Study Group on Antihypertensive Agents: Effects of treatment on morbidity in hypertension: I. Results in patients with diastolic blood pressures averaging 115 through 129 mm Hg. JAMA *202*:1028, 1967.

*2. Veterans Administration Cooperative Study Group on Antihypertensive Agents: Effects of treatment on morbidity in hypertension: II. Results in patients with diastolic blood pressure averaging 90 through 114 mm Hg. JAMA *213*:1143, 1970.

*3. Veterans Administration Cooperative Study Group on Antihypertensive Agents: Effects of treatment on morbidity in hypertension: III. Influence of age, diastolic pressure, and prior cardiovascular disease; further analysis of side effects. Circulation *45*:991, 1972.

 4. Hamilton M, Thompson EN, and Wisniewski TKM: The role of blood-pressure control in preventing complications of hypertension. The Lancet *1*:235, 1964.

*5. Report of Inter-Society Commission for Heart Disease Resources: Guidelines for the detection, diagnosis, and management of hypertensive populations. Circulation *44*:A263, 1971. (Revised August 1972.)

 6. Kannel WB, Castelli WP, McNamara PM, and Sorlie P: The Framingham Study: Some factors affecting morbidity and mortality in hypertension. Milbank Mem Fund Q *47*:116, 1969.

 7. Gubner RS: Systolic hypertension: A pathogenetic entity. Significance in therapeutic considerations. Am J Cardiol *9*:773, 1962.

 8. Gifford RW Jr: Renovascular hypertension—when to operate, when to treat medically. Postgrad Med *52*:110, 1972.

 9. Tarazi RC: Diuretic drugs: mechanisms of antihypertensive action. In: Hahnemann Symposium on Hypertension. New York, Grune and Stratton, 1971 (in press).

10. Jain AK, Ryan JR, and McMahon FG: The effect of single morning doses of alpha methyldopa on blood pressure. Clin Path and Thera *14*:137, 1973.

11. Gifford RW Jr and Tween DC: Spurious elevation of urinary catecholamines during therapy with alpha-methyl-dopa. JAMA *182*:493, 1962.

12. Prichard BNC and Gillam PMS: Treatment of hypertension with propranolol. Br Med J *1*:7, 1969.

*See Appendix for complete study.

13. Tarazi RC and Dustan HP: Beta adrenergic blockade in hypertension; practical and theoretical implications of long-term hemodynamic variations. Am J Cardiol *29*:633, 1972.
14. Hansson L, Olander R, Aberg H, Malmcrona R, and Westerlund A: Treatment of hypertension with propranolol and hydralazine. Acta Med Scand *190*:531, 1971.
15. Zacest R, Gilmore E, and Koch-Weser J: Treatment of essential hypertension with combined vasodilation and beta-adrenergic blockade. N Engl J Med *286*:618, 1972.
16. Frohlich ED, Tarazi RC, and Dustan HP: Hyperdynamic β-adrenergic circulatory state. Arch Intern Med *123*:1, 1969.
17. Seller EM and Koch-Weser J: Protein binding and vascular activity of diazoxide. N Engl J Med *281*:1141, 1969.
18. Miller WE, Gifford RW Jr, Humphrey DC, and Vidt DG: Management of severe hypertension with intravenous injections of diazoxide. Amer J Cardiol *24*:870, 1969.
19. Gifford RW Jr: Treatment of hypertensive emergencies including use of sodium nitroprusside. Mayo Clin Proc *34*:387, 1959.
20. Franciosa JA, Guiha NH, Limas CJ, Rodriguera E, and Cohn JN: Improved left ventricular function during nitroprusside infusion in acute myocardial infarction. The Lancet *1*:650, 1972.

Chapter 6

New Techniques for Improving Patient Compliance

Frank A. Finnerty, Jr., M.D.

Hypertension

6

New Techniques for Improving Patient Compliance*

Frank A. Finnerty, Jr., M.D.

Professor of Medicine
Georgetown University Medical Division
District of Columbia General Hospital
Washington, D.C.

A Brief Overview of the Problem

Detecting hypertension is easy. Recording blood pressure is painless and takes less than one minute. Medical treatment is readily available and relatively simple to administer. And there is ample proof that effective therapy can reduce morbidity and mortality.[1]

Yet, we physicians have not identified the more than 11 million Americans who have hypertension and don't know it. And we are not giving adequate treatment to about 80 percent of those we have identified.

How can this appalling situation exist? There are several reasons, and here are three of the most important:

1. Many physicians do not record blood pressure as a routine part of a patient visit.
2. Many physicians treat only those patients with the more severe elevations of blood pressure.
3. Most patients with hypertension are completely asymptomatic and resist taking medication unless they are truly motivated.

Recording Problems

Too many physicians do not include a blood pressure recording as a routine part of a patient visit. Indeed, some physicians, notably psychiatrists, dermatologists, and ophthalmologists, do not have a sphygmomanometer in active use.

*See Appendix for forms and instructions.

This state of affairs is in marked contrast to an ideal situation in which a blood pressure recording would be a routine part of a visit to physicians, dentists, or specialists in any medical facility.

The hypertension problem, regrettably, is not confined to office or clinic practice. A recent study of ours,[2] not yet published, revealed a significant problem in a nearby city hospital. A nurse from our study group recorded blood pressures in 1300 patients in the hospital, but not on the medical or obstetrical services.

She found that 400 patients (31 percent) had a blood pressure reading higher than 150/100 mm Hg. Reflecting the statistical experience outside a hospital setting, she found that 285 of these 400 patients (71 percent) did not know they were hypertensive. And she learned that only 8 percent were receiving drug therapy for their high blood pressures.

Treatment Problems

Many physicians agree that effective treatment of the most severe types of hypertension reduces morbidity and mortality, but they are not convinced that effective therapy can be beneficial for patients with less severe elevations of blood pressure.

The cavalier attitude that some physicians take regarding patients with moderate elevations of blood pressure was demonstrated by the recent studies of Dr. James A. Schoenberger and his colleagues dealing with an industrial population in Chicago.[3]

They found that 58.9 percent of newly identified hypertensive patients denied prior knowledge of the diagnosis, yet 90 percent of the women and 75 percent of the men had seen their doctors in the preceding two years.

The message embodied in the Veterans Administration Cooperative Studies* and other studies is that effective control of arterial blood pressure can significantly reduce morbidity and mortality. Apparently that message has not been effectively communicated. Indeed, Dr. Schoenberger found that a smaller percentage of hypertensive patients was being treated after publication of the Veterans Administration Cooperative Studies than before publication.

Another aspect of the treatment problem is that many university centers tend to place a higher priority on the diagnosis of unusual curable forms of hypertension and, perhaps, less than adequate emphasis on therapy. This emphasis on diagnosis has often led to the practice of routinely performing expensive and sophisticated tests on newly discovered hypertensives.

*See Appendix for complete studies.

In my experience, the time and expense of diagnostic work has often failed to reveal the causative factor, and has frequently delayed the start of effective therapy.

The American Heart Association notes that the prevalence of curable hypertension is so low in patients over 35 years of age that the cost and effort of an elaborate workup is not justified unless the physician has reason to suspect its presence.[4]

Patient Problems

Discovering that a person has hypertension and placing him on drug therapy is not enough—in and of itself. The benefits of therapy will not be realized—strokes, congestive heart failure, heart attacks, and renal failure will not be prevented or minimized —unless the patient remains under medical care and regularly takes his medication.

It has been my experience, both in private practice and in the clinic, that patients, particularly asymptomatic patients, will not remain under medical care and take medication unless they are properly motivated. And proper motivation can only result from a good doctor-patient relationship.

Recent experience with an inner city patient population has shown us that a well-trained, understanding, paramedical person can substitute for the doctor in this relationship. Once this relationship has been established, patients readily accept both education and motivation, and, fortunately, the paramedical person can devote the time required.

Our training and expertise as physicians have centered around the challenge of complicated diagnostic problems, or treating patients in emergency-crisis situations. The long-term, routine care of hypertensive patients does not have that same sense of urgency or satisfaction for us.

We have come to train and rely on nurses in the coronary intensive care unit. Now, we must also become aware of the value of such personnel in the routine follow-up care of hypertensive patients.

Once a physician has initially evaluated a hypertensive patient, placed him on a therapeutic regimen, and guided him to a control status, the patient can be monitored by a nurse or a health assistant working closely with the nurse. We have found that a nurse or health assistant is challenged by this assignment. They take great pride in carrying out duties in every detail, and easily establish a meaningful relationship which allows them to educate and motivate the patient to remain under long-term medical care.

Researching the Patient Problem

To gain an insight into the tremendous problem of patient noncompliance, a sociologist and I recently conducted a survey among patients who dropped out from hypertension clinics in an inner city.[5] Early in the research we learned that patients dropped out *not* because they were uneducated, *not* because they didn't care about their health, and *not* because they could not afford the medication.

Rather, these patients abandoned the clinic because they were treated like cattle, herded from one room to another, left waiting for hours, then examined by a different doctor on each visit.

Their major complaints centered around two points:

1. The amount of time they spent at the clinic.
2. The lack of a medical relationship at the clinic.

The average waiting time for the doctor's examination was 2.5 hours, and the average waiting time at the pharmacy after examination was another 1.8 hours. Since most of the patients used public transportation, travel time was considered as one more frustrating element of the problem.

In contrast to the long waiting time before and after the examination, the average time spent with the physician was only 7.5 minutes. This was often not enough time for the patient to have questions answered or to learn more about the disease, and obviously there was no opportunity to establish a good doctor-patient relationship. This unsatisfactory doctor-patient relationship was further weakened because typically the patient was examined by a different physician on each visit.

Applying the Research Results

To decrease the high "dropout rates," our group reorganized the hypertension clinic several years ago, using the patients' complaints as our guidelines. We had three major objectives:

1. Develop a personal relationship with the patient.
2. Provide comprehensive health care on a 24-hour basis.
3. Provide convenient services for the patient.

A specially trained nurse, assisted by paramedical personnel, directed the clinic under the supervision of a physician. Emphasis was placed on personalized care. The warm, personal atmosphere of our clinic was immediately apparent to the patient when the receptionists greeted him with a "Good morning, Mr. Allen."

First visit

After a few basic facts were obtained, e.g., age, address, telephone number, etc., the patient was sent to an interviewer who took the initial medical history. This interviewer, as with most of our paramedical personnel, has a high school education and was trained "on the job" to extract meaningful information from the patient.

Using special forms, a cardiovascular history was obtained in 15-20 minutes. If there were any questions regarding accuracy of information, or if there were communication problems, the nurse-director was consulted. The interviewer recorded the blood pressure at the beginning and the end of the interview.

Another paramedical person drew a blood sample for determinations of glucose, creatinine, and potassium. A urine sample was sent to the laboratory, a 12-lead electrocardiogram was taken by another paramedical person, then the patient was sent for a chest x-ray.

This initial visit usually took between 30 and 40 minutes, not counting transit time to another building where the x-ray was taken.

The physician did not examine the patient at the first visit unless the diastolic pressure was more than 120 mm Hg or the patient was obviously sick or insisted on seeing the physician. Antihypertensive therapy was not initiated at the first visit. The patient was scheduled for a return appointment in a week's time for the initial physical examination and evaluation by the physician.

Second visit

At the second visit, the patient's blood pressure was again recorded by "his interviewer" before and after a short interview. He was then referred to the physician who had in hand the patient's electrocardiogram, chest x-ray, and the laboratory data. After questioning the patient on the positive points in his history, the physical examination was performed, and antihypertensive therapy initiated as required. The average time spent by the physician for this initial evaluation was 12 to 15 minutes. The medication was issued by the paramedical pharmacist and a subsequent appointment made.

Later visits

On subsequent visits the patient was always seen by the same paramedical interviewer who routinely recorded the blood pressure at the beginning and end of the interview. She weighed the patient, recorded the heart rate, and took a short interval history regarding any unusual symptoms or occurrences since the last visit. She also asked special questions regarding possible drug-induced side effects. Until the blood pressure reached normal limits, the patient was routinely referred to the physician for re-evaluation and change in therapy as required. These physician visits usually took two to five minutes.

When the patient reached a stabilized situation, i.e., with his blood pressure normal, no side effects, and no need for change in therapy, the interviewer did not refer the patient to the physician. Stabilized patients were seen by the nurse-director who verified the situation and then referred the patient to the paramedical pharmacist where his supply of medication was replenished and another appointment made. Patients who were on thiazide diuretics had blood drawn at intervals of three months for laboratory determinations of potassium, glucose, creatinine, and uric acid.

Obviously, if at any time a toxic reaction occurred, or if it were obvious that more or less medication was needed to control the blood pressure, or if any interim illness had occurred, the patient was referred to the physician.

During the initial clinic visit, the patient was informed that, within reason, we would provide total health care on a 24-hour basis. If the patient also had diabetes (and 20 percent of our patients did), developed influenza, or had an upper respiratory infection, he was referred to the clinic physician for appropriate care. Patients were able to receive care during nonclinic hours by using a direct telephone line answering service which enabled them to contact one of our "on-call" physicians or nurses.

To provide broader health service, our paramedical pharmacist was trained as a health counselor. She encouraged the smoking patient to abandon the habit. She furnished literature written in simple, understandable language, and gave him additional reasons for not smoking. If the patient was obese, she provided dietary instructions, also written in simple language.

Our Experience

This nurse-directed clinic went a long way toward eliminating overcrowding and easing the strain on patients and doctors that often accompany programs that require a doctor to examine every patient at every visit.

With a trained nurse, assisted by two paramedical people,

all working under the supervision of a physician, a clinic could easily handle 30 to 40 patients per day. Doubling the paramedical personnel could easily double the number of patients our clinic could handle. Considering that a cost ratio of roughly 8 to 1 exists between physician to paramedical personnel, this arrangement led to a substantial economic saving while it freed the doctor for more challenging tasks.

Three years' experience has convinced us that the long-term care of the hypertensive patient can be carried out ideally by specially trained nurses and paramedical personnel. The patient acceptance of this program is apparent in our ongoing research. The dropout rate decreased from 42 percent in the period 1966-69 (before we started our new clinic program) to 8 percent in 1970-71.

During the past year, as part of the National Heart and Lung Institute sponsored Hypertension Detection and Follow-up Program, we compared our personalized care with standard medical care in a prospective fashion.[6]

Two hundred and eighty-four newly discovered hypertensive patients, identified in supermarkets, were randomly placed into three groups:

Group A:	98 patients who were followed with personalized care in our special clinic.
Group B:	81 patients who received standard care in the general medical clinic, with special reminder of clinic appointments on the day before the appointment.
Group C:	105 patients who received standard care in the general medical clinic.

After an average follow-up of 8 months, the results are somewhat startling.

	Group A (98 Pts)	*Group B* (81 Pts)	*Group C* (105 Pts)
Percent of patients who came to clinic at least one time.	100	42	50
Percent of patients still in program.	84	33	17
Percent of patients with normal diastolic blood pressure.	70	10	17

The key to the success of this program lies in the basic assumption that the vast proportion of hypertensive patients have mild or moderate elevations of blood pressure that will readily respond to simple therapy. Indeed, 80 percent of the patients in *Group A* whose blood pressure was brought to normal received only one tablet per day.

Under these circumstances, much of the clinic time was spent in establishing a meaningful relationship with the patient and motivating him to take his medication, follow instructions, and to remain under medical care for the rest of his life.

Conclusion

It is not our intent to advocate that the treatment of all patients with hypertension be relegated to the specially trained nurse or paramedical person. Certainly those patients with moderately severe or severe disease must be under the constant attention of the physician since they frequently require complicated therapeutic regimens, careful dosage adjustments, monitoring of electrolytes and kidney function, and, at times, hospitalization. This small group of patients should be under the direct care of the physician until blood pressure has returned to normal, and a stable therapeutic regimen has been established.

It is hoped, however, that these pilot studies will stimulate other physicians, both in hospitals and in private practice, to identify and treat more hypertensive patients, and use specially trained nurses and paramedical personnel in their long-term management.

References

*1. Veterans Administration Cooperative Study Group on Antihypertensive Agents: Effects of treatment on morbidity in hypertension: II. Results in patients with diastolic blood pressure averaging 90 through 114 mm Hg. JAMA *213*:1143, 1970.

2. Finnerty FA Jr: Unpublished data.

3. Schoenberger JA, Stamler J, Shekelle RB, and Shekelle S: Current status of hypertension control in an industrial population. JAMA *222*:559, 1972.

4. American Heart Association: Hypertension: Office Evaluation. Pamphlet, 1972.

5. Finnerty FA Jr, Mattie EC, and Finnerty FA III: Hypertension in the inner city; Part I. Analysis of clinic dropouts. Circulation *47*:73, 1973.

6. Finnerty FA Jr, Shaw LW, and Himmelsbach CK: Hypertension in the inner city; Part II. Detection and follow-up. Circulation *47*:76, 1973.

*See Appendix for complete study.

Appendix

Blood Pressure
Measurement Aids*

This section contains three practical items that can be reproduced or adapted for your own office use:
1. "First Visit Interview Form." (Adapted from procedures used by Dr. Finnerty's Hypertension Clinic.)**
2. Instructions for use of above forms by paramedical personnel.
3. Concise and practical "at home" guide for instructing the patient in measuring his own blood pressure.

*We thank Dr. Finnerty and *Patient Care* for permission to reproduce this material.
**See Chapter 6.

Patient Interview Form

See page 139 for instruction for use.

FIRST VISIT

1. Name: (PRINT IN BLOCK CAPITALS)

_____

(Mr., Miss, Mrs.)   Last   First   Middle

2. Age:

_____

3. Date of Birth

_____

    Month   Day   Year

4. Time arrived:

_____:_____

Hour Minute   (a.m. or p.m.)

COMPLETE ITEMS 5 AND 6 AT TERMINATION OF VISIT BEFORE PARTICIPANT LEAVES

5. Review of completed form:

_____Every item on each page is complete and legible.

_____Name of participant is correct.

_____Participant is "N" (Normal) and has been advised accordingly.

_____Participant is "H" (Hypertensive):

In which case,

_____A second visit has been scheduled. Date:_____Time:_____

_____Appointment slip has been given.

_____Chest x-ray has been scheduled. Date:_____Time:_____

_____ECG has been completed.

6. Time visit completed:_____

                  Date   Time   a.m./p.m.

This section completed by:_____

This section completed by receptionist. (Rest of form completed by interviewer.)

Now I would like to record your blood pressure and measure your height and weight.

7. Blood Pressure

a. Pulse: Beats in 30 seconds_____ × 2 =_____beats/minute.

b. First Reading:_____

              Systolic   Diastolic (5th Phase)   SUM*

Second Reading:_____

              Systolic   Diastolic (5th Phase)   SUM   SUM (averaged)

NOTE: IF SUM is less than 180, advise the participant accordingly and end the visit.

      IF SUM is 180 to 248, continue and complete the First Visit form and interview.

      IF SUM is 250 or greater, notify the physician, and complete First Visit interview.

8. Height:_____ 9. Weight:_____

    Inches   Pounds

REMARKS:

Observer: _____

*Dr. Finnerty uses the "SUM" of the systolic and diastolic pressures as a technique when working with paramedical personnel.

10. Has any close relative (father, mother, brothers, sisters, children) ever had any of the following diseases?

	Yes	No	DK*	Relationship
Heart attack	☐	☐	☐	_____
Other heart disease	☐	☐	☐	_____
High blood pressure	☐	☐	☐	_____
Stroke	☐	☐	☐	_____
Diabetes	☐	☐	☐	_____
Kidney disease	☐	☐	☐	_____

11. Now some questions about your own health.
Do you have any conditions or health problems at the present time?

	Condition or Health Problem	Duration
(1)	_____	_____
(2)	_____	_____
(3)	_____	_____
(4)	_____	_____

12. I would like to know about some specific conditions you may have had:

	Yes	No	DK
a. Has a doctor ever told you that you had kidney stones or other kidney trouble?	☐	☐	☐
b. Has a doctor ever told you that you had gout?	☐	☐	☐
c. Has a doctor ever told you that you had cirrhosis or liver disease?	☐	☐	☐
d. Has a doctor ever told you that you had tuberculosis?	☐	☐	☐
e. Has a doctor ever told you that you had intestinal bleeding or ulcers?	☐	☐	☐
f. Has a doctor ever told you that you had cancer?	☐	☐	☐

What part of the body was affected?
☐ Breast   ☐ Gastro-intestinal tract
☐ Lung   ☐ Genito-urinary system
☐ Skin   ☐ Other, specify:_____

_____

13. a. Do you have attacks of headache, racing of your heart, and sweating all at once?

Yes	No	DK
☐	☐	☐

*"DK" is abbreviation for "Don't Know."

Comments:

131

Now thinking about the past several months, have you been troubled with:

Comments:

	Yes	No	DK
13. b. skin rash or bruising	☐	☐	☐
c. headaches so bad that you had to stop what you were doing?	☐	☐	☐
d. faintness or light-headedness when you stand up quickly?	☐	☐	☐
e. your heart beating fast or skipping beats?	☐	☐	☐
f. blacking out or losing consciousness?	☐	☐	☐
g. swelling or tenderness of your breasts?	☐	☐	☐
h. recurrent stomach pains?	☐	☐	☐
i. waking up too early and having difficulty getting back to sleep?	☐	☐	☐

Within the past several months:

	Yes	No	DK
j. have your stools been black or tarry?	☐	☐	☐
k. have you noticed bright red blood in your stools?	☐	☐	☐

FOR WOMEN SKIP TO m.

	Yes	No	DK
l. have you noticed a decrease in sexual ability?	☐	☐	☐
m. have you often felt so depressed (sad or blue) that it interfered with your work, recreation, or sleep?	☐	☐	☐

FOR MEN SKIP TO 15.

132

14. a. Have you ever been pregnant?

No   DK   Yes

☐   ☐   ☐
         │
         ▼
         (1) How many live-born children? ┌──────┐
                                           └──────┘

         (2) How many miscarriages or stillbirths? ┌──────┐
                                                     └──────┘

         (3) Have seizures or convulsions occurred
             during any pregnancy?

                   Yes   No   DK
                   ☐   ☐   ☐

         (4) Has high blood pressure or toxemia complicated
             any pregnancy?

                   Yes   No   DK
                   ☐   ☐   ☐

   b. Have you had a menstrual period within the past six weeks?

   Yes   No

   ☐   ☐
   │   │
   │   ▼
   │   What is the reason?
   │
   │   ☐ Post-menopause, natural
   │   ☐ Post-menopause, other ──────────► SKIP TO 15.
   │   ☐ Known pregnancy
   │   ☐ Possible pregnancy
   │   ☐ Other, specify:_____
   ▼
   c. Are you currently taking birth control pills?

                   Yes   No   DK
                   ☐   ☐   ☐

---

15. a. (1) Have you ever had any pain or discomfort in your chest?

        Yes   No
        ☐   ☐

           IF NO, have you ever had any pressure or heaviness in
           your chest?

           Yes   No
           ☐   ☐

              IF NO TO BOTH OF THESE QUESTIONS, skip
              to 16.

        IF YES TO EITHER OF THESE TWO QUESTIONS, continue to
        (2).If any answer given below is marked *, skip to 15b;
        do NOT finish 15a.

Comments:

133

(2) Do you get this pain or discomfort when you walk uphill or hurry?

Yes   No*   Never walk uphill or hurry
☐   ☐   ☐

(3) Do you get this pain or discomfort when you walk at an ordinary pace on the level?

Yes   No
☐   ☐

(4) What do you do if you get this pain while you are walking?

☐ Stop or slow down

☐ Take a nitroglycerin

☐ Continue at same pace*

(5) If you stand still what happens to the pain?

Relieved   Not relieved*
☐   ☐

(6) How soon is the pain relieved?

10 minutes or less   More than 10 minutes*
☐   ☐

		Yes	No
(7) Will you show me where it was?	(a) Sternum (middle or upper)	☐	☐
	(b) Sternum (lower)	☐	☐
	(c) Left anterior chest	☐	☐
	(d) Left arm	☐	☐

Did you feel it anywhere else?

Yes   No
☐   ☐

IF YES, record additional information on the diagram above.

NOTE: IF YES to (a); or (b); or (c) and (d), history is positive for angina.

15. b. (1) Have you ever had a severe pain across the front of your chest lasting half an hour or more?

Yes   No
☐   ☐

IF NO, skip to 15c;   do NOT finish 15b.

IF YES, history is positive for possible infarction.

Comments:

134

(2) Did you see a doctor because of this pain?

Yes   No

☐   ☐

IF YES, what did he say it was?_____

_____

(3) How many of these attacks have you had? (Record number of attacks.)

	Date	Duration
Tell me about your first attack:	_____	_____
Your last attack:	_____	_____

15. c. If any answer given below is marked *, SKIP TO 16; do NOT finish 15c.

(1) Do you get pain in either leg on walking?

Yes   No*

☐   ☐

(2) Does this pain ever begin when you are standing still or sitting?

Yes*   No

☐   ☐

(3) In what part of your leg do you feel it?

Pain includes calf/calves   Pain does not include calf*

☐   ☐

IF calves not mentioned, ask "Anywhere else?" If calves still not mentioned, indicate "Pain does not include calf," above.

(4) Do you get this pain when you walk uphill or hurry?

Yes   No*   Never walk uphill or hurry

☐   ☐   ☐

(5) Do you get this pain when you walk at an ordinary pace on the level?

Yes   No

☐   ☐

(6) Does the pain ever disappear while you are still walking?

Yes*   No

☐   ☐

Comments:

135

(7) What do you do if you get this pain while you are walking?   Comments:

        Stop or slacken pace   Continue at same pace*

           ☐   ☐

(8) What happens to the pain if you stand still?

          Relieved   Not relieved*

           ☐   ☐

(9) How soon is it relieved?

        10 minutes   More than 10 minutes

           ☐   ☐

    NOTE: If 10 or less, history is positive for intermittent claudication.

---

16. a. Do you get shortness of breath that requires you to stop and rest?

Yes   No
☐   ☐

       IF NO, skip to 16 b.

IF YES, do you get it walking on level ground or climbing a single flight of stairs?

Yes   No
☐   ☐

16. b. Do you get shortness of breath when you are lying down flat?

Yes   No
☐   ☐

       IF NO, skip to 16 c.

IF YES, does this shortness of breath improve when you sit up, or do you use extra pillows at night to prevent it?

Yes   No
☐   ☐

16. c. Do you get severe shortness of breath which wakes you up when lying down asleep?

Yes   No
☐   ☐

---

17. a. (1) Do you usually cough first thing in the morning (on getting up) in the winter? (Include a cough with first smoke or on first going out of doors. Exclude clearing throat or a single cough.)

Yes   No
☐   ☐

(2) Do you usually cough during the day—or at night—in the winter? (Ignore an occasional cough.)

Yes ☐ No ☐

IF NO TO BOTH QUESTIONS (1) & (2), skip to 17b.

(3) Do you cough like this on most days (or nights) for as much as three months each year?

Yes ☐ No ☐

17. b. (1) Do you usually bring up any phlegm from your chest first thing in the morning (on getting up) in the winter? (Include: phlegm with the first smoke, phlegm on first going out of doors, and swallowed phlegm. Exclude phlegm from the nose.)

Yes ☐ No ☐

(2) Do you usually bring up any phlegm from your chest at least twice during the day—or at night—in the winter?

Yes ☐ No ☐

IF NO TO BOTH QUESTIONS (1) & (2), skip to 17c.

(3) Do you bring up phlegm like this on most days (or nights) for as much as three months each year?

Yes ☐ No ☐

IF YES, have you had phlegm like this for 3 years or more?

Yes ☐ No ☐

17. c. (1) Does your chest ever sound wheezing or whistling?

Yes ☐ No ☐

IF YES, do you get this most days—or nights?

Yes ☐ No ☐

(2) Have you ever had attacks of shortness of breath with wheezing?

Yes ☐ No ☐

IF YES, is (was) your breathing absolutely normal between attacks?

Yes ☐ No ☐

Comments:

137

18. Now I would like to ask you about medications you may be taking now or have taken in the past.

a. Has any medication ever caused you to have a skin rash or other kind of allergic reaction?

Yes No

☐   ☐

IF YES, describe medications, reaction, and circumstances:

_____

_____

_____

_____

NOTE: Positive responses should be brought to the attention of and verified by a physician.

b. Have you taken any medications or drugs or treatments, including special diet, today or in the past two weeks?

Yes No

☐   ☐

IF YES, describe:

Reason for medication	When started	Identification
(1) _____	_____	_____
(2) _____	_____	_____
(3) _____	_____	_____
(4) _____	_____	_____
(5) _____	_____	_____

Ask participant to bring all medications to next visit to insure proper identification, if not already done.

Comments:

This interview completed by:_____

138

Procedures and Instructions for Taking Patient's Initial Medical History*

This form should be prepared from the appointment list in advance of the scheduled visit, by entry of the essential identifying information. When the patient arrives, he or she should be greeted by the receptionist, identified by name, and the prepared form initiated. Items 2, 3, and 4 should be completed immediately. Items 7, 8, and 9 (measurement of blood pressure, height, and weight) should be completed as soon as possible after the participant has been seated for five minutes. At the location for blood pressure measurement, depending upon the results, the participant found to be normotensive is advised accordingly and his visit terminated after appropriate discussion.

If the patient is found to be hypertensive, then the entire First Visit form is to be completed. The patient is interviewed to complete items 10 through 18. He visits the laboratory for collection of blood and urine specimens, has an ECG, and is either given a chest x-ray or is scheduled for an x-ray appointment prior to the second visit.

With the exception of initiation of the First Visit form and measurement of blood pressure, height, and weight, the sequence of the additional procedures required at this visit is flexible. The completed form should then be reviewed in detail. The time of completion of the visit should be recorded.

Detailed instructions are as follows:

Item 2.

Age in years as of the last birthday is to be recorded.

Item 3.

When the patient arrives for the first visit, he is greeted and identified, and the date entered on the form according to the standard procedures (e.g., March 12, 1973 written as 03 12 73).

*For use with Patient Interview Form on page 130

Item 4.

Immediately after recording the date, note the time the patient arrived, verifying this with the patient in the event of any delay in contact with the receptionist after the arrival at the premises (which is the time to be recorded). This will permit documentation of the length of patient's visit.

The patient is then guided to the location where pulse, blood pressure, height, and weight are measured, and asked to be seated. He remains seated until the blood pressure measurement has been completed.

Items 5 and 6 (see pages 145 and 146).

Item 7.

The pulse and blood pressure are measured after the patient has been seated at the measurement location for a minimum of five minutes. The entries are recorded in the standard manner.

At the completion of Item 9, the observer who has recorded the blood pressure readings checks to insure that the SUM is correct, reads the three possible actions to be taken, and acts appropriately:

If SUM is less than 180, the patient should be advised that this normal confirmatory reading has shown that the pressure is not consistently high enough to require treatment. However, it should be checked at a clinic or doctor's office once a year to insure that it is still at a safe level; if higher, it should be treated in accordance with the judgment of the patient's physician.

If SUM is 180 to 248, the patient should be advised that the blood pressure is found at a level where treatment may be very helpful. Further evaluation is necessary, and the next step is an interview to learn more about his health—especially as it may have been affected by high blood pressure.

If SUM is 250 or greater, the patient should be advised that the blood pressure is found at a level where treatment is very important, and where additional information about his health should be obtained very promptly so that treatment can be arranged. The interviewer should leave the room and contact a physician at once, arranging for completion of as much of the baseline evaluation information as possible. The interviewer should then return to the room and explain that the next step is an interview from which more can be learned about the patient's health, especially as it may have been affected by high blood pressure.

REMARKS should be entered according to the observer's judgment, especially in reference to *any* circumstance during blood pressure measurement which was an unavoidable departure from the standard measurement procedure or in any other way may have affected the recorded measurement. For example, such remarks would document irregularity of the pulse, absence of the right arm, unusual background noise, or repetition of a reading because of unavoidable technical difficulties.

The observer then checks to insure that the page is complete, enters his name at the bottom of page, and assists the patient in moving to the location of the interview or to the receptionist to close the visit, as appropriate.

The interview which follows consists of Items 10 through 18, to be administered, as written, by the appropriate staff member. The text of these items includes statements (to be used by the interviewer) which explain what the immediate or following questions are about and which provide a smooth transition from one topic to the next.

Where unusual circumstances in an interview may appear to affect the recorded response, or where information is volunteered which, in the interviewer's judgment, should be recorded for the physician's review, the space under "Comments" should be used. This space is *not* intended for recording extraneous information merely because it has been volunteered.

Item 10.

For any condition checked "Yes," the relationship(s) of the affected relative(s) should be entered. If this relationship is unknown, enter "DK" on the line provided. For any condition checked "No" or "DK" (Don't Know), the line for "Relationship" should be left blank. Note that, as elsewhere, "DK" is the code used when the *patient* is uncertain of the answer. This code is not to be used when the *interviewer* is uncertain; if this is the case, further questions are required to clarify the patient's meaning so that his answer may be recorded accurately.

Item 11.

The space provided should be used to enter only conditions or problems at the present time, as stated by the patient. If the duration is unknown, enter "DK" under "Duration"; if it is only approximately stated, indicate this—e.g., "*about* 6 months." If there is no such condition or problem at this time, enter "None" on line (1) under "Condition or Health Problem."

Item 12.

Check the correct response as given. Regarding cancer, if the response is "Yes," the subsequent question must be asked and the response checked as given. Note that more than one type of cancer may be reported; each should be recorded.

Item 13.

Check the correct response as given. Note that Items 13b through 13m all refer to "the past several months." For some patients, it may be helpful to repeat for later items the lead phrases at 13b and 13j. Note that Item 13l applies to men only.

Item 14.

This item applies to women only. Item 14a refers to *past* history only; if there is uncertainty about possible pregnancy at present, this would apply only under 14b. If the response is "Yes," then parts (1) through (4) are asked. The numbers of live born children (one twin birth=02, etc.), or miscarriages or stillbirths are recorded in the standard manner, using "DK" if the number is not known (presumably this applies to (2) only).

Item 14b determines current menstrual status and the possibility of pregnancy. If the response is "Yes," skip directly to 14c; if "No," ask for the reason. The response to this question must be interpreted in one (and *only* one) of the categories provided. If interruption or cessation of a regular menstrual cycle is explained by known menopause or known pregnancy, skip to Item 15; if not, the interpretation should be "Possible pregnancy" unless a specific "Other" condition is reported. In either of these latter cases, Item 14c is asked.

Item 14c is asked when required, as stated above, and the response recorded as given.

Item 15.

Parts a, b, and c constitute a standard cardiovascular questionnaire used widely to assess chest pain of effort, chest pain of possible myocardial infarction, and intermittent claudication. The sequence of questions, and rules for interrupting the sequence to skip ahead, must be followed exactly within each part. In this way, only enough questions are asked to exclude the presence of each of these three conditions; for example, a participant responding "No" to both questions of Part a (1) is asked none of the remaining questions in Part a, and none of the questions in Part b. A patient who gives none of the starred (*) answers to Part a (2) through (6) is asked to point to his own torso and locate the pain; the responses are recorded by the interviewer by specific location. After any starred answer has been given, the remaining questions within that part of the Item *must not* be asked.

In Part a, all responses are recorded as given, or as interpreted by the interviewer; question (7) is completed by marking on the sketch the location(s) of the pain as well as by checking each listed location "Yes" or "No" according to the patient's description.

In Part b, the response to the first question(1) is recorded as shown. The second question (2), if answered "Yes," must include the doctor's reported description of the pain or, if not known, "DK," on the lines provided. The third question(3) is asked, and the number (e.g., 03) is entered. The first (or only) attack is documented as shown. "Date" should be by calendar year, or "DK" entered. "Duration" refers to the episode of pain and must be 30 minutes or more, perhaps several hours—*this is uninterrupted pain only, and not the total duration of illness or hospitalization.* If more than one attack is recorded in the box, the last (most recent) one is described similarly in the space provided.

In Part c, the same scheme is used as in Part a, and the procedure of interviewing is the same. Note that question (3) is asked only in an open, undirected manner; if the calf is not mentioned literally, or unmistakably demonstrated by the patient, in response to the first inquiry, the interviewer gives one additional chance for this condition to be volunteered, by asking "Anywhere else?" If still not volunteered, the starred response is checked and, as always for a starred response, one skips the remainder of this part of Item 15.

Item 16.

The three Parts of this Item document symptoms suggesting the presence of congestive heart failure. Only if the first question of Part a or Part b is answered "Yes" is a second question asked for fuller description of the symptom. All responses are checked as given.

Item 17.

This Item is an adaptation of a standard questionnaire concerning symptoms of respiratory disease—cough, phlegm production, and wheezing. In addition to the text of the standard questions, parenthetical guides to interpretation of responses are given. Further, optional wording is given which makes the questions applicable to persons whose working hours are during the night rather than in the daytime. (For persons usually awake during daytime hours, the nighttime reference should be omitted.) At several points, secondary questions are skipped. With these provisions, the appropriate questions are asked and the interviewer's interpretations as "Yes" or "No" recorded by checking the appropriate boxes.

Item 18.

This Item determines both any history of recognized adverse drug reactions, as well as any drugs recently used. If the patient's response to Part a is not clearly "Yes" or "No," this should be stated under "Comments" to insure that the reviewing physician will inquire further about this very important matter. Note that any medication indicated by the patient as possibly causing some adverse reaction must be recorded and brought to the attention of the attending physician for further review and verification.

Part b includes any medication, drug, or treatment, including diet. Thus vitamins, aspirin, laxatives, low-calorie diets, and physical therapy would all be included; strictly cosmetic treatments (facials, steambaths, etc.) would be excluded, as examples. As far as possible, actual medications should be specifically identified by inspection, comparison with photo catalogs (as in the Physicians' Desk Reference), and/or tracing of prescriptions by number, when applicable. These measures are of great importance to insure that treatment recommendations are not made in ignorance of other treatment currently provided from other sources. Accordingly, if the response to Part b is "Yes," and included are medications *not* brought to this clinic visit, the patient should be urged once again to bring such medications to the second visit.

The interview portion of the form is signed by the interviewer. The electrocardiogram (ECG), laboratory specimens, and x-ray (or an appointment for x-ray) are to be completed next, and the interviewer should guide the patient to the appropriate location. When these procedures have been completed, and recorded as re-

144

quired, the patient returns to the receptionist who completes the remaining items.

Item 5.

The review of the completed form and procedures is the responsibility of the receptionist. For all patients, completeness, legibility, and name are carefully checked. If the participant is "N" (Normotensive), this is again noted and verified that he has been advised accordingly. If the patient is "H" (Hypertensive), the remaining points are reviewed to insure their completeness *before* the patient leaves. The following information should then be provided to insure a clear understanding of the plans for the next visit:

It should be explained that the patient should come back in one week for a physical examination by the doctor (or physician assistant if this is the case). It should be explained that at the time of the second visit, the results of the blood and urine tests, the cardiogram, and the chest x-ray will be explained to the patient and that he will be advised what to do in terms of getting further treatment.

The patient should expect the second visit to take approximately one-and-a-half to two hours. At that time, another blood test will be done. Part of this blood test will be a blood sugar test for the detection of the tendency for diabetes. Hence, *it is important that the patient not eat or drink anything for at least 3 hours prior to his second appointment;* in this way, his blood sugar can be tested in a state of fasting. Even a candy bar, chewing gum, or coffee with cream and sugar can raise the blood sugar, so *it is important NOT to take ANYTHING but water by mouth for three hours prior to the appointment.* Also, the person will be given a specially sweetened drink at this visit, which gives the most sensitive test for diabetes. A second blood sugar will be drawn an hour after this drink has been administered.

For persons whose SUM was 220 or greater at the first visit, additional explanation must be given that it will be necessary to dilate their eyes to get a good look at their eye grounds. These persons should be told that their blood pressure is at such a level that it sometimes causes changes in the eyes, and that it is very important to get a good look in their eyes to see whether or not any of these changes have occurred. This knowledge will be extremely important in deciding how they are to be treated. To get a good look in their eyes it will be important to put a medicine in their eyes that will dilate the pupils. This medicine may make the vision blurred for several hours. Therefore *it is important that they not drive themselves to the second visit*, but that they either be brought by someone or take public transportation. If necessary, taxi vouchers should be offered to be sure that the person has a way to come for his appointment, rather than driving himself.

Item 6.

Finally, the time at which the patient is free to leave should be recorded. Note that this may not be the time of actual departure (e.g., he may be waiting for another household member, etc.). *The total time attributed to the visit is thus from the actual arrival to the potential departure* (i.e., the time the patient is *free* to leave).

The first visit is completed when the reviewer of the record has signed at the bottom of the First Visit interview form.

Instructions to patient for measuring his own blood pressure:

From PATIENT CARE, April 15, 1973.

Measuring your blood pressure

Blood pressure actually entails two measurements: the systolic and diastolic blood pressure. In order to understand how this works, think of the heart as a pump. Every time your heart beats, blood is pumped through the arteries to all parts of your body.

The blood pressure cuff put around your arm is inflated and squeezes the arteries so that the blood pumped to your arm is momentarily stopped, and the heart beat can't be heard through the stethoscope, which is put on your arm below the cuff. Then air pressure is gradually released from the cuff. When the heart is heard pumping the blood through the arteries, the reading on the meter at this moment is called the systolic blood pressure.

As the pressure continues to be reduced, the sound of the heart pumping gradually fades. When it can no longer be heard, the compressed arteries are again round; the reading on the meter now is called the diastolic pressure. It is the pressure which is constantly on the arteries, and is considered to be more important than the systolic blood pressure.

The systolic blood pressure is recorded first. Thus, for example, 120/80 means a systolic blood pressure of 120 and a diastolic pressure of 80.

Now that you have been shown how to take your own blood pressure, and understand what it means, you can take your own readings at home. Here are a few reminders:

»Take your blood pressure three times a day whenever possible—preferably in the morning upon arising, during the afternoon (if this can't be done on the job, take it upon arriving home), and at bedtime. Each time, take the blood pressure while standing and while lying down. Be sure to rest your arm on a support of some kind. It should not be elevated, nor should your shirt sleeve be tightly rolled up.

»When you inflate the blood pressure cuff, it should be 20-30 points higher than your present blood pressure, which is _____.

»Don't be in a hurry; release the cuff pressure slowly.

»The stethoscope bell should be put on the front surface of the upper arm directly above the elbow.

»Remember, the meter's reading at the first sharp sound you hear as you release pressure from the cuff should be considered the systolic blood pressure reading; the meter's reading at the last sharp sound you hear through the stethoscope is the diastolic blood pressure reading.

»Write both the standing and lying systolic and diastolic blood pressure readings and the times they were taken on the reverse side of this form.

Bring this form to my office when you come for your next office visit.

Your blood pressure record form

Date	Time of day	Standing Systolic	Diastolic	Lying down Systolic	Diastolic

FIRST WEEK

Date	Time of day	Standing Systolic	Diastolic	Lying down Systolic	Diastolic

SECOND WEEK

Date	Time of day	Standing Systolic	Diastolic	Lying down Systolic	Diastolic

THIRD WEEK

148

The Landmark Studies*

This section of the Hypertension Handbook contains three papers describing the research of the Veterans Administration Cooperative Study Group on Antihypertensive Agents and two covering the well-known Framingham Study. Also included is the Report of Inter-Society Commission for Heart Disease Resources.

Veterans Administration Cooperative Study Group on Antihypertensive Agents: Effects of Treatment on Morbidity in Hypertension
    Results in Patients With Diastolic Blood Pressures Averaging 115 Through 129 mm Hg
    Results in Patients With Diastolic Blood Pressure Averaging 90 Through 114 mm Hg
    Influence of Age, Diastolic Pressure, and Prior Cardiovascular Disease; Further Analysis of Side Effects

The Framingham Study
    "Epidemiologic Assessment of the Role of Blood Pressure in Stroke"
    "Role of Blood Pressure in the Development of Congestive Heart Failure"

Report of Inter-Society Commission for Heart Disease Resources
    Guidelines for the Detection, Diagnosis, and Management of Hypertensive Populations

*We thank the authors and journals for permission to reproduce these studies.

Reprinted From The Journal of the American Medical Association
December 11, 1967 Volume 202
Copyright 1967, American Medical Association

Effects of Treatment on Morbidity in Hypertension

Results in Patients With Diastolic Blood Pressures Averaging 115 Through 129 mm Hg

Veterans Administration Cooperative Study Group on Antihypertensive Agents

A group of 143 male hypertensive patients with diastolic blood pressures (at the clinic) averaging between 115 and 129 mm Hg were randomly assigned to either active (hydrochlorothiazide plus reserpine plus hydralazine hydrochloride) or placebo treatment. Twenty-seven severe, complicating events developed in the placebo-treated patients as compared to two in the active group. Four deaths occurred in the placebo-treated group and none in the actively treated patients. Other complications in the placebo group included grade 3 or 4 hypertensive retinopathy, congestive heart failure, increasing azotemia, cerebrovascular thrombosis, transient ischemic attacks, cerebral hemorrhage, myocardial infarction, and severely elevated blood pressure. Severe complications in the active-treatment group were one cerebrovascular thrombosis and one case of multiple drug toxicity. Male patients with diastolic blood pressures averaging 115 mm Hg or above represent a high-risk group in which antihypertensive therapy exerts a significant beneficial effect.

The value of antihypertensive drug treatment in malignant hypertension has been amply demonstrated.[1-6] However, its effectiveness in preventing morbidity and mortality in less severe forms of hypertension has been disputed.[7-9] Adequately controlled, prospective studies are needed to evaluate this question in patients with essential hypertension.[9] An investigation of this type was initiated by the Veterans Administration Cooperative Study Group on Antihypertensive Agents in 1963. The design of the study, including the precautions employed to maintain adherence to protocol and avoidance of dropouts, has been described in a previous communication.[10] The present report is concerned with the results obtained in the patients

without signs of accelerated hypertension at admission whose diastolic blood pressures prior to treatment averaged 115 through 129 mm Hg.

Plan of Investigation

All patients were hospitalized for the initial work-up. Male patients whose diastolic blood pressures from the fourth through the sixth day of hospitalization averaged 90 through 129 mm Hg without treatment were considered for admission to the prerandomization trial period.

Severity was evaluated in five categories. These were the average diastolic blood pressure during hospitalization and the degree of clinically detectable hypertensive damage in the following four target organs: the optic fundi, the brain, heart, and kidneys. Severity of damage in each category was graded on a scale from 0 (no detectable abnormality) to 4 (most severe changes). The criteria used for grading severity have been described in detail elsewhere.[11] After doubling the scores for the average diastolic blood pressure and the severity of damage to the optic fundi, the scores obtained in each category were summed to obtain a total severity index. Patients with total scores of 2 through 7 were classified as mild, 8 through 15 as moderate, and 16 or above as severe, the latter being excluded from the trial.

Also excluded from the study were patients with surgically curable hypertension, uremia, and concomitant fatal diseases such as carcinoma. Patients with hemorrhages, exudates, or papilledema in the optic fundi, history of cerebral or subarachnoid hemorrhage, dissecting aneurysm, or congestive heart failure resistant to digitalis and mercurial diuretics were excluded. Additional exclusions included patients who wished to return to the care of their private physicians, those who for geographical or

For complete list of participants, see page 1033.
Reprint requested to 50 Irving St NW, Washington, DC 20422 (Dr. Edward D. Freis).

other reasons would be unable to attend clinic regularly, and patients of dubious reliability such as alcoholics, vagrants, and poorly motivated patients.

Prerandomization Trial Period.—Following discharge from the hospital, the patients entered a prerandomization trial period of two to four months' duration. They received two placebos, known to the physician but not to the patient, and were seen in the clinic at monthly intervals.

Riboflavin (5 mg) was incorporated into one of the placebos. Riboflavin produces a yellow fluorescence of the urine when the latter is viewed under ultraviolet light. At each visit, a urine specimen was examined for fluorescence. Patients were required to return all bottles of medication, at which time the tablets were counted to assess the patient's reliability. To qualify for admission to the study, the patients were required to have no "violations" on two successive clinic visits. A violation consisted either of failure to appear at the regularly scheduled clinic appointment, or failure of the urine to exhibit fluorescence, or a tablet count (of either of the two types of placebos) which was outside the acceptable range. The upper limit of the acceptable range was defined as the return of no more than a 10% excess of the calculated number of tablets remaining if all doses had been taken as prescribed, while the lower limit was a return of five tablets less than the same calculated number. Nearly one half of the patients accepted into the trial period were excluded prior to randomization because of failure to pass the above tests of reliability.

Also excluded were patients who during the trial period exhibited diastolic blood pressures (while in the sitting position) averaging below 90 or above 129 mm Hg. Thus, the final decision to accept the patient into the study was based on both reliability and the level of diastolic blood pressure determined in the clinic during the trial period.

Postrandomization Period.—At the time of randomization, a sealed envelope was opened which assigned the patient to one of two possible regimens—active antihypertensive medications or their placebos. A table of random numbers was utilized by the statistician in determining the assignments. Patients classified by severity scores as having mild hypertension were randomized in a separate stratification from those with moderate hypertension. The double-blind technique was employed by utilizing a series of complex code numbers to disguise the identity of the randomized treatments and by making active drugs and placebos identical in appearance. It is realized, however, that blood pressure levels and side effects made the maintenance of such a double-blind study difficult and imperfect.

The active drugs were incorporated in the two tablets as follows: tablet A contained 50 mg hydrochlorothiazide plus 0.1 mg reserpine, and tablet B contained hydralazine hydrochloride. Tablet B was available in two strengths, 25 and 50 mg. Placebos were made up to correspond with each tablet of the active drugs.

Table 1.—Background of Randomized Patients

Characteristic	No. Placebo Treated	No. Actively Treated
Total randomized	70	73
White	35	31
Negro	35	42
Family history of hypertension		
None	19	23
Present	48	49
Unknown	3	1
Cardiac symptoms		
None	48	52
Present	22	21
Heart size by roentgenogram		
Ungerleider normal	39	44
Ungerleider enlarged	31	29
Electrocardiogram		
Left ventricular hypertrophy absent	48	49
Left ventricular hypertrophy present	22	24
Prior cardiovascular thrombosis	5	6
Occipital headaches	12	10
Diabetes absent	65	65
Diabetes present	5	8

Table 2.—Measurement Data

Characteristic	Placebo Mean	Placebo SD	Active Mean	Active SD
Age (yr)	51.4	10.8	50	8.7
Height (in)	69	2.6	68.7	2.9
Weight (lb)	182.9	34.5	185.2	36.7
Duration known hypertension (yr)	5.4	4.4	5.3	4.7
Average hospital diastolic pressure (mm Hg)	105.8	8.4	106.5	8.4
Average clinic systolic (mm Hg)	186.8	17.2	185.6	15.4
Average clinic diastolic (mm Hg)	121	4.7	121.2	5
Severity grades (0-4)°				
Fundi (hypertensive)	1.2	...	1.3	...
Fundi (sclerotic)	1.3	...	1.4	...
Cardiac	1.2	...	1	...
Central nervous system	0.4	...	0.3	...
Renal	0.5	...	0.3	...
Blood glucose, fasting (mg/100 cc)	96.8	20.6	97.7	18.9
Blood glucose, 2-hr postprandial	118	41.5	116.1	54.3
Cholesterol (mg/100 cc)	251.3	59.5	242	51.5

°Detailed criteria for grades 0 through 4 are given in reference 11.

Table 3.—Trends of Diastolic Blood Pressure

Time of Observation	Placebo No. Patients Observed°	Placebo Average Diastolic, mm Hg	Active No. Patients Observed	Active Average Diastolic, mm Hg
Prerandomization	70	121	73	121.2
At 4 months	57	118.5	68	93.1
8	50	120.3	64	92.2
12	44	118.8	58	91.6
16	33	118.5	47	92.1
20	27	115.2	40	89.4
24	23	119.7	32	91.5

°The decline in the number of patients observed is due primarily to the fact that patients were admitted over a 2½-year period. Hence, many were not in the study long enough to be observed at the longer time periods.

Treatment was begun with either tablet A, one twice daily, plus the 25-mg tablet B, one tablet three times daily, or else with the placebos of both of these tablets. At the next visit, tablet B was increased to the 50-mg strength. Thus, the regular maintenance daily dose to patients randomized to the active regimen was 100 mg of hydrochlorothiazide, 0.2 mg of reserpine, and 150 mg of hydralazine hydrochloride. However, if there were hypotensive reactions or other severe side effects, doses could be reduced to a tolerable level.

In order to further minimize losses due to drug

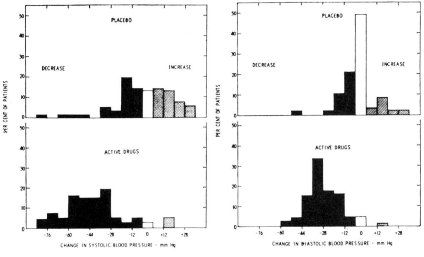

Changes in systolic (*left*) and diastolic blood pressure (*right*) after four months of treatment in 57 patients given placebos (*above*) and 68 patients treated with hydrochlorothiazide plus reserpine plus hydralazine (*below*).

group have since been given active treatment.

The total number of high-risk patients randomized was 143. Of this total, 70 received placebos, and 73 received active antihypertensive drugs during the randomization trial. Their average age was 51 years with a range of 30 to 73 years. The average weight was 83.5 kg (184 lb). Seventy-seven patients were Negroes and 66 whites. There were no significant differences with regard to age, weight, duration of known hypertension, or family history of hypertension, between the placebo- and active-treatment groups (Tables 1 and 2). There were more Negro and diabetic patients in the actively treated than in the placebo group, but the differences were not significant. The various indices of severity such as hospital and clinic blood pressure; funduscopic, cardiac, central nervous system, and renal abnormalities were essentially similar in the two groups.

The 143 patients were admitted into the study from April 1964 to December 1966. Observations on all these patients ended in May 1967. Thus, there is considerable variation in the duration of observation (Table 3). Nevertheless, 38% of the patients were observed for two years or more. The duration of the postrandomization phase of the study averaged 15.7 months for the placebo-treated patients and 20.7 for the active-drug group. Twenty-six of the placebo patients were in the postrandomization period of the study for less than one year as compared to 15 of the active group. Twenty-three placebo-treated patients exceeded a two-year period of postrandomization follow-up as opposed to 32 of the actively treated patients. The briefer period of follow-up of the patients in the placebo group was caused by the larger number of terminating events which developed in this group.

Modification in Treatment Regimens.—Of the 73

toxicity, two special A tablets were available on request. One contained hydrochlorothiazide without reserpine for patients becoming depressed or having active peptic ulcer or other reserpine-associated severe side effects. The other contained reserpine without hydrochlorothiazide for toxicity associated with the latter, such as hyperglycemia or acute gout. These special A tablets were available in both active and placebo forms.

The patients visited the clinic at monthly intervals for the first two months following randomization and at bimonthly intervals henceforth. Additional interim visits were scheduled if needed. Tablet counts were made at all clinic visits and fluorescence tests of the urine were made at alternate visits. Annual examinations included complete physical examination, roentgenogram of the chest, electrocardiogram, blood chemistry, and renal function tests. General medical care measures and symptomatic treatment, with the exception of known active antihypertensive drugs, were employed in all patients.

Characteristics of Patients

Only the patients whose diastolic blood pressures averaged 115 to 129 mm Hg during the last two prerandomization clinic visits are included in the present report. For this high-risk group the study was ended in May 1967. The patients with lower prerandomization diastolic readings are continuing in the study and will be reported on later. The study was terminated in the 115 mm Hg and above group at an earlier date than expected when it became apparent that the risk rate increased sharply at these levels of diastolic blood pressure and that the clinical course of such patients appeared to be favorably influenced by antihypertensive drug treatment. Therefore, all patients in this high-risk

Table 4.—Incidence of Mortality and Morbidity

	Placebo-Treated Patients	Actively Treated Patients
Deaths	4	0
Class A events	10	0
Subtotal	14	0
Other treatment failures	7	1
Total terminating events	21	1
Class B events (nonterminating)	6	1
Total	27	2

patients randomized to active antihypertensive drugs, 45 received the standard maintenance doses of hydrochlorothiazide, 50 mg plus reserpine 0.1 mg twice daily, and hydralazine hydrochloride, 50 mg three times daily, throughout their participation in the study. Dosages were reduced in the remaining patients because of low blood pressure levels with the standard regimen or because of side effects such as severe headache or weakness. There were no cases of systemic lupus erythematosus. Two patients were transferred to the special A tablets, one because of depression and the other because of a hyperglycemic reaction.

Sixty-six of the 70 placebo-treated patients received standard maintenance dosages. Reduced doses of tablet B were given to two patients because of presumed hydralazine-induced side effects. Special tablet A placebos were substituted in two other patients because of depression.

Dropouts.—The total number of dropouts was 12 or 8.4%. Nine occurred during the first two months following randomization. Seven had been randomized to placebos and five to active drugs. Thus, the dropout rate was small and was approximately equally divided between the active- and placebo-treated patients.

Changes in Blood Pressure.—Systolic and diastolic blood pressures fell promptly and significantly in the actively treated patients and remained at these reduced levels throughout the trial. The pro-

spective trends for diastolic blood pressure recorded with the patients in the sitting position are shown in Table 5. After 24 months of active treatment, the reduction from prerandomization levels of clinic blood pressure averages 43 mm Hg systolic and 29.7 mm Hg diastolic. By contrast, the placebo-treated patients showed no significant changes in average blood pressure levels following randomization (Table 3). The distribution of individual changes are shown in the Figure. There is a marked shift to the left into the "decrease" zone for the treated patients as compared with the placebo group. This marked shift is evident for both systolic and diastolic changes. Also apparent is the wide variation in individual responses.

Assessable Morbid Events

As shown in Table 4 assessable morbid events occurred in 27 placebo-treated versus two actively treated patients. Using the chi-square test, and assuming that the treatment has no effect, this result is statistically significant at the $P<.001$ level. If the possible effect of the 12 patient dropouts is considered and the most adverse assumption made, namely, that the seven placebo-treated patients would have had no countable event if they had stayed in the study and the five patients taking active drugs each would have had a countable event (a most unlikely occurrence!), then the score would have been 27 to 7. But even this con-

Table 5.—Terminating Events

No. Placebo	Age	Race	Prerandomized Blood Pressure, mm Hg	Time in Randomized Trial, Months	Class of Events	Nature of Terminating Event
1	57	W	185/126	16	A, D	Dissecting aortic aneurysm
2	59	W	214/120	6	A, D	Dissecting aortic aneurysm
3	55	N	177/117	2	B, D	Sudden death
4	65	W	230/127	2	B, D	Ruptured abdominal aortic aneurysm
5	65	N	211/121	4	A	Cerebral hemorrhage; bloody xanthrochromic spinal fluid
6	49	W	192/123	24	A	Fundi striate hemorrhage and papilledema
7	69	W	225/123	12	A	Fundi striate hemorrhage and papilledema
8	53	W	180/122	2	A	Fundi striate hemorrhage and soft exudates
9	68	W	214/117	12	A	Fundi striate hemorrhage and soft exudates
10	37	N	211/122	8	A	Fundi bilateral striate hemorrhage
11	45	N	200/121	2	A	Fundi bilateral striate hemorrhage and congestive heart failure
12	50	W	180/118	17	A	Fundi bilateral striate hemorrhage and congestive heart failure
13	67	N	215/120	2	A	Elevated BUN level to 71 mg/100 cc
14	55	W	186/125	5	A	Rehospitalization, basal diastolic pressure average 136 mm Hg
15	46	W	170/125	10	TF	Fundi single soft exudate
16	53	W	196/128	24	TF	Rehospitalization, basal diastolic pressure average 128 mm Hg
17	69	W	188/116	24	TF	Fundi hemorrhage and exudate but also diabetic
18	44	N	193/127	16	TF	Rehospitalization, basal diastolic pressure average 100 mm Hg
19	68	W	197/121	26	TF	Fundi hemorrhage and soft exudates plus BUN level 70 mg/100 cc but also diabetic
20	34	N	165/117	13	TF	Creatinine level increase 1.1 to 3 and BUN level 18 to 28 mg/100 cc in young patient
21	60	N	205/115	4	B, TF	Cerebrovascular accident, paralysis, and invalidism
Active 22	47	W	167/118	7	TF	Hyperglycemia, depression

A = class A event, D = death, TF = treatment failure, and B = class B event

Table 6.—Class B (Nonterminating) Events

Patient No.	Age	Race	Preran-dom BP, mm Hg	Time in Trial, mo Before Events	Time in Trial, mo After Events	Nature of Events
1	48	W	182/117	4	24	Myocardial infarction
2	45	N	165/115	18	10	Myocardial infarction
3	46	W	175/121	11	9	Congestive heart failure
4	68	W	180/120	20	9	Congestive heart failure
5	59	N	217/119	2	4	Cerebrovascular thrombosis
6	45	W	181/120	5†	15	Transient ischemic attacks
7	66	W	188/124	1	26	Cerebrovascular thrombosis

Patients 1 through 6 received placebos; patient 7 received active therapy.
†Subsequent ischemic attacks at 13 and 15 months after random-ization.

servative hypothetical "result" is statistically significant at the .001 level.

When deaths and class A hypertensive complications are combined, such events occurred in 14 placebo-treated patients as compared to none in the group receiving antihypertensive drugs. The total number of patients with terminating events, which includes deaths, class A events, and other treatment failures, was 21 in the placebo group versus one in the actively treated group.

Terminating Events in Placebo-Treated Patients. —The 21 placebo-treated patients having complications which required discontinuation of the protocol assigned treatment are listed in Table 5. The average age of these patients was 55.2 years, which was four years older than the average age of the total randomized population. Thirteen of the terminating events occurred in whites and eight in Negroes. The average clinic blood pressure of the 21 patients prior to randomization was 196.9/121.5 mm Hg, a slightly higher systolic average than that found in the entire group at risk.

The shortest period from randomization to terminating event was 2 months, the longest 26 months and the average 11 months. Terminating events were well distributed among the 15 participating hospitals, 14 contributing one or more events.

1. *There were four deaths,* all of which were related to cardiovascular diseases. Dissecting aortic aneurysm occurred in two, ruptured abdominal aneurysm in one, and sudden death at home in one (Table 5). No autopsy was obtained in the latter instance. The diagnosis of dissecting aortic aneurysm was verified either at surgical exploration or at autopsy. The diagnosis of ruptured abdominal aortic aneurysm with fatal hemorrhage was verified at autopsy.

2. *Class A events* were those hypertensive complications as defined in the protocol which required treatment with known active agents and permanent removal from protocol assigned therapy. They included the following: funduscopic evidence of grade 3 or 4 hypertensive retinopathy (multiple striate hemorrhages or soft exudates in

more than one quadrant, or bilateral papilledema), doubling of blood urea nitrogen (BUN) to levels above 60 mg/100 cc; dissecting aortic aneurysm; cerebrovascular hemorrhage as opposed to thrombosis; subarachnoid hemorrhage; congestive heart failure persisting despite digitalis and mercurial diuretics; and elevation of diastolic blood pressures to 140 mm Hg or higher on three repeated visits and average rehospitalization diastolic pressure to 130 mm Hg or higher.

The case histories of patients having terminating events were reviewed by a panel of four members consisting of two participants and two consultants. The panel determined in each case whether the criteria for a class A event as defined in the protocol were fulfilled. Terminating events which did not fully meet these criteria were classified as treatment failures as described below.

There were ten class A events in which the patients lived. Two of these were considered irreversible, and eight proved to be reversible following active antihypertensive treatment. One of the irreversible events was a cerebrovascular hemorrhage as evidenced by hemiplegia, stiff neck, and bloody and xanthrochromic spinal fluid. The other occurred in an azotemic patient whose renal function deteriorated rapidly.

Seven of the eight reversible class A events included grade 3 or 4 changes in the optic fundi. In two, striate hemorrhages and papilledema were present. In two others, multiple bilateral striate hemorrhages and cotton wool exudates were visualized; in two additional patients bilateral striate hemorrhages and resistant congestive heart failure were present simultaneously; and in the seventh patient, striate hemorrhages were present bilaterally but without exudates (Table 5). The remaining reversible class A event was associated with severely elevated blood pressure, the diastolic pressure during rehospitalization averaging 136 mm Hg.

3. *Treatment failures* were those events which did not meet the specific criteria for any one class A event as defined in the protocol. Nevertheless, because the complications were considered to be life threatening, protocol drugs were removed and treatment instituted with known antihypertensive agents. Seven of the terminated placebo-treated patients were classified as treatment failures. In two, multiple striate hemorrhages and soft exudates were seen in the optic fundi, but these patients also had diabetes mellitus. That the retinopathy probably was primarily associated with hypertension is suggested by the fact that, in both instances, the changes in the fundi cleared within two months after initiation of treatment with known antihypertensive agents. In a third nondiabetic patient only one cotton wool exudate and no striate hemorrhages were observed.

Two patients were classified as treatment failures because the diastolic blood pressures in the clinic were frequently recorded above 140 mm Hg but averaged below 130 mm Hg during rehospitalization. Additionally, a 34-year-old patient was removed from protocol therapy because previously normal levels of BUN and serum creatinine increased to 28 and 3 mg/100 cc respectively at the time of annual examination. The final treatment failure was a cerebrovascular accident diagnosed as thrombosis rather than hemorrhage, but which resulted in complete invalidism and inability to return to the clinic.

Terminating Event in Actively Treated Patients.—The single terminating events in the 73 patients who received active drugs occurred in a patient with multiple drug toxicity. Five months before termination the patient was found to have a blood glucose level of 450 mg/100 cc and a serum potassium value of 2.5 mEq/liter. Both abnormalities disappeared when the special A tablet containing only reserpine was substituted. However, five months later he had a mental depression.

Nonterminating (Class B) Morbid Events.— Class B events (Table 6), as opposed to class A events, were those which did not require permanent discontinuation of protocol treatments. Patients with developing B events could be treated with known antihypertensive agents for as long as six months, after which, protocol treatment had to be reinstituted. Class B events included organic complications associated with atherosclerosis, such as cerebrovascular thrombosis (as contrasted to hemorrhage which was considered a class A event) or myocardial infarction. Congestive heart failure which responded to routine therapy with digitalis or mercurials and did not require antihypertensive agents also was classified as a B event.

Seven patients, in addition to those described above under terminating events, had class B complications during the course of the trial (Table 6). These events occurred in six placebo-treated patients and in one actively treated. In the placebo-treated group myocardial infarction accompanied by diagnostic electrocardiographic and serum transaminase changes occurred in two patients. Congestive heart failure occurred in two others, the symptoms and signs of which cleared following treatment with digitalis. Cerebrovascular thrombosis was diagnosed in the fifth case, and the sixth had repeated transient episodes of left-sided hemiparesis. The single class B event in the active-treatment group occurred in a 68-year-old man who had hypotensive levels of blood pressure accompanied by a left-sided hemiparesis.

Comment

Although essential hypertension is generally regarded as a slowly progressive disorder, such did not appear to be the case in these male patients with clinic diastolic blood pressures of 115 mm Hg or higher. An extremely high incidence of severe complications, especially early funduscopic manifestations of accelerated hypertension occurred in the placebo-treated group. A similar high incidence of severe hypertensive complications occurring in placebo-treated patients over a two-year period of observation was reported by Wolff and Lindeman.[12] They attributed this in part to the fact that their clinic population was primarily a lower-income Negro group. However, in the present report more whites than Negroes had hypertensive complications despite equal numbers of each race randomized to placebos.

The majority of prior reports on the effects of antihypertensive drug treatment in essential hypertension have not contained randomized control groups. Hodge et al[11] utilized as their control the patients who refused to undertake treatment. They found a 50% reduction in mortality in the treated group over a period of 1 to 8 years of observation in patients with grade 2 hypertensive retinopathy. Leishman's untreated patients were those who declined or who were considered unsuitable for sympathectomy.[11] He found morbidity and mortality reduced by two thirds in the treated group. Hood and his associates[13] using a nonrandomized untreated control group concluded that mortality was considerably reduced by treatment in essential hypertension.

A prospective, randomized control study was carried out by Wolff and Lindeman in 87 patients.[12] Twelve percent defaulted. Over a two-year period the incidence or morbid events in the treated patients was one third of that observed in the placebo group. Hamilton[16] alternately assigned 61 patients with clinic diastolic blood pressures averaging 110 mm Hg or higher to active treatment and placebo. Thirty were treated with antihypertensive agents and 31 were not. Over an eight-year period of follow-up, 16 of the untreated patients had complications, primarily strokes, as compared to five of the treated group. Of the latter, four exhibited poor blood pressure control. If they are excluded, only one of the treated patients had a severe complication.

The evidence provided by these earlier studies plus the present report leaves little doubt as to the value of antihypertensive drug therapy in essential hypertension associated with clinic diastolic blood pressures of 115 mm Hg or more. It appears that the majority of such patients can be managed satisfactorily with combinations of thiazides, reserpine, and hydralazine,[17] none of which require more than minor dosage adjustments.

Generic and Trade Names of Drugs

Hydralazine hydrochloride—*Apresoline Hydrochloride.*
Hydrochlorothiazide—*Aquarius, Esidrix, Hydril, Hydrodiuril, Oretic.*
Reserpine—*Rauloydin, Raurine, Rau-Sed, Reserpoid, Sandril, Serfin, Serpasil, Serpate, Vio-Serpine.*

Participants

Members of Study Group: Edward D. Freis, MD, *Chairman;* Luis A. Arias, MD; Mark L. Armstrong, MD; Alston W. Blount, MD; Massimo Calabresi, MD; C. Hilmon Castle, MD; Leo Elson, MD; Rudolph E. Fremont, MD; Michael A. Harris, MD; John D. Kyriacopoulos, MD; David Littman, MD; Alan F. Lyon, MD; Gloria D. Massaro, MD; Donald McCaughan, MD; Henry W.

Overbeck, MD; Eliseo C. Perez-Stable, MD; Eli A. Ramirez, MD; and J. R. Thomas, MD.

Participating Veterans Administration Hospitals: Bronx; Brooklyn; Dearborn, Mich; Iowa City; Jackson, Miss; Memphis; Nashville; Oklahoma City; Pittsburgh; Richmond, Va; Salt Lake City; San Juan, PR; Washington, DC; West Haven, Conn; and West Roxbury, Mass.

Biostatisticians: Russell B. Tewksbury, ScD. and Lawrence W. Shaw.

Consultants and Associates: Walter M. Kirkendall, MD; David W. Richardson, MD; and Louis Lasagna, MD.

The special medications used in this investigation were prepared by William E. Wagner, MD. of Ciba Pharmaceutical Co., Summit, NJ.

References

1. Perry, H.M. Jr., and Schroeder, H.A.: The Effect of Treatment on Mortality Rates in Severe Hypertension. A Comparison of Medical and Surgical Regimens, *Arch Int Med* 102:418-425 (Sept) 1958.

2. Dustan, H.P., et al: The Effectiveness of Long-Term Treatment of Malignant Hypertension. *Circulation* 18:644-651 (Oct) 1958.

3. Harrington, M.; Kincaid-Smith, P.; and McMichael, J.: Results of Treatment in Malignant Hypertension. *Brit Med J* 2:969-980 (Nov 14) 1959.

4. Sokolow, M., and Perloff, D.: Five-Year Survival of Consecutive Patients With Malignant Hypertension Treated With Antihypertensive Agents, *Amer J Cardiol* 6:858-863 (Nov) 1960.

5. Björk, S., et al: The Effect of Active Drug Treatment in Severe Hypertensive Disease, *Acta Med Scand* 169:673-689 (June) 1961.

6. Mohler, E.R., and Freis, E.D.: Five-Year Survival of Patients With Malignant Hypertension Treated With Antihypertensive Agents, *Amer Heart J* 60:329-335 (Sept) 1960.

7. Perera, G.A.: Antihypertensive Drug Versus Symptomatic Treatment in Primary Hypertension: Effect on Survival, *JAMA* 173:11-13 (May 7) 1960.

8. Goldring, W., and Chasis, H.: Antihypertensive Drug Therapy: An Appraisal, *Arch Int Med* 115:523-525 (May) 1965.

9. Relman, A.S.: in Ingelfinger, F.J.; Relman, A.S.; and Finland, M. (eds.): *Controversy in Internal Medicine*, Philadelphia: W.B. Saunders Co., 1966, pp 101-102.

10. Freis, E.D.: in Gross, F. (ed.): *Antihypertensive Therapy: Principles and Practice, an International Symposium*, New York: Springer-Verlag New York, Inc., 1966, pp 345-354.

11. A Double-Blind Control Study of Antihypertensive Agents: I. Comparative Effectiveness of Reserpine and Hydralazine, and Three Ganglionic Blocking Agents. Veterans Administration Cooperative Study on Antihypertensive Agents, *Arch Intern Med* 106:81-96 (July) 1960.

12. Wolff, F.W. and Lindeman, R.D.: Effects of Treatment in Hypertension: Results of a Controlled Study, *J Chronic Dis* 19:227-240 (March) 1966.

13. Hodge, J.V.; McQueen, E.G.; and Smirk, H.: Results of Hypotensive Therapy in Arterial Hypertension, *Brit Med J* 1:1-7 (Jan 7) 1961.

14. Leishman, A.W.D.: Hypertension—Treated and Untreated—A Study of 400 Cases, *Brit Med J* 1:1361-1368 (May 30) 1959.

15. Hood, B., et al: Analysis of Mortality and Survival in Actively Treated Hypertensive Disease, *Acta Med Scand* 174 (pt 4): 393-406, 1963.

16. Hamilton, M., in Gross, F. (ed.): *Antihypertensive Therapy, Principles and Practice, an International Symposium*, New York: Springer-Verlag New York, Inc., 1966, pp 196-211.

17. Double Blind Control Study of Antihypertensive Agents: III. Chlorothiazide Alone and in Combination With Other Agents: Preliminary Results, Veterans Administration Cooperative Study on Antihypertensive Agents, *Arch Intern Med* 110:230-236 (Aug) 1962.

Reprinted from the Journal of the American Medical Association
August 17, 1970 Volume 213
Copyright 1970, American Medical Association

Effects of Treatment on Morbidity in Hypertension

II. Results in Patients With Diastolic Blood Pressure Averaging 90 Through 114 mm Hg

Veterans Administration Cooperative Study Group on Antihypertensive Agents

Three hundred and eighty male hypertensive patients with diastolic blood pressures averaging 90 to 114 mm Hg were randomly assigned to either active antihypertensive agents or placebos. The estimated risk of developing a morbid event over a five-year period was reduced from 55% to 18% by treatment. Terminating morbid events occurred in 35 patients of the control group as compared to 9 patients in the treated group. Nineteen deaths related to hypertension or atherosclerosis occurred in the control group and 8 in the actively treated group. In addition to morbid events, 20 control patients developed persistent diastolic levels of 125 mm Hg or higher. Treatment was more effective in preventing congestive heart failure and stroke than in preventing the complications of coronary artery disease. The degree of benefit was related to the level of prerandomization blood pressure.

In a previous publication in this journal[1] the Veterans Administration Cooperative Study Group on Antihypertensive Agents reported on the beneficial effects of antihypertensive drugs on morbidity in patients with moderately severe hypertension. These were patients with initial diastolic blood pressures averaging 115 through 129 mm Hg who had been randomized into a prospective double-blind trial of active antihypertensive drugs vs placebos. Twenty-seven patients developed assessable events in the control group as compared to two patients in the group receiving active antihypertensive agents. This striking result favoring treatment was in agreement with the results of other prospective trials[2,3] in patients with hypertension of similar severity.

In hypertension of lesser severity, however, there are little or no controlled data available on the value of antihypertensive drug therapy. Resolution of this question is of great importance not only because of the large number of patients with mild hypertension but also because the potential benefits of drug treatment have been questioned especially in this group of hypertensive patients.[4] The present report presents the results of a prospective, controlled trial of drug treatment on morbidity and mortality in a group of 380 patients with mild or moderate hypertension whose initial

For complete list of participants, see page 1152.
Reprint requests to 50 Irving St NW, Washington, DC 20422 (Dr. Freis).

161

diastolic blood pressure averaged 90 through 114 mm Hg.

Plan of Investigation

The clinical trial included 523 male veterans who, while not receiving antihypertensive treatment, exhibited diastolic blood pressures averaging 90 through 129 mm Hg. Randomization of patients began in April 1964. However, in May 1967, the study was terminated in the subgroup of 143 patients whose diastolic blood pressures averaged 115 through 129 mm Hg prior to randomization. Termination of the study of this group as previously reported[1] was necessitated by the high incidence of morbid events in the control as compared to the treated patients, demonstrating at a relatively early date a highly significant ($P < 0.001$) effect of treatment. Such a significant difference was not evident at the time, however, in the patients whose diastolic blood pressures averaged below 115 mm Hg prior to randomization. These latter patients were continued in the randomized trial until 1969 and are the subject of the present communication.

The experimental design has been described in previous reports.[1,5] Initially all patients were hospitalized for diagnosis and evaluation of the severity of their hypertension. Patients whose diastolic blood pressure averaged 90 through 129 mm Hg during the fourth through sixth hospital day were accepted for further follow-up. Patients whose diastolic averages fell below 90 mm Hg or rose above 129 mm Hg during this period of hospitalization were excluded.

Following hospitalization the patients entered a prerandomization observation period of two to four months' duration during which time they received placebos of antihypertensive agents. The patients whose diastolic blood pressures during the last two clinic visits of the observation period averaged 90 through 129 mm Hg were entered into the trial, providing there were no other reasons for exclusion. Blood pressure was measured by a physician with the patient in a sitting position.

Other reasons for excluding patients from the trial, in addition to diastolic blood pressure, are detailed in other reports.[1,5] Such reasons included a history of a severe hypertensive complication such as a cerebral or subarachnoid hemorrhage, hypertensive neuroretinopathy, dissecting aneurysm, or renal failure, but did not include atherosclerotic complications such as coronary artery disease or cerebrovascular thrombosis. Also excluded were (1) patients with surgically curable hypertension, (2) with unrelated fatal diseases such as malignant tumors, (3) those unwilling or unable to return to clinic, and (4) poorly motivated or otherwise uncooperative or unreliable patients.

The outpatient prerandomization observation period provided a further opportunity to check on the reliability of the patients. Riboflavin, which produces bright yellow fluorescence of the urine, was incorporated in the placebos. At each clinic visit a urine specimen was examined under ultraviolet light. In addition, pill counts were made at each clinic visit. No patient was accepted into the randomized trial unless the urine exhibited fluorescence and the pill counts were within a stipulated range, at each of two successive visits during the prerandomization observation period.

Accepted patients were then randomly assigned double-blind to either active drugs or placebos. Active drugs consisted of two types of tablets, one being a combination tablet containing 50 mg hydrochlorothiazide and 0.1 mg reserpine which was given twice daily. The other was 25 mg of hydralazine hydrochloride given three times daily. The latter medication was raised to 50 mg three times daily if the diastolic blood pressure remained at 90 mm Hg or higher. Obviously, practically all of the patients in the placebo group had their "doses" raised to this level. Provision was made for reduction of doses if hypotensive reactions or other disturbing side effects occurred. Patients in the control group received placebos identical in taste and appearance to the active drugs. Indicated symptomatic treatment, including drugs other than antihypertensive agents, was permitted in all patients.

Postrandomization clinic visits were at monthly intervals for the first two months and at bimonthly intervals thereafter. Annual examinations included taking a history and a physical examination, roentgenogram of the chest, electrocardiogram, pertinent chemical analyses of the blood, and renal function tests. Additional interim visits could be scheduled when indicated.

Characteristics of Patients

Three hundred and eighty patients with diastolic blood pressures averaging 90 through 114 mm Hg were randomized into the trial. Of this number, 186 received active drugs while 194 were given placebos. Tables 1 and 2 indicate that the two groups were comparable according to the indicated variables. The median ages were 49.2 and 48.1 years and the average ages were 52.0 and 50.5 years in the control and treatment groups, respectively. Negro patients comprised 42% of the control group and 41% of the treated group. Blood pressure as measured in the clinic during the posthospitalization observation period prior to randomization averaged 165.1/104.7 mm Hg in the control group and 162.1/103.8 mm Hg in the treated patients. There were no significant differences between the control and treated pa-

162

tients with regard to findings from renal function tests, fasting blood sugar value, serum cholesterol value, uric acid level, and left ventricular enlargement as assessed by x-ray films and electrocardiography. By all factors measured the two groups were comparable.

Duration of Observation

Patients were entered into the trial from April 1964 to September 1968, and the study was terminated in October 1969. Thus, the earliest entrants were observed for 5.5 years and the latest entrants for a minimum of 1 year. The average potential duration of observation, disregarding losses and terminations, was 3.9 years for the control group and 3.7 years for the treated patients. However, because of the losses and terminations due to elevated diastolic blood pressure described below, the actual duration of postrandomization observation was 3.3 years for the control group and 3.2 years for the treated patients.

Changes in Blood Pressure

Systolic and diastolic blood pressure fell promptly and significantly in the treated patients and remained at reduced levels throughout the trial. The changes in blood pressure at the fourth month of observation in the treated and control patients are depicted in Fig 1. The mean change in systolic blood pressure was an increase of 4.2 mm Hg in the control group and a fall of 27.2 mm Hg in the treated patients from the levels recorded during the prerandomization observation period. The mean change in diastolic blood pressure was a rise of 1.2 mm Hg in the control patients and a fall of 17.4 mm Hg in the treated group during this same interval. The distribution of the changes in blood pressure as shown in Fig 1 indicates a marked shift to

Table 1.—Background of Randomized Patients: Numeration Data

Characteristic	Control Group No.	Control Group %	Treatment Group No.	Treatment Group %	Total
Total randomized	194		186		380
Negro	81	42	76	41	157
Other°	114	58	109	59	223
Heart size by roentgenogram					
Ungerleider enlarged	42	22	53	29	95
Electrocardiogram					
Left ventricular hypertrophy	32	16	30	16	62

*In addition to whites, this group includes four patients of Asiatic extraction, two in the control group and two in the treated group.

Table 2.—Measurement Data Prior to Randomization

Characteristic	Control Group Mean	Treatment Group Mean
Age (yr)	52.0	50.5
Age (median, yr)	49.2	48.1
Height, cm (ft, in)	175.3 (5, 9)	172.7 (5, 8)
Weight, kg (lb)	82.0 (180.9)	79.8 (176.1)
Duration known hypertension (yr)	4.4	4.6
Average hospital diastolic pressure (mm Hg)	101.3	100.2
Average hospital systolic pressure (mm Hg)	157.5	154.0
Average clinic diastolic pressure (mm Hg)	104.7	103.8
Average clinic systolic pressure (mm Hg)	165.1	162.1
Total severity score°	6.7	6.8
Renal score (0-4)	0.2	0.2
Cardiac score (0-4)	0.8	0.9
CNS† score (0-4)	0.3	0.3
Serum creatinine (mg/100 cc)	1.26	1.24
BUN (mg/100 cc)	15.6	16.2
Serum potassium (mEq/liter)	4.4	4.4
PSP‡ excretion (% in 2 hr)	58.8	60.0
Fasting blood glucose (mg/100 cc)	96.5	100.4
Cholesterol (mg/100 cc)	250.1	245.0
Uric acid (mg/100 cc)	6.3	6.0

*Detailed criteria for grades 0 through 4 given in reference 6.
†CNS signifies central nervous system.
‡PSP signifies phenolsulfonphthalein.

the left into the "decrease" zone for the treated patients as compared to the control group. Also apparent is the wide variation in individual responses particularly with regard to systolic blood pressure.

Losses Other Than Assessable Events

Deaths Due to Unrelated Conditions.—Four patients died of disorders unrelated to hypertension. Two of the patients were in the control group. One died of generalized carcinomatosis demonstrated at autopsy and the other of uremia secondary to carcinoma of the urinary bladder. One patient in the treated group died of a subdural hematoma following a skull fracture and another of penicillin anaphy-

laxis. Postmortem examination was carried out in both of these patients.

Losses Due to Drug Toxicity.—Two patients in the treatment group developed reactions thought to be due to drug toxicity. The first patient developed orbital edema with fever and malaise. Roentgenogram of the chest revealed infiltrates in the lungs. There was no dermatitis or arthritis. Lupus cells were not found in the blood although the antinuclear antibody test was positive. Protocol drugs were discontinued because of the possibility of lupus syndrome associated with hydralazine. The second patient developed purpura one month after beginning active drug treatment. Findings from examination in the hospital, including biopsy, were con-

Morbidity in Hypertension **1145**

163

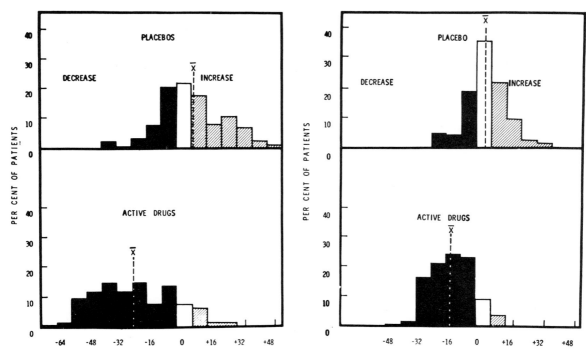

1. Changes in systolic (left) *and diastolic blood pressure* (right) *after four months of treatment in patients given placebos* (top) *and in patients treated with active drugs* (bottom). *Mean of changes* ($\bar{X}$).

sistent with anaphylactoid purpura. The purpuric lesions cleared two weeks after protocol treatment was discontinued and reappeared within three days after administration of active drugs began again. Protocol treatment was, therefore, discontinued.

Drop-Outs.—Fifty-six or 15% of the 380 randomized patients were classified as drop-outs during the course of the trial. Of this number 27 had been randomized to receive placebos and 29 to receive active drugs. The average period of follow-up prior to dropping out was 17.6 months with a range from less than 1 month to 49 months. Six patients moved away from the area of the clinic. Two were lost from follow-up because of closure of one participating clinic. Four returned to the care of their private physicians. Fifteen

complained of side effects prior to dropping out. Nine of these patients had been receiving drugs, and six were taking placebos. Five patients had psychiatric or alcoholic problems of such severity as to make continued protocol treatment impractical. In the remaining patients the reason for drop-out could not be determined. It should be noted that three of the patients taking placebos sustained nonterminating morbid events prior to their dropping out.

Assessable Morbid Events

The records of the patients reported as having assessable morbid events were reviewed by two consulting physicians who had not participated in the trial. All assessable events were reviewed except those related to the development of

electrocardiographic signs of left ventricular hypertrophy or of roentgenographic evidence of cardiac enlargement, which will be reported in a subsequent communication. All available data pertaining to each organic complication, except the type of protocol treatment and the level of blood pressure, were presented to the reviewers and their decisions regarding the occurrence and classification of an event according to the definitions given in the protocol (see list of assessable events at the end of the communication) were accepted as final.

Table 3 summarizes the assessable events by major categories. Such events occurred in 98 of the 380 randomized patients, 76 in the control group and 22 in the treated patients. Of this number 20 control patients developed an increase in

164

diastolic blood pressure to levels exceeding 124 mm Hg on three separate clinic visits and persisting for 3 weeks or longer. Since these patients were removed from the trial only because of persistent blood pressure elevations and not for an organic complication, they will not be included in the subsequent assessment of effectiveness of treatment in preventing morbid events.

The remaining 78 patients had organic complications subdivided as follows: 56 of 194 or 28.9% of the control group and 22 of 186 or 11.8% of the treated patients. The most striking evidence of benefit of treatment was manifested in the count of class A events (hypertensive complications defined in the protocol which required removal of the patient from the study.[1] There were none among the treated patients but 14 among the controls. These included five class A deaths (Table 4) plus nine other class A events (Table 5). When other cardiovascular (class B) deaths and treatment failures were added, the comparisons were still impressive, 35 of 194 patients or 18.0% amongst the controls and only 9 of 186 or 4.8% in the treated group (Table 3). The effectiveness of treatment (difference in percent incidence of complications between control and treated groups divided by the percent incidence in the control group) in preventing terminating organic complications was 73% (Table 3). The decision to discontinue the trial was based on this favorable evidence supplemented by the life-table analyses described below which suggested that the benefit of treatment was continuing through time and was not solely concentrated in the first year or two of treatment.

Terminating Events. — DEATHS RELATED TO CARDIOVASCULAR DISEASE.—Twenty-seven patients died of hypertensive or atherosclerotic complications, 19 occurring in the

Table 3.—Summary of Assessable Events

	Control Group		Treated Group		% Effectiveness*
	No.	%	No.	%	
Terminating morbid events†	35	18.0	9	4.8	73
Nonterminating B events	21		13		
Total morbid events	56	28.9	22	11.8	59
Terminated on account of elevated blood pressure	20		0		
Total assessable events	76	39.2	22	11.8	70
No. patients randomized	194	100.0	186	100.0	

*See text.
†Includes cardiovascular deaths, class A events, and treatment failures except those due to diastolic levels >124 mm Hg.

Table 4.—Causes of Death

Cause	Control Group	Treated Group
Deaths due to class A events		
Cerebrovascular hemorrhage	3	0
Subarachnoid hemorrhage	1	0
Dissecting aneurysm	1	0
Deaths due to class B events		
Myocardial infarction	3	2
Sudden death	8	4
Cerebrovascular thrombosis	3	1
Ruptured atherosclerotic aneurysm	0	1
Total related deaths*	19	8

*Does not include four unrelated deaths, two in the control group and two in the treated group (see text).

Table 5.—Terminating Morbid Events Other Than Death

Type of Event	Control Group	Treated Group
Class A events		
Uncontrolled cardiac failure	5	0
Dissecting aortic aneurysm	1	0
Subarachnoid hemorrhage	1	0
Fundi, striate hemorrhages	1	0
Acute hypertensive encephalopathy	1	0
Subtotal	9	0
Treatment failures		
Cerebrovascular thrombosis, severe	4	0
Progressive azotemia	1	0
Fundi, one striate hemorrhage and ? early papilledema	1	0
Fundi, one striate hemorrhage and ? encephalopathy	1	0
Hypotension	0	1
Subtotal	7	1
Total	16	1

control group and 8 in the treated patients (Table 4). Five deaths associated with class A or hypertensive events (see list of assessable events at the end of the communication) were cerebral hemorrhage in four and dissecting aortic aneurysm in one, all occurring in the control group of patients. Deaths resulting from class B events were associated predominantly with coronary artery disease. Eleven patients in the placebo group and 6 in the treated group had either a documented myocardial infarction or a "sudden death." Cerebrovascular thrombosis as opposed to hemorrhage was the cause of death in three control patients and in one treated patient. The remaining

Table 6.—Nonterminating Class B Events

Type	Control Group	Treated Group
CVA, thrombosis or TIA*	8	4
Congestive heart failure†	6	0
Myocardial infarction	2	5
Atrial fibrillation	2	3
Heart-block	1	1
Serum creatinine, persistent, >2.0 mg/100 cc	1	0
Proteinuria, persistent, >1+	1	0
Total	**21**	**13**

*Cerebrovascular accident, either a thrombosis (clinical diagnosis) or transient ischemic attack with objective neurological signs.
†Controlled by administration of digitalis and short-term diuretics.

Table 7.—Classification of Morbid Events by Diagnostic Categories

Diagnosis	Total Events		Terminating Events	
	Control	Treated	Control	Treated
Cerebrovascular accident	20	5	12	1
Coronary artery disease	13	11	11	6
Congestive heart failure	11	0	5	0
"Accelerated" hypertension	4	0	4	0
Renal damage	3	0	1	0
Other	5	6	2	2
Total	**56**	**22**	**35**	**9**

death in the treated group was caused by a rupture of an atherosclerotic aneurysm of the aorta.

OTHER CLASS A EVENTS.—Nine patients in the control group as opposed to none in the treated group developed nonfatal class A events (Table 5). Five of the patients had congestive heart failure which could not be controlled by administration of digitalis, sodium restriction, and the intermittent administration of diuretics. In the four remaining patients there was one instance of each of the following complications: dissecting aortic aneurysm, subarachnoid hemorrhage, multiple striate retinal hemorrhages, and acute hypertensive encephalopathy with accompanying neurological signs.

OTHER TERMINATING EVENTS.—Additional organic complications, which did not fulfill the criteria for class A events but which were nevertheless of sufficient severity to require terminating protocol treatment occurred in eight patients of which seven were in the control group. These are listed in Table 5 under the subtitle "treatment fail-ure." Four were associated with cerebrovascular accidents diagnosed clinically as thrombosis rather than hemorrhage but which resulted in such severe incapacity that the patients were unable to attend the clinic. Two additional control patients were removed from the study because of the appearance of a single striate retinal hemorrhage associated in one with symptoms suggesting acute hypertensive encephalopathy, and, in the other, with questionable early papilledema. The remaining control patient exhibited increasing azotemia. One patient in the treated group was removed from the study because of hypotension following a myocardial infarction which resulted in his inability to tolerate the antihypertensive regimen. It is noteworthy that of the 17 nonfatal terminating events (class A and others) 16 occurred in the control group and only one in the treated patient (Table 5).

Nonterminating (Class B) Events.—Class B events include organic complications which require no or only temporary suspension of proto-col treatment (see list of assessable events listed at the end of the communication). Objectively demonstrable atherosclerotic complications predominate as class B events, but the category also includes congestive heart failure responsive to routine therapy other than administration of antihypertensive drugs and certain less severe manifestations of renal disease.

Nonfatal class B events occurred in 21 of the control patients and in 13 of the treated patients (Table 6). Six patients developed congestive heart failure controllable by digitalis and short-term administration of diuretics. It is noteworthy that all six of these patients were in the control group. Also, the incidence of nonterminating cerebrovascular accidents was twice as great in the control as in the treated patients. However, nonfatal myocardial infarction occurred in five of the treated patients as opposed to two of the control group. The incidence of atrial fibrillation and conduction defects was essentially the same in the two groups.

Life-Table Analysis.—The benefit of treatment is more precisely analyzed using life-table methods (Fig 2). This method has the following advantages: (1) it adjusts for the fact that patients enter the study at different times and thus are observed for varying lengths of time; (2) the method adjusts for any differences in losses to observation between the control and treated groups; and (3) most important, it determines whether the benefit of treatment occurs early or late or is continuing through time. The distance separating the control and treatment lines is a measure of the degree of benefit.

It is clear from Fig 2 that the benefit of treatment manifested itself early and continued throughout the entire five years of follow-up. The life-table analysis of either terminating or all morbid events indi-

Morbidity in Hypertension

166

Table 8.—Incidence of Morbid Events With Respect to Level of Prerandomization Blood Pressure

	Control Group			Treated Group			
Prerandomization Blood Pressure, mm Hg	Patients Randomized	Patients With "Morbid Event"		Patients Randomized	Patients With "Morbid Event"		% Effectiveness
		No.	%		No.	%	
Systolic <165	98	15	15.3	108	10	9.3	40
Systolic 165+	96	41	42.7	78	12	15.4	64
Total	**194**	**56**		**186**	**22**		
Diastolic 90-104	84	21	25.0	86	14	16.3	35
Diastolic 105-114	110	35	31.8	100	8	8.0	75
Total	**194**	**56**		**186**	**22**		

Table 9.—Incidence of Morbid Events With Respect to Age and Race

	Control Group			Treated Group			
	Patients Randomized	Patients With "Morbid Event"		Patients Randomized	Patients With "Morbid Event"		% Effectiveness
		No.	%		No.	%	
Age (on admission)							
<50 yr	99	15	15.2	102	7	6.9	55
50 & over	95	41	43.2	84	15	17.9	59
Total	**194**	**56**		**186**	**22**		
Race							
Negro	81	21	25.9	76	8	10.5	54
Other	113	35	31.0	110	14	12.7	59
Total	**194**	**56**		**186**	**22**		

cates that the benefit increased with time. For example, with respect to "all morbid events" it may be seen that at three years the estimated cumulative incidence of morbidity in the control group is twice as great as in the treated patients. This suggests that treatment was about 50% effective at three years. At five years the spread between the two curves was substantially greater indicating an increasing degree of benefit with the passage of time. Specifically, at five years the cumulative incidence rate of events for the control group rises to 55%. By contrast, for the treated group the indicated incidence of events at five years is only 18%. It can be estimated, therefore, that over a five-year period treatment prevented 37% morbidity (55% minus 18%), and this represents a 67% effectiveness (37/55).

The standard errors at five years were 6.3% for the control patients and 4.0% for the treated group. The significance of the difference between the two rates of 55% and

18% yielded a t-value of 5.0 which is highly significant. A crude estimate gave confidence limits of 49% to 81% for the observed 67% effectiveness.

Relationship of Treatment to Other Factors.—RELATIONSHIP TO DIAGNOSTIC CATEGORIES.—It is revealing to examine the incidence of morbid events as related to treatment when the events are classified according to diagnostic categories (Table 7). Thus, in the control vs the treated groups, the prevalence of congestive heart failure was 11:0, of renal deterioration 3:0, and of "accelerated" hypertension (hypertensive neuroretinopathy or encephalopathy) 4:0. The number of cerebrovascular complications also seemed to be considerably influenced by treatment since the ratio of cerebrovascular events in the control vs treated patients was 20:5, and, of the more severe or terminating cerebrovascular events, it was 12:1. On the other hand, assessable events caused by coronary artery disease (myocardial infarction or

sudden death) were nearly the same in the two groups, 13 in the control and 11 in the treated, although fatal coronary events were somewhat greater in the control group.

RELATIONSHIP TO PRERANDOMIZATION BLOOD PRESSURE.—The beneficial effect of treatment was most evident in the patients with higher initial levels of blood pressure. With respect to diastolic blood pressure the effectiveness of treatment was 75% in the patients with prerandomization diastolic blood pressure averaging 105 through 114 mm Hg as opposed to only 35% in the group averaging 90 through 104 mm Hg (Table 8). A similar although somewhat less striking trend was noted with respect to systolic blood pressure, the effectiveness of treatment being 64% in patients with initial systolic levels averaging 165 mm Hg and above as opposed to 40% in the group with lower initial systolic blood pressure.

RELATIONSHIP TO AGE.—The majority of the patients developing

Morbidity in Hypertension **1149**

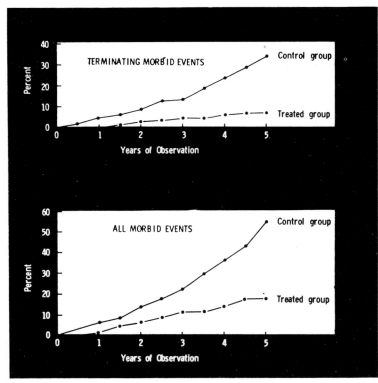

2. *Estimated cumulative incidence of morbidity over a five-year period as calculated by life-table method. Terminating morbid events* (top) *and all morbid events* (bottom).

morbid events were in the older age group. Of the 56 control patients developing morbid events 41 were 50 years of age or older at the time of admission to the study, while only 15 were below age 50. A similar distribution was found with respect to the treated patients. The percent effectiveness of treatment was approximately the same in the younger and older groups (Table 9). However, because of the lower number of events in the patients below age 50 the estimated effectiveness of treatment cannot be accepted with the same degree of confidence as in the older patients.

RELATIONSHIP TO RACE.—The in-cidence of morbid events was no greater in Negro patients. In fact, in the control group the incidence of events was slightly lower in Negroes, 25.9% as opposed to 31.0% of the other patients. A similar relationship was noted in the treated patients (Table 9). The percent effectiveness of treatment was essentially the same in the two racial groups.

Side Effects

In the treated group of patients dosage adjustments frequently were required because of hypotensive and other symptoms. A complete analy-sis of these and other side effects

will be made in a subsequent com-munication. The two patients lost to protocol because of drug toxicity have been described above. In addi-tion, in the present report only those side effects requiring removal of either reserpine or hydrochloro-thiazide from the treatment regimen will be considered.

Administration of either reserpine or hydrochlorothiazide or their placebos was withdrawn because of side effect in 29 patients. Reserpine and hydrochlorothiazide were ad-ministered combined in a single tablet. In order to avoid losses to protocol because of side effects pre-sumably caused by one or the other of the two agents, provision was made to permit substitution of a tablet which contained either reser-pine or hydrochlorothiazide alone and omitted the offending medica-tion. These special tablets were made available on request of a participating physician. Similar-appearing placebo tablets were made available for the control pa-tients and the physician did not know whether the substitution rep-resented active drugs or placebos.

In the majority of the 29 patients substitution of the special tablet was necessitated by presumed res-erpine-induced side effects. Mental depression occurred in 12 patients. However, only seven of these pa-tients had been receiving active drugs while the remaining five had been randomly selected to receive placebos. Ten patients developed peptic ulcer of which six had been taking active drugs and four place-bos. In two patients substitution was made because of impotence; one of these two had been randomly selected to receive the placebo regi-men. The remaining six patients all were receiving active treatment. Their side effects included sleep-iness, severe nasal stuffiness, gout, seizures presumably caused by hy-potension, and abnormal results from the glucose tolerance test.

Comment

The effectiveness of treatment was clearly demonstrated in the patients with prerandomization systolic blood pressures above 164 or diastolic pressure above 104 mm Hg. The difference in the incidence of morbid events between control and treated patients was less clear cut in the patients with blood pressures below these levels. This may be due to the fact that organic complications appear slowly in mild hypertension as indicated by the considerably lower incidence of such events in patients with blood pressures below 165/105 mm Hg.

As would be expected, a greater incidence of organic complications occurred in the older than in the younger patients. Of considerable importance is the observation that treatment was found to be effective in reducing the number of such complications in these older patients. Although the indicated effectiveness of treatment was essentially the same in patients above and below age 50 years, the results were not as convincing in the younger group because of the low incidence of morbid events in both the control and treated patients. It should be mentioned, however, that in the group of 20 control patients, not counted as having morbid events but who were removed from the study because of persistent elevation of diastolic blood pressure greater than 124 mm Hg, 14 so removed were below 50 years of age.

Treatment was most effective in preventing hypertensive complications and least effective in preventing atherosclerotic complications, particularly those associated with coronary artery disease. Complications such as congestive heart failure, renal damage, cerebrovascular hemorrhage, and accelerated hypertension occurred only in the control group. On the other hand, the incidence of complications associated with coronary artery disease was essentially the same in the control and treated patients.

Because of the gradual progression of atherosclerosis, the negative result with regard to prevention of myocardial infarction and sudden death cannot be taken as evidence that treatment is ineffective. Continuation of the present study was not justified because of the favorable evidence with regard to prevention of hypertensive complications. If follow-up had been longer, and if administration of antihypertensive drugs had been started at an earlier age, a significant difference might have been demonstrated. The average age of the patients was 51 years and hypertension could have been present for many years prior to randomization. Atherosclerosis of the coronary arteries, therefore, may have been well established at the time of entrance into the study. Further trials are needed in a more selected population to determine whether antihypertensive treatment helps prevent coronary artery disease.

It is of interest to compare the results of the present series of patients whose initial diastolic blood pressures averaged 90 through 114 mm Hg with the results previously reported in the patients whose diastolic blood pressures at the beginning of study averaged 115 through 129 mm Hg.[1] The benefit of treatment was quickly manifested in the latter series. Thirty-eight percent of the control patients in that series developed assessable events over an average period of only 15.7 months of postrandomization follow-up, whereas such events occurred in only 3% of the treated patients. A considerably longer period of follow-up was required to demonstrate a significant benefit of treatment in the presently reported series of patients with lower levels of diastolic blood pressure.

The distribution as to type of events also was different in the two groups of patients divided according to level of initial diastolic blood pressure. In the control patients with initial diastolic levels of 115 through 129 mm Hg accelerated hypertension with hypertensive neuroretinopathy was the most frequent complication. In the present series cerebrovascular disease, congestive heart failure, and coronary artery disease were the most frequent morbid events occurring in the control group. Of the four control patients who died in the previously reported series of patients with high diastolic pressures, three deaths were caused by dissecting or ruptured aortic aneurysm whereas the most common causes of death in the series of patients with lower diastolic pressures were strokes, myocardial infarcts, and sudden death.

It should be emphasized that the present study dealt with a selected population. Many uncooperative and unreliable patients were identified and eliminated from the trial on the basis of pill counts, urine fluorescence test results, and irregularity of clinic attendance during a prerandomization observation period. Treatment obviously would not have been as effective in a group of patients less carefully selected with regard to their desire to cooperate. The population was further limited in that it excluded female patients and patients with labile hypertension whose diastolic blood pressures averaged lower than 90 mm Hg during the fourth through the sixth day of hospitalization. Finally, the incidence of morbid events in the group below age 50 was relatively low. Further studies are needed to evaluate the effectiveness of treatment in labile hypertension and in the prevention of atherosclerotic complications, particularly coronary artery disease. Such studies would seem to require larger numbers of younger patients who can be followed up for long periods of time.

Within the limits defined by this study, however, the present results leave little doubt that antihypertensive drug treatment is beneficial. The present results together with those previously reported in patients with initial diastolic blood pressures of 115 through 129 mm Hg[1] indicate clearly that the higher the level of blood pressure the greater the degree of benefit of such therapy. Certain complications such as congestive heart failure, hypertensive neuroretinopathy,[1] strokes, and renal deterioration were reduced or essentially eliminated in the treated patients. In addition, treatment prevented elevation of diastolic blood pressure to levels where the risk of developing hypertensive complications is greatly increased. The effectiveness of the treatment in preventing such progression is indicated by the fact that while persistent elevation of diastolic blood pressure exceeding 124 mm Hg occurred in approximately 10% of the control patients, they were completely absent in the treated group.

Participants

Permanent Members of the Study Group: Massimo Calabresi, MD; C. Hilmon Castle, MD; Leo Elson, MD; Edward D. Freis, MD, *Chairman;* Rudolph E. Fremont, MD; Michael A. Harris, MD; David Littman, MD; Eli A. Ramirez, MD; and J. R. Thomas, MD.

Other Members: Luis A. Arias, MD; Mark L. Armstrong, MD; Alston W. Blount, MD; Thomas A. Bruce, MD; Ovid B. Bush, Jr., MD. *deceased;* Eugene C. Clark, MD; Annette Fitz, MD, R. M. Freeman, MD; Edward D. Frohlich, MD; Arthur Gear, MD; John D. Kyriacopoulos, MD; Alan F. Lyon, MD; Gloria D. Massaro, MD; Donald McCaughan, MD; Jean Morgan, MD; Henry W. Overbeck, MD; Eliseo C. Perez-Stable, MD; Mitchell Perry, MD; Roger Sutton, MD; and James Taguchi, MD.

Participating Veterans Administration Hospitals: Allen Park, Michigan; Birmingham, Ala; Brooklyn, NY; Dayton, Ohio; Iowa City; Jackson, Miss; Memphis; Nashville, Tenn; Oklahoma City; Pittsburgh; Richmond, Va; Salt Lake City; St. Louis; San Juan, PR; Washington, DC; West Haven, Conn; and West Roxbury, Mass.

Biostatisticians: Russell B. Tewksbury, ScD, and Lawrence W. Shaw.

Central Office Coordinator: Harold W. Schnaper, MD.

Consultants: Jacques Genest, MD; Ray W. Gifford, Jr., MD; Walter M. Kirkendall, MD; Louis Lasagna, MD; David W. Richardson, MD; and Robert W. Wilkins, MD.

The special medications used in this investigation were prepared by William E. Wagner, MD, of Ciba Pharmaceutical Co., Summit, NJ.

References

1. Effects of treatment on morbidity in hypertension: Results in patients with diastolic blood pressures averaging 115 through 129 mm Hg. Veterans Administration Cooperative Study Group on Antihypertensive Agents. *JAMA* 202:1028-1034, 1967.
2. Hamilton M: Selection of patients for antihypertensive therapy, in Gross F (ed): *Antihypertensive Therapy: Principles and Practice, an International Symposium.* New York, Springer-Verlag Inc, 1966, pp 196-211.
3. Wolff FW, Lindeman RD: Effects of treatment in hypertension: Results of a controlled study. *J Chronic Dis* 19:227-240, 1966.
4. Relman AS: Comment on who needs drugs for hypertension in Ingelfinger FJ; Relman AS; Finland M (eds): *Controversy in Internal Medicine.* Philadelphia, W B Saunders Co, 1966, pp 101-102.
5. Freis ED: Organization of a long-term multiclinic therapeutic trial on hypertension, in Gross F (ed): *Antihypertensive Therapy: Principles and Practice, an International Symposium,* New York. Springer-Verlag Inc, 1966, pp 345-354.
6. A double-blind control study of antihypertensive agents: I. Comparative effectiveness of reserpine and hydralazine, and three ganglionic blocking agents, Veterans Administration Cooperative Study Group on Antihypertensive Agents. *Arch Intern Med* 106:81-96, 1960.

Assessable Events

Abbreviated definitions of terminating events (class A and treatment failures) and nonterminating (class B) events.

Class A Events

1. Striate hemorrhages in more than one retinal quadrant or cotton wool exudates or papilledema.
2. Cerebral or subarachnoid hemorrhage.
3. Dissecting aortic aneurysm.
4. Inability to control congestive heart failure without using antihypertensive agents.
5. Elevation of blood urea nitrogen level (BUN) by more than 50% of previous level and exceeding 59 mg/100 cc.
6. Acute hypertensive encephalopathy requiring hospitalization.

Treatment Failures

1. Diastolic blood pressure exceeding 124 mm Hg on each of three successive visits and persisting for three weeks or longer.
2. Assessable organic complications not fulfilling criteria for class A events but of sufficient severity to require discontinuation of protocol regimen.

Class B Events

Cardiac

1. Myocardial infarction documented by characteristic electrocardiogram or serum enzyme changes.
2. Congestive heart failure controllable by routine therapy other than antihypertensive agents including digitalis, restricted activity, low salt diet, and intermittent diuretics.
3. Atrial fibrillation or flutter or ventricular tachycardia without evidence of quinidine or digitalis intoxication.
4. Heart-block such as bundle-branch block, second or third degree heart-block or first degree heart-block with P-R interval of 0.28 seconds or more.
5. Left ventricular enlargement by ECG or roentgenogram.
6. Pulmonary embolism or infarction.

Central Nervous System

1. Cerebrovascular thrombosis or embolism.
2. Transient ischemic attacks with objective neurological changes during the attack.

Aorta

1. Arteriosclerotic aneurysm.

Renal

1. Doubling of BUN (but to below 60 mg/100 cc) or creatinine levels to values above normal limits not due to primary renal disease.
2. Proteinuria (2+ or more in three or more specimens) in absence of congestive heart failure, primary renal disease, or lower urinary tract disease.
3. Persistent hematuria (> 5 cells per high power field centrifuged sediment) not due to primary renal or lower urinary tract diseases.

Morbidity in Hypertension

Reprinted from *Circulation*
May 1972 Volume 45
Copyright 1972 American Heart Association

Effects of Treatment on Morbidity in Hypertension

III. Influence of Age, Diastolic Pressure, and Prior Cardiovascular Disease; Further Analysis of Side Effects

VETERANS ADMINISTRATION COOPERATIVE STUDY GROUP

ON ANTIHYPERTENSIVE AGENTS

SUMMARY

Additional data are presented from the Veterans Administration Cooperative Study with respect to the 194 control and 186 treated male patients with initial diastolic blood pressures averaging 90–114 mm Hg. Attack rates and effectiveness of treatment were examined with respect to the following risk factors present at entry: (1) cardiovascular-renal (CVR) abnormalities, the prevalence of which was higher than in the general population of hypertensive patients; (2) diastolic blood pressure; and (3) age. Both attack rates and effectiveness of treatment increased directly with the number of these risk factors present at entry. Age and presence of CVR abnormalities at entry appeared to strongly influence subsequent attack rates, whereas entry level of blood pressure had a relatively smaller effect on attack rates. On the other hand, "effectiveness of treatment" appeared to be most influenced by the initial level of blood pressure. Patients with prerandomization diastolic blood pressure in the range of 90 to 104 mm Hg derived relatively little benefit from treatment unless they had CVR abnormalities at entry or were over 50 years of age. A longer period of follow-up would be needed to assess the value of treatment in the lower risk subgroups.

With respect to side effects, the incidence of mild hypokalemia, hyperuricemia, and elevated fasting blood sugar was significantly higher in the treated group. These and other side effects should be weighed against the benefit to be expected from treating hypertensive patients at low risk.

From the Veterans Administration Hospital, Washington, D. C.

Permanent Members of the Study Group: Massimo Calabresi, M.D., C. Hilmon Castle, M.D., Leo Elson, M.D., Edward D. Freis, M.D. (Chairman), Rudolph E. Fremont, M.D., Michael A. Harris, M.D., David Littman, M.D., Eli A. Ramirez, M.D., and J.R. Thomas, M.D.

Other Members: Luis A. Arias, M.D., Mark L. Armstrong, M.D., Alston W. Blount, M.D., Thomas A. Bruce, M.D., Ovid B. Bush, Jr., M.D. (deceased), Eugene C. Clark, M.D., Annette Fitz, M.D., R. M. Freeman, M.D., Edward D. Frohlich, M.D., Arthur Gear, M.D., John D. Kyriacopoulos, M.D., Alan R. Lyon, M.D., Gloria D. Massaro, M.D., Donald McCaughan, M.D., Jean Morgan, M.D., Henry W. Overbeck, M.D., Eliseo C. Perez-Stable, M.D., Mitchell H. Perry, M.D., Roger Sutton, M.D., and James Taguchi, M.D.

Biostatisticians: Russell B. Tewksbury, Sc.D. (deceased), Paul D. Williams, M.S., and Lawrence Shaw, A.M.

Central Office Coordinator: Harold W. Schnaper, M.D.

Participating Veterans Administration Hospitals: Allen Park, Michigan, Birmingham, Alabama, Brooklyn, New York, Dayton, Ohio, Iowa City, Iowa, Jackson, Mississippi, Memphis, Tennessee, Nashville, Tennessee, Oklahoma City, Oklahoma, Pittsburgh, Pennsylvania, Richmond, Virginia, Salt Lake City, Utah, St. Louis, Missouri, San Juan, Puerto Rico, Washington, D. C., West Haven, Connecticut, and West Roxbury, Massachusetts.

Address for reprints: Dr. Edward D. Freis, Veterans Administration Hospital, 50 Irving Street, N.W., Washington, D.C. 20422.

Received September 28, 1971; revision accepted for publication December 21, 1971.

173

THE VETERANS Administration Cooperative Study Group previously reported on the results of a randomized, double-blind clinical trial in 194 control and 186 treated male patients with initial diastolic blood pressures averaging 90 through 114 mm Hg followed prospectively for periods up to 5.5 years, average 3.3 years.[1] Treatment consisted of a combination of hydrochlorothiazide, reserpine, and hydralazine. There were 19 deaths related to cardiovascular disease in the control group and eight in the treated series. Life table analysis indicated that the risk of a morbid event, fatal or nonfatal, over a 5-year period was reduced from 55 to 18% by treatment. Congestive heart failure, stroke, and progressive renal damage were sharply reduced or eliminated in the treated patients. However, the incidence of myocardial infarction and sudden death was essentially the same in the control and treated groups. In addition to assessable morbid events, 20 control patients versus none of the treated group developed persistent diastolic elevations of 125 mm Hg or higher.

In the initial report the patients were incompletely characterized as to the prevalence of cardiovascular abnormalities prior to randomization. The present report determines the relationship between prior cardiovascular damage and the effectiveness of treatment. The influences of age and blood pressure also are analyzed in more detail than in the original paper. The prerandomization blood pressures given in this and in the initial report[1] represent the average of the readings taken by the physician during the last two outpatient visits preceding randomization. Finally, additional data with respect to side effect and dose modifications are presented.

Influence of Age

The median ages were given in the initial report[1] as 49.2 years for the control group and 48.1 years for the treated series.

Additional data are presented in table 1. Fifty-one percent of the control and 55% of the treated group were less than 50 years of age. Approximately one fourth of the patients were in the 50–59-year age group. The 60 and above age group included 22.1% of the control and 20.5% of the treated patients, the oldest patient being 75 years of age.

The prerandomization blood pressures for the different age groups are shown in table 2. Systolic blood pressure was related directly to age, and averaged 154 mm Hg in the patients under 40 years of age and rose with age to 178 mm Hg in the 70–75-year age group. Mean diastolic blood pressures, however, were essentially the same at all ages. There were no significant differences in blood pressure in the control and treated patients.

Information on the duration of known hypertension indicated that 48% had recognized hypertension for 5 years or more, and 29% had hypertension for 9 years or more. The relatively high prevalence of hypertension of long duration may be explained in part by the age distribution and in part by the fact that the sample included only patients with "fixed" hypertension, namely those with diastolic blood pressures averaging 90 mm Hg or more from the fourth through the sixth day of hospitalization.

The incidence of morbid events during the study by age at randomization is listed in table 3. As would be expected, the incidence of major complications rose with age. In the control group, 15.2% of the patients under age 50 years developed morbid events following randomization as compared to 62.8% of the patients above age 59 years. In the treated patients, the percentage incidence of morbid events was 6.9 and 28.9%, respectively, in these two age groups. Treatment appeared to be effective in all age groups. The effectiveness of

Table 1

Age Distribution of Patients

Age (years)	Control		Treated		Total	
	No.	%	No.	%	No.	%
24–39	22	11.3	32	17.2	54	14.2
40–49	77	39.7	70	37.6	147	38.7
50–59	52	26.8	46	24.7	98	25.8
60–69	28	14.5	23	12.5	51	13.4
70–75	15	7.7	15	8.0	30	7.9
Total	194	100.0	186	100.0	380	100.0

Table 2

Relationship between Age and Blood Pressure prior to Randomization

Age (years)	Control group Systolic	Control group Diastolic	Treated group Systolic	Treated group Diastolic	Total Systolic	Total Diastolic
24–39	151.6	104.4	155.2	103.4	153.7	103.8
40–49	159.5	104.5	159.2	105.2	159.4	104.8
50–59	169.5	105.2	163.2	104.7	166.5	105.0
60–69	176.2	104.9	169.7	101.4	173.3	103.3
70–75	173.7	100.4	182.9	106.0	178.3	103.2
All ages	164.8	104.4	162.7	104.4	163.8	104.4

Mean blood pressure (mm Hg)*

*Average of last two clinic visits prior to randomization.

Table 3

Incidence of Morbid Events with Respect to Age at Randomization

Age (years)	Control group No. rand	Control group With events No.	Control group With events %	Treated group No. rand	Treated group With events No.	Treated group With events %	Effectiveness of treatment* (%)
<50	99	15	15.2	102	7	6.9	55
50–59	52	14	26.9	46	4	8.7	68
60+	43	27	62.8	38	11	28.9	54
Total	194	56	28.9	186	22	11.8	59

*Difference between percent incidence of events in control and treated groups divided by percent incidence in control group.

Table 4

Incidence of Assessable Events by Age and Diagnostic Category

Diagnostic category	<50 C	<50 T	50–59 C	50–59 T	60+ C	60+ T	Total events C	Total events T
Cerebrovascular accident	5	1	5	1	10	3	20	5
Congestive heart failure	1	0	1	0	9	0	11	0
Accelerated hypertension or renal damage	5	0	2	0	0	0	7	0
Coronary artery disease*	4	4	4	2	5	5	13	11
Atrial fibrillation	0	2	0	1	2	0	2	3
Dissecting aneurysm	0	0	1	0	1	0	2	0
Other†	0	0	1	0	0	3	1	3
Total morbid events	15	7	14	4	27	11	56	22
Diastolic > 124 mm Hg	15	0	3	0	2	0	20	0

Abbreviations: C = control group; T = treated group.

*Myocardial infarction or sudden death.

†Includes in treated group one patient terminated because of hypotensive reactions, one death from ruptured atherosclerotic aneurysm, and one patient with second-degree heart block. In control group includes one patient with left bundle-branch block.

treatment in preventing morbid events was estimated from the difference in the percentage incidence of major complications between control and treated patients divided by the percentage incidence in the control patients (table 3). Treatment was 55% effective in the subsample below 50 years of age, 68% in the 50–59-year age group, and 54% in the patients aged 60 years and over.

The relationship between age and type of morbid event is shown in table 4. In the control group the most frequent complications in the oldest age group were cerebrovascular accidents and congestive heart failure. The latter was uncommon below age 60 years. However, increasing hypertension or progressive renal damage occurred predominantly in the control patients below age 50 years. Coronary artery disease occurred in all age groups but its percentage incidence was more common in the patients aged 60 years or over (tables 1, 4). Unlike the other categories, the complications of coronary artery disease did not appear to be affected by treatment.

Influence of Prior Cardiovascular Abnormalities

The prevalence of cardiovascular-renal abnormalities found prior to randomization is summarized in table 5. In grading the optic fundi, "hypertensive" and "sclerotic" changes were evaluated separately. Grade 1 hypertensive changes were defined as a probable decrease in arteriolar caliber with an A-V ratio of approximately 1:2, while grade 2 changes indicated a definite decrease in arteriolar caliber ranging from an A-V ratio less than 1:2 to threadlike arterioles. Because of the difficul-

ty and variability in differentiating grade 1 from normal, only the grade 2 changes are reported. Such changes occurred in 31% of the control and 25% of the treated patients. Grade 2 sclerotic as opposed to hypertensive changes were defined as scattered prominent A-V nicks or asymmetric irregularity of arteriolar segments. Such changes were reported in 24% of patients.

Background charactistics were analyzed to determine the presence of cardiac, central nervous system (CNS), or renal abnormalities. All patients with severity grades[2] greater than zero with respect to any of these target organ systems were included with the following exceptions: headache, if this was the only CNS abnormality, and dyspnea on heavy effort if it was the only cardiac abnormality; optic fundi scores also were not included. Patients with dyspnea on ordinary activity, angina, left ventricular enlargement (LVE), cardiomegaly by X-ray, neurologic symptoms other than headache, or renal score greater than zero were included. On the basis of these criteria, 55% of the control group and 60% of the treated patients exhibited one or more abnormalities in the major target organ systems (table 5).

Ungerleider criteria[3] were used for determining cardiomegaly from the standard posterior-anterior X-ray of the chest. By these criteria, 22% of the control group and 28% of

Table 5

Prevalence of Cardiovascular-Renal Abnormalities prior to Randomization

Abnormality	Control group No.	Control group %	Treated group No.	Treated group %	Total No.	Total %
Optic fundi-grade 2 (hypertensive changes)*	60	31.0	46	24.8	106	27.9
Any cardiac, CNS, or renal abnormality*	107	55.2	112	60.2	219	57.6
Cardiomegaly (X-ray)*	42	21.7	53	28.5	95	25.0
LVE (ECG)*	32	16.5	30	16.1	62	16.3
Renal grade 1*	23	11.9	23	12.4	46	12.1
Renal grade 2*	4	2.1	4	2.1	8	2.1
Myocardial infarct	14	7.2	13	7.0	27	7.1
Congestive heart failure*	12	6.2	17	9.1	29	7.6
Cerebral thrombosis	10	5.2	9	4.8	19	5.0
Patients randomized	194	100.0	186	100.0	380	100.0

*Defined in text.

the treated patients were considered to exhibit cardiomegaly prior to randomization.

The electrocardiographic criteria for left ventricular enlargement (LVE) required that the patient exhibit both voltage changes (S in V_1 or V_2 plus R in V_5 or $V_6 > 35$ mm) and flat, biphasic, or negative T waves in leads I, aV_L, and V_5 or V_6. Sixteen percent of both the control and treated groups exhibited LVE by these criteria prior to randomization.

Renal damage was graded as follows. Grade 1 included any two of the following: specific gravity of 1.020 or less in all of three separate overnight urine collections, proteinuria of 1+ or more in any one of these specimens, and phenosulfonphthalein (PSP) excretion of less than 45% in a pooled 2-hour specimen. Grade 2 changes included any two of the following: specific gravity of 1.015 or less, proteinuria 1+ or more in all of three daily specimens, and PSP excretion of 30% or less. Grade 3 indicated all three of the above changes. Grade 4 denoted the presence of azotemia.

The frequency of grades 1 and 2 renal changes was the same in control and treated groups with 12% exhibiting grade 1 and 2% exhibiting grade 2 changes (table 5). None of the patients exhibited grade 3 changes. There were four patients in the control group and three in the treated series in whom the blood urea nitrogen was reported as being in the range of 25 to 32 mg/100 ml. However, the serum creatinine value was normal in four of these patients, and they did not develop morbid events following randomization. Of the remaining three patients, one died of a carcinoma of the urinary bladder, another developed congestive heart failure, while the third, who had chronic glomerulonephritis (GN) with serum creatinine of 2.4 mg/100 ml initially, was later removed from the trial because of elevated diastolic blood pressure.

Five patients, two in the control and three in the treated group, were diagnosed as having primary renal disease. Chronic glomerulonephritis was diagnosed in four and bilateral medullary sponge kidney in one. One of the two control patients with chronic GN was removed because of elevated diastolic

blood pressure (see above) while the other developed a cerebral thrombosis. In the three actively treated patients with primary renal disease there were no morbid events.

Included in the study were some patients who had previous major events. Seven percent of the 380 patients, equally divided between control and treated groups, had sustained a myocardial infarction prior to randomization. Six percent of the control group and 9% of the treated patients had a past history of cardiac decompensation but were not in congestive heart failure at the time of randomization. Five percent of patients in both the control and treated groups had a clinical diagnosis of cerebral thrombosis. Patients with a history of other major complications of hypertension such as cerebral or subarachnoid hemorrhage, persistent congestive heart failure requiring continuous diuretics, accelerated phase of hypertension, or acute hypertensive encephalopathy were not admitted into the trial.

Cardiovascular-renal abnormalities were more frequent in the older patients (table 6). In those under 50 years of age, 46% presented with one or more abnormalities as opposed to 65% of the 50–59-year age group and 78% of the patients above age 59 years.

The presence of prior cardiovascular damage greatly increased the risk of developing morbid events following randomization (table 7). In the patients with either myocardial infarction, congestive heart failure, or cerebral thrombosis prior to randomization, subsequent major complications occurred in 53% of the control and 26% of the treated group during the postrandomization period. In those with evidence of cardiac, CNS, or renal damage but without a major complication preceding randomization, the incidence of subsequent morbid events was 33% in the control patients and 8% in the treated group. Effectiveness of treatment for the combined subsamples presenting with prerandomization abnormalities was 64% (table 7).

The incidence of morbid events was much less in the control series of patients presenting without abnormalities. In this subsample, 16% of the control patients developed a major

Table 6

Relationship between Age and Presence of Cardiac, CNS, or Renal Abnormality prior to Randomization

Age (years)	Control group			Treated group			Total		
	No. rand	With abnormality		No. rand	With abnormality		No. rand	With abnormality	
		No.	%		No.	%		No.	%
<40	22	9	40.9	32	13	40.6	54	22	40.7
40–49	77	29	37.7	70	41	58.6	147	70	47.6
50–59	52	34	65.4	46	30	65.2	98	64	65.3
60+	43	35	81.4	38	28	73.7	81	63	77.8
Total	194	107	55.2	186	112	60.2	380	219	57.6

Table 7

Incidence of Morbid Events with Respect to Prerandomization Cardiac, CNS, or Renal Abnormality

Status prerandomization	Control group			Treated group			Effectiveness of treatment (%)
	No. rand	With events		No. rand	With events		
		No.	%		No.	%	
With abnormality:							
Prior MI, CHF, CVA	34	18	53.0	38	10	26.4	50
All other	73	24	32.9	74	6	8.1	75
Subtotal	107	42	39.3	112	16	14.3	64
No abnormality	87	14	16.1	74	6	8.1	50
Total	194	56	28.9	186	22	11.8	59

complication as opposed to 8% of the treated. The difference is not statistically significant although the trend indicating 50% effectiveness of treatment is similar to that found in the group with preexisting abnormalities.

It should be emphasized that 20 control patients were removed from the trial prior to any morbid event because of elevations of diastolic pressures to more than 124 mm Hg which persisted for 3 weeks or longer.[1] Seven of the 20 patients had a prerandomization clinic diastolic blood pressure lower than 105 mm Hg. Fifteen of the 20 were less than 50 years of age; 10 of the 20 had no evidence of cardiac, CNS, or renal abnormality. Since at this level of diastolic blood pressure the risk of developing subsequent events without treatment is very high,[4] the removal of these patients prior to the development of a morbid event probably resulted in an underestimate of the effectiveness of treatment in all subgroups but especially in the subgroup under age 50 years and the group presenting without cardiac, CNS, or renal abnormalities.

Among the 27 fatalities occurring during the randomized trial, 17 deaths were associated with myocardial infarction or occurred suddenly; of these, 11 occurred in the control group and six in the treated patients. With respect to other risk factors in these 17 patients, six of the control and two of the treated patients had prerandomization serum cholesterol levels greater than 260 mg/100 ml. Two control patients and one treated patient exhibited fasting blood sugar levels above 110 mg/100 ml. There was no evidence of hypokalemia during the annual examinations in any of the patients who had sudden death.

Congestive heart failure occurred in 11 of the control patients. In five it represented a recurrence, while in six the initial attack occurred following randomization. Although 17 of the treated patients had a history of congestive heart failure prior to randomization, none developed recurrences during the postrandomization period.

Influences on Therapeutic Effectiveness

Because of the separate effects of level of diastolic blood pressure,[1] age, and prior cardiovascular abnormalities on the incidence of

Table 8

Attack Rates and Effectiveness of Treatment in Relation to Any One or Two Risk Factors at Entry

Risk factors at entry	Control group No. rand	Control group Attack rate*	Treated group No. rand	Treated group Attack rate*	Effectiveness of treatment (%)
By single risk factor					
Diastolic pressure:					
90–104 mm Hg	84	0.263	86	0.144	45
105–144 mm Hg	110	0.309	100	0.096	69
Age:					
<50 years	99	0.145	102	0.064	56
50+ years	95	0.439	84	0.184	58
CVR abnormalities:					
Without abnormality	87	0.161	74	0.081	50
With abnormality	107	0.393	112	0.143	64
By two risk factors					
CVR abnormalities and diastolic B P:					
Without abnormality					
90–104 mm Hg	36	0.145	38	0.114	21
105–114 mm Hg	51	0.173	36	0.046	73
With abnormality					
90–104 mm Hg	48	0.352	48	0.168	52
105–114 mm Hg	59	0.426	64	0.124	71
CVR abnormalities and age:					
Without abnormality					
<50 years	61	0.098	48	0.040	59
50+ years	26	0.311	26	0.157	50
With abnormality					
<50 years	38	0.222	54	0.085	62
50+ years	69	0.487	58	0.196	60
Age and diastolic B P:					
<50 years					
90–104 mm Hg	43	0.121	46	0.088	27
105–114 mm Hg	56	0.164	56	0.043	74
50+ years					
90–104 mm Hg	41	0.413	40	0.208	50
105–114 mm Hg	54	0.459	44	0.163	64

*By regression data. See text.

Abbreviation: CVR = cardiovascular-renal abnormalities.

morbid events it seemed of interest to assess the influence of various combinations of these factors. Subdivision of the patient population into small subgroups increases the likelihood of large errors in observed rates due to random fluctuations. Therefore, rates were estimated by the use of multiple regression technics which, like curve fitting, smooth out some of the random fluctuations in the observed data.

The multiple regression technic likewise can provide improved estimates for the larger subgroups (all patients presenting with a given risk factor). Thus, the technic has been used to restate the attack rates for subgroups previously described, e.g., the younger group versus the older group. Such improved estimates are shown in the first section of table 8. Of course, the calculated "effectiveness of treatment" is modified to some degree.

With regard to combinations of risk factors the results indicate that the greatest benefit of treatment was achieved in the subgroups with diastolic blood pressure of 105–114 mm Hg

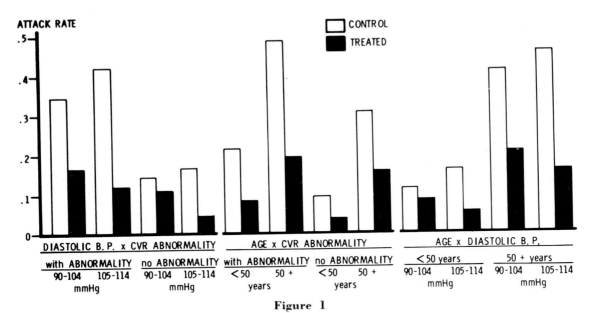

Figure 1

Attack rates computed by multiple regression data for control (clear columns) and treated (black columns) patients.

Table 9

Attack Rates and Effectiveness of Treatment in Relation to the Prevalence of Risk Factors at Entry

Risk factors at entry*	Control group		Treated group		Effectiveness of treatment (%)
	No. rand	Attack rate†	No. rand	Attack rate†	
None	24	0.066	22	0.069	—
Any one	68	0.171	66	0.087	49
Any two	62	0.363	64	0.138	62
All three	40	0.509	34	0.173	66

*Risk factors are (1) age over 50 years, (2) CVR abnormalities, and (3) diastolic blood pressure 105–114 mm Hg.
†By regression data.

regardless of evident cardiovascular-renal disease and irrespective of age (table 8, fig. 1). Treatment was least effective in two subgroups: those with initial diastolic blood pressure below 105 mm Hg and no cardiovascular, CNS, or renal abnormalities; and those below age 50 years with similar levels of blood pressure. These results, of course, may be considerably influenced by the relatively brief period of follow-up.

Table 9 indicates attack rates and effectiveness of treatment in relation to prevalence of the three risk factors at entry irrespective of

the type of risk factor. Both attack rates and effectiveness of treatment are lowest when no risk factors are present and increase progressively with increasing prevalence of risk factors.

Side Effects

The initial report[1] indicated that two treated patients were removed from the trial because of presumed toxic reactions, one being anaphylactoid purpura, the other suspected, but unproven, lupus syndrome. In addition, there were 30 patients in whom the suspected offending drug or its placebo was discontinued because of presumed drug-related side effects. Twelve of these patients developed mental depression, of whom seven were in the treated group and five in the control group. Ten patients developed peptic ulcer; six had been taking active drugs and four placebos. Two patients, one on active drugs the other on placebos, had a change in regimen because of impotence. The remaining six patients all were receiving active treatment. Their side effects included excessive sleepiness, severe nasal stuffiness, gout, seizures presumably caused by hypotension, and an abnormal glucose tolerance test.

Biochemical Side Effects

Hypokalemia. As indicated in table 10, the distribution of serum potassium levels prior to randomization was nearly identical in the control and treated patients with only 1% of the control and 2% of the treated patients exhibiting subnormal values. At the first annual examination, however, the percent distributions in the treated group shifted toward lower values of serum K while the control group remained essentially unchanged. At the end of 1 year, 2% of the control and 23% of the treated group exhibited subnormal values. However, only 1% of the treated patients exhibited a serum K level below 2.5 mEq/liter. A similar trend was found at the second annual examination, although there were no patients in the treated group who had a serum potassium level below 2.5 mEq/liter.

Of the patients completing two annual examinations, approximately half of the 23 treated patients who exhibited serum K levels under 3.5 mEq/liter at the first annual examination remained hypokalemic at the second annual examination. Five of the patients exhibiting subnormal serum K values at the first annual examination received potassium supplements. Three of these exhibited normal serum K values at the second annual examination, while two remained mildly hypokalemic.

Serum Uric Acid. At the initial examination, 13% of the control group and 11% of the treated patients exhibited uric acid levels of 8.0 mg/100 ml or higher (table 11). At the first annual examination patients with elevations of 8.0 mg/100 ml or higher accounted for 16% in the control and 30% in the treated series; at the second annual examination the percentages were 19 in the control and 25 in the treated. In the 40 treated patients exhibiting hyperuricemia after 1 year, 18 had uric acid levels remaining at 8.0 mg/100 ml or higher at the second annual examination. Five of the patients exhibiting uric acid elevations at the first annual examination were placed on either allopurinol or probenecid; the uric acid remained elevated in three and fell below 8.0 mg/100 ml in two at the second annual examination. As indicated in the previous report,[1] two actively treated patients experienced their first attack of gout during the postrandomization period.

Fasting Blood Sugar. The data with regard to fasting blood sugar (FBS) are incomplete due to the fact that the 2-hour postprandial blood sugar was substituted for FBS at a few hospitals during the first 3 years of the trial.

Table 10

Percent Distribution of Serum Potassium Levels on Initial and First and Second Annual Examinations

Serum K (mEq/liter)	Initial (%)		First annual (%)		Second annual (%)	
	C	T	C	T	C	T
2.0–2.4	0	0	0	1	1	0
2.5–3.4	1	2	2	22	2	20
3.5–4.4	49	51	52	63	59	58
4.5+	50	47	46	14	38	22
Total patients	194	186	168	167	137	137

Abbreviations: C = control group; T = treated group.

Table 11

Percent Distribution of Serum Uric Acid Levels on the Initial and First and Second Annual Examinations

Serum uric acid (mg/100 ml)	Initial (%)		First annual (%)		Second annual (%)	
	C	T	C	T	C	T
<6.0	43	55	41	23	37	31
6.0 – 7.9	44	34	43	47	44	43
8.0 – 9.9	11	10	15	25	16	16
10.0 – 11.9	2	1	1	3	2	7
>11.9	0	0	0	2	1	2
Total patients	194	186	168	167	137	137

Abbreviations: C = control group; T = treated group.

The prevalence of FBS values of 110 mg/100 ml or higher was essentially the same in the control and treated groups prior to randomization (table 12). One year after randomization, however, the prevalence was 20.8% in the treated series as compared to 15.6% in the control, and 2 years after randomization it was 30.0% in the treated and 17.0% in the control patients. FBS levels of 120 mg/100 ml were found in 7.0% of the treated patients prior to randomization, 12.5% at the first annual, and 14.6% at the second annual examination.

Because of the difference in total patients available for examination at the end of the first and second year of follow-up (table 12), the data also were analyzed using as denominators only the patients who completed both the first and second annual examinations. The results still indicated a greater percentage of patients with elevated FBS in the treated as compared to the control group of patients.

There was no significant correlation between reduction in serum K and the increase in FBS in the treated group of patients. After 1 year of treatment mean serum K was 3.91 SD 0.57 mEq/liter in 119 treated patients with FBS levels below 110 mg/100 ml and 3.89 SD 0.57 mEq/liter in 40 treated patients with FBS levels of 110 mg/100 ml or higher. After 2 years, the serum K levels were 4.04 SD 0.58 and 3.98 SD 0.91 mEq/liter, respectively, in the two groups.

Changes in Doses of Protocol Drugs

At the time of randomization a combination of hydrochlorothiazide 50 mg and reserpine 0.1 mg twice daily plus hydralazine 25 mg three times daily[5] were administered to all patients in the treated group.* Obviously, this therapeutic regimen will result in a higher incidence of side effects than the usual method of initiating treatment with a single antihypertensive agent. Therefore, provision was made

---

*The special medications used in this study were prepared by Dr. William E. Wagner of Ciba Pharmaceutical Co., Summit, New Jersey.

Table 12

Percent Distribution of Fasting Blood Sugar Levels on the Initial and First and Second Annual Examinations

Fasting blood sugar (mg/100 ml)	Initial (%)		First annual (%)		Second annual (%)	
	C	T	C	T	C	T
<110	85.2	85.4	84.4	79.2	83.0	70.0
110–119	6.5	7.6	9.5	8.3	8.1	15.4
120+	8.3	7.0	6.1	12.5	8.9	14.6
Total patients	169	172	148	144	123	123

Abbreviations: C = control group; T = treated group.

Circulation, Volume XLV, May 1972

Table 13

Dose Changes in a Representative Subsample of 56 Control and 68 Treated Patients

Dose change	No. of patients		Reasons for change (treated group only)			
	Control	Treated	Hypotension*	Angina	Headache	Other
Hydralazine reduced	3	6	4	0	1	1
Hydralazine omitted	0	8	5	1	2	0
Thiaserp† reduced	0	6	6	0	0	0
Both reduced	0	5	4	1	0	0
Thiaserp reduced and hydralazine omitted	1	8	7	1	0	0
Special Thiaserp‡	1	1	0	0	0	1
Other	4	2	2	0	0	0
Total	9§	36	28	3	3	2
% of sample	16	53	41	4.5	4.5	3

*Diastolic below 90 mm Hg with weakness, lethargy, faintness, etc.

†Combination tablet containing 50 mg hydrochlorothiazide and 0.1 mg reserpine. Standard dose 1 tablet twice daily.

‡Thiaserp without reserpine.

§Reasons for changing doses of placebos were as follows: angina in three patients, headache in one, nasal stuffiness in one, skin rash in one, and multiple complaints in two.

for reducing doses or for discontinuing one of the three drugs in the presence of hypotensive symptoms or other side effects.

A sample of 124 patients was taken of the 380 randomized into the trial. Their case records were examined for modifications in doses and for the reason for the changes. The sample was chosen in a way which would contribute proportionate numbers from each of the participating clinics and would span the time period during which the patients were entered into the trial.

Doses were modified in nine (16%) of the control sample and in 36 (53%) of the treated sample (table 13). In the placebo group the reasons for changing doses included the following side effects: headache, nasal stuffiness, angina, skin rash, and multiple complaints. In the treated group 28 of the 36 patients whose regimens were modified had their doses reduced mainly because of hypotensive symptoms of weakness, lethargy, or faintness associated with a fall of diastolic blood pressure to levels usually well below 90 mm Hg. These symptoms abated following appropriate reductions in doses. Side effects other than hypotensive symptoms leading to changes in doses included angina in three patients, headache in three, nervousness in

one, and nasal stuffiness in one patient. Thus, the incidence of side effects *other than hypotension* leading to changes in doses was not significantly different in the control and treated groups. Hypotensive symptoms probably would have been far less if treatment had been initiated with a single antihypertensive agent.

Incidence of Subjective Side Effects

Subjective side effects in the same subsample of 124 patients were evaluated from a physician's interview checklist contained on the clinic visit report forms. The reports for the last two visits during the prerandomization trial period and all postrandomization visits were reviewed.

Probably because of different value judgments used by the various clinic physicians there was considerable variation from one hospital to another regarding the frequency with which specific complaints were reported. Since the same physician always saw a particular patient it seemed valid to compare the postrandomization against the prerandomization period for each patient. In any particular patient only those side effects were counted which were complained of solely during the postrandomization period and which were not noted prior to randomization.

The results indicate a surprising number of patients complaining of specific side effects in the group of patients randomized on placebos. For example, of 52 patients in the control group who did not complain of nightmares prior to randomization, six reported this "side effect" at some time following randomization (table 14). For the specific complaints of nightmares, arthritis, angina, and headache, the incidence actually was greater in the control group of patients than in the treated group. The incidence was nearly equal for both control and treated groups for the side effects of depression, skin rash, impotence, and "other complaints." A possible explanation for the high incidence of "side effects" is that the physician may have paid more attention to the side effects interview following randomization.

The only side effects occurring with greater frequency in the treated group of patients were lethargy or weakness, nasal stuffiness, ulcer symptoms, and first appearance of any complaint. The latter refers to the patients who had no complaints of any kind prior to randomization but who reported one or more side effects following randomization.

It also seemed important to examine the incidence of side effects after appropriate maintainence doses of the antihypertensive drugs had been obtained. Therefore, data relating to the reporting of specific side effects omitting the first two postrandomization visits (third and subsequent visits only) also are presented in table 14. For these latter visits the reporting of complaints of ulcer symptoms, lethargy or weakness, and nasal stuffiness were insignificantly different in the control and treated groups of patients. It is interesting that during these visits the reporting of angina and headache was considerably higher for the control as compared to the treated group of patients.

Discussion

The incidence of morbid events in the present study was higher than would be expected in the general population of hypertensive patients. The reasons for this probably include the following: (1) patients with hypertension on admission but whose diastolic blood pressure averaged below 90 mm Hg during the fourth through sixth day of hospitalization were excluded; (2) more than half of the patients presented with cardiovascular or renal abnormalities; (3) in almost 30% of the patients hypertension was known to be present for 10 years or longer; and (4) while

Table 14

Incidence of Specific Side Effects among a Subsample of 56 Control and 68 Treated Patients

Side effect	Control group					Treated group				
	Without prev complaint* (no.)	With complaint postrand				Without prev complaint* (no.)	With complaint postrand			
		Any visit		After 2nd visit			Any visit		After 2nd visit	
		No.	%	No.	%		No.	%	No.	%
Nightmares	52	6	12	4	8	65	4	6	2	3
Depression	53	5	9	5	9	67	6	9	5	7
Skin rash	55	5	9	4	7	64	5	8	5	8
Arthritis	50	19	38	16	32	63	17	27	15	24
Impotence	46	13	28	10	22	62	18	29	13	21
Angina	49	12	24	9	18	64	8	13	6	9
Headache	38	13	34	8	21	52	13	25	4	8
Ulcer symptoms	55	5	9	5	9	68	8	12	6	9
Lethargy or weakness	46	12	26	8	17	64	25	39	13	20
Nasal stuffiness	48	14	29	10	21	63	22	35	10	16
Other complaints	47	20	43	16	34	58	25	43	18	31
Any complaint†	24	16	67	15	63	40	33	82	31	78

*Patients who did not have the specific complaint prior to randomization.

†Patients without any of the above complaints prior to randomization, and those who subsequently developed some complaint.

only one fifth of the patients were above 60 years of age such patients contributed half of the morbid events.

The incidence of morbid events in the control group was greater in patients with initial levels of diastolic blood pressure averaging 105–114 mm Hg than in those with 90–104 mm Hg at entry. The effectiveness of treatment was much greater for those with the higher initial blood pressure levels. In the present communication it is shown that preexisting cardiovascular disease markedly increases the risk of developing events in the control group and that the effectiveness of treatment over the limited period of observation was greater in those with such evidence of prior disease.

Termination of the trial was necessitated by the clear-cut evidence of benefit in the treated group as compared to the controls. Since the patients without evidence of cardiovascular disease were at reduced risk, follow-up was of too brief duration for the occurrence of many events or to obtain a statistically significant difference between control and treated groups in this subsample. However, the observed 50% effectiveness of treatment in the "no abnormality" group, which was not substantially different from the 64% effectiveness found in the group with abnormalities, is consistent with a protective effect of treatment.

The results of the present trial justify more intensive efforts to identify and maintain under adequate treatment patients with any signs of cardiovascular damage or with diastolic blood pressure averaging in excess of 104 mm Hg. Evidence from surveys carried out in representative population groups[6, 7] indicate that many of these patients are either unaware of their hypertension or are not receiving adequate treatment.

Additional evidence will be required, however, to determine whether the benefits of treatment outweigh its disadvantages in lower risk patients, such as in those with mild hypertension and no evidence of vascular disease, particularly in women, and in patients with labile hypertension. Toxic reactions may occur with any of the presently available antihypertensive agents, and side effect, particularly biochemical changes associated with thiazides and related diuretics, are relatively common. Modifications of doses often are required because of other disturbing side effects. While the risk associated with these various side effects appears small, it must be considered in relation to the benefit to be expected in treating patients whose risk of developing complications due to hypertension also is relatively low. If patients are not treated, however, they should be followed periodically to determine whether the hypertension progresses to a more severe stage. Such follow-up appears to be particularly important in younger patients. In the present study, 15 of the 20 control patients whose diastolic blood pressures became severely elevated were below 50 years of age; seven had an initial diastolic blood pressure below 105 mm Hg.

In the present sample of patients, antihypertensive treatment appeared to be effective in reducing the complications associated with hypertension except for myocardial infarction and sudden death. This result is not necessarily inconsistent with the statistical evidence that elevated blood pressure is one of the "risk factors" associated with an increased incidence of coronary heart disease. It is possible that a larger sample size or a longer period of follow-up might have revealed differences not apparent in the present study. Also, a greater degree of protection might have been afforded if treatment had been instituted at an earlier stage of hypertension. Therapeutic trials are needed in a different population of hypertensive patients in order to resolve this question.

Acknowledgments

We wish to thank Drs. Jacques Genest, Ray W. Gifford, Jr., Walter M. Kirkendall, Louis Lasagna, David W. Richardson, and Robert W. Wilkins for valuable consultation and advice.

References

1. VETERANS ADMINISTRATION COOPERATIVE STUDY GROUP ON ANTIHYPERTENSIVE AGENTS: Effects of treatment on morbidity in hypertension. II: Results in patients with diastolic blood

pressure averaging 90 through 114 mm Hg. JAMA **213**: 1143, 1970

2. VETERANS ADMINISTRATION COOPERATIVE STUDY GROUP ON ANTIHYPERTENSIVE AGENTS: A double-blind control study of antihypertensive agents. I: Comparative effectiveness of reserpine, reserpine and hydralazine, and three ganglionic blocking agents, chlorisondamine, mecamylamine and pentolinium tartrate. Arch Intern Med (Chicago) **106**: 81, 1960

3. UNGERLEIDER HE, GUBNER R: Evaluation of heart size measurements. Amer Heart J **24**: 494, 1942

4. VETERANS ADMINISTRATION COOPERATIVE STUDY GROUP ON ANTIHYPERTENSIVE AGENTS: Effects of treatment on morbidity: Results in patients with diastolic blood pressures averaging 115 through 129 mm Hg. JAMA **202**: 1028, 1967

5. VETERANS ADMINISTRATION COOPERATIVE STUDY GROUP ON ANTIHYPERTENSIVE AGENTS: A double-blind control study on antihypertensive agents. III: Chlorothiazide alone and in combination with other agents. Arch Intern Med (Chicago) **110**: 230, 1962

6. WILBER JA: Detection and control of hypertensive disease in Georgia, U.S.A. *In* The Epidemiology of Hypertension, edited by Stamler J, Stamler R, Pullman TN. New York, Grune & Stratton, 1967, p 439

7. STAMLER J, ET AL.: Detection of susceptibility to coronary disease. Bull NY Acad Med **45**: 1306, 1969

Reprinted from the Journal of the American Medical Association
October 12, 1970 Volume 214
Copyright 1970, American Medical Association

Epidemiologic Assessment of the Role of Blood Pressure in Stroke

The Framingham Study

William B. Kannel, MD; Philip A. Wolf, MD; Joel Verter, MS; and Patricia M. McNamara

Control of hypertension, labile or fixed, systolic or diastolic, at any age, in either sex appears to be central to prevention of atherothrombotic brain infarction (ABI). Prospectively, hypertension proved the most common and potent precursor of ABI's. Its contribution was direct and could not be attributed to factors related both to stroke and hypertension. Asymptomatic, causal "hypertension" was associated with a risk of ABI about four times that of normotensives. The probability of occurrence of an ABI was predicted no better with both blood pressure measurements or the mean arterial pressure than with systolic alone. Since there was no diminishing impact of systolic pressure with advancing age, the concept that systolic elevations are, even in the aged, innocuous is premature. Comparing normotensives and hypertensives in each sex, women did not tolerate hypertension better than men.

Identification of potential stroke victims for preventive medical or surgical management would seem essential if the impact of this common and devastating illness is to be substantially reduced. The economic and human merit of avoiding or postponing the occurrence of stroke in a population which is living longer hardly requires emphasis. It is imperative that the high-risk individual be detected early and management instituted before crippling brain damage occurs.

No factor has been identified which contributes more potently than hypertension to the development of cerebrovascular accidents (CVAs) involving the brain in general, and to the occurrence of atherothrombotic brain infarction (ABI), the most common variety of stroke. The key to the prevention of CVAs would, therefore, appear to be the early detection and control of hypertension. Since there is a very long latent period in hypertensive disease before its cerebral sequelae appear, it is important to study the disease prospectively, beginning at least in middle age, if an undistorted picture of the evolution of hypertension as a precursor of stroke is to be achieved.

This has been possible in Framingham, Mass, where 5,209 men and women between the ages of 30 and 62 years classified while still asymptomatic according to their blood pressure have been followed up biennially over 14 years for the occurrence of strokes in general and ABI in particular. Guidelines for the prophylactic management of asymptomatic hypertension may be ascertained from a detailed investigation of the relation of blood pressure to the development of strokes.

While the relation of hypertension to the development of stroke is well established, there is much that

From the Heart Disease Epidemiology Study, Framingham, Mass, and the National Heart Institute, Washington DC. (Dr. Kannel and Miss McNamara); the Neurology Department, Boston University School of Medicine, Boston (Dr. Wolf); and the Biometrics Research Section, National Heart Institute, Bethesda, Md (Mr. Verter).

Read before the Section on Preventive Medicine at the 118th annual convention of the American Medical Association, New York, July 16, 1969.

Reprint requests to 25 Evergreen St, Framingham, Mass 01701 (Dr. Kannel).

remains to be learned concerning the pathogenetic mechanism involved. Some of the accepted notions concerning the details of the relationship between blood pressure and stroke appear ill-founded. A detailed examination is made of the relation of asymptomatic hypertension in general and in particular the relative contribution of the systolic vs the diastolic component of the blood pressure to the development of strokes and ABIs specifically over 14 years in a general population sample of men and women initially between the ages of 30 and 62 years.

Methods

The method of sampling, composition of the study group, diagnostic criteria, and examination procedures have been described in detail elsewhere.[1-3]

At Framingham, Mass, the National Heart Institute has been conducting a prospective longitudinal study of factors related to the development of cardiovascular disease and stroke since 1949. A probability sample by household of two thirds of the adult population, aged 30 to 62 years, based on an annual town census for voting purposes maintained by the town, was chosen for study. It was possible to bring in for examination 68.6% of the 6,510 selected. A group of 740 persons who originally volunteered were added to supplement the initial group of sampled respondents after analysis revealed a similar distribution of attributes and morbidity and mortality experience.[3] In brief, blood pressures were obtained at the time of each biennial examination from the left arm with the subject seated. The diastolic pressure was recorded at the point of distinct muffling of sound. The point of disappearance was also recorded when this differed from the point of muffling. These blood pressures were obtained at each examination. The bulk of the analysis reported here relates to the

blood pressures obtained by the physician at the initial examination. When otherwise specified, blood pressures obtained at subsequent biennial examinations were also used.

Diagnostic Criteria.—When clinical blood pressure categories were employed, hypertension was arbitrarily designated present when at least two blood pressures during a clinic visit were recorded at 160/95 mm Hg or greater. Normotension was considered present at pressures under 140/90 mm Hg. The rest were considered borderline.

Minimal criteria for a stroke or cerebrovascular accident consisted of the abrupt onset of a focal neurologic deficit such as hemiparesis, aphasia, or homonymous hemianopia. Also included were sudden changes in sensorium in association with a bloody spinal fluid under increased pressure with a relative absence of lateralizing focal neurologic signs, but occurring in the presence of nuchal rigidity. The stroke was judged an ABI when focal neurologic findings appeared in the absence of a source for embolus or a bloody spinal fluid. All hospital protocols were reviewed by a qualified neurologist and also by the research staff of the Framingham Study to ascertain that minimal criteria were met. When possible, hospitalized patients suspected of having had strokes were examined by the staff neurologist during the acute stage.

Surveillance of the population for the occurrence of strokes was reasonably comprehensive and included a brief neurological examination of each participant biennially with confirmation of all suspected cases by a second observer and by a neurologist in consultation; examination of each study participant admitted to the hospital with even a suspicion of CVA (beginning in 1965); reevaluation of the condition of each surviving stroke victim on regularly scheduled return visit to

the clinic; and review of all pertinent information concerning the circumstances of each death in the study population for the possibility of stroke whether this was listed as the cause of death or not. Also, spouses of subjects were routinely queried concerning the health of their spouse in general, and in regards to stroke in particular. In addition, 263 subjects participating in the study were, at the time of their regularly scheduled return visit subjected to an extensive detailed examination by a neurologist. No additional cases were uncovered that had not already been identified by the standard procedure.

It is unlikely that many overt strokes have escaped detection in this population sample. Follow-up of the population sample has been reasonably complete with less than 2% completely lost to follow-up after 14 years.

Analysis of the relation of blood pressure to stroke is presented for cerebrovascular accidents of all types combined and for ABI the commonest variety of stroke. The method of analysis employed to assess the net contribution of each component of the blood pressure consisted of discriminant analysis. Thus, the ability of systolic vs diastolic blood pressure to discriminate potential cases of CVA from those remaining free of it was tested by determining standardized mean deviations (ie, mean blood pressure cases minus mean blood pressure of noncases divided by the standard deviation) for systolic and diastolic pressure. The sign gives the direction of the association and the size of the value the strength of the association.

Age-adjusted incidence according to blood pressure level was computed employing morbidity ratios: cases observed divided by cases expected multiplied by 100. The expected number of cases was calculated by applying the age-specific incidence rates for CVA in the total

190

study cohort to the age composition of each blood pressure category in the population at risk.

Results

In 14 years of follow-up 65 men and 70 women developed focal neurological deficits of abrupt onset meeting the minimal criteria for a stroke. Among these, the conditions of 39 men and 47 women were diagnosed as atherothrombotic brain infarctions accounting for some 60% of all strokes. As might be expected, the incidence increased with age in each sex. However, in neither CVA in general nor in ABI in particular, was there a male predominance. The incidence of ABI was quite similar in the two sexes with women possibly appearing more vulnerable in the older age groups (Fig 1). This sex ratio is quite different from that occurring in coronary heart disease or peripheral vascular disease where a distinct male predominance is the rule although with advancing age a closing gap in incidence between the sexes is noted. Coronary heart disease and ABI occurred with a similar incidence in women, while coronary disease was distinctly more common than ABI in men.

Hypertensives in this population shared an increased propensity to each of the major atherothrombotic diseases. The blood pressure relationship was, with the exception of congestive failure, more striking for CVA than for the other cardiovascular disease outcomes (Fig 2) Risk of stroke in general and of ABI in particular, was distinctly related to antecedent blood pressure status with conventional clinical criteria. Although the number of ABIs is small, there is an intriguing similarity in the age-sex trends in blood pressure and ABI with a male predominance at younger ages and a female predominance at older ages (Fig 1). It will be of interest to learn whether these relationships persist when larger numbers of ABI

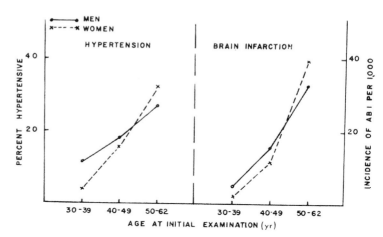

1. *Prevalence of hypertension and incidence of ABI by age and sex. Men and women aged 30 to 62 years at entry.*

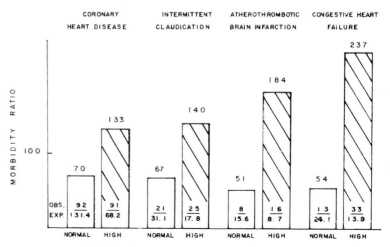

2. *Risk of cardiovascular disease (14 years) according to blood pressure status. Men aged 30 to 62 years at entry.*

become available to allow more precise estimates of incidence. Surprisingly, the relative risk of hemorrhagic strokes (intracerebral and subarachnoid) was no greater than that noted for nonhemorrhagic ones (Fig 3).

A detailed examination of the relation of each component of the blood pressure to risk of stroke was possible for the nonhemorrhagic variety, in particular ABI. An examination of the gradients of risk of ABI in persons classified first according to their systolic and then their diastolic blood pressure revealed rather similar gradients of risk. When this was examined for

Table 1.—Slope of Average Annual Incidence of Cerebrovascular Accident and Brain Infarction According to Systolic vs Diastolic Pressure*

Age (yr)	Men — Cerebrovascular Accident				Women			
	Systolic Slope	SE	Diastolic Slope	SE	Systolic Slope	SE	Diastolic Slope	SE
35-44	...	...	...	...	−0.019	0.029	−0.013	0.044
45-54	0.036†	0.011	0.034	0.019	0.029‡	0.011	0.052‡	0.020
55-64	0.045†	0.008	0.075†	0.015	0.045†	0.008	0.067†	0.015
	Brain Infarction							
35-44	...	...	...	...	...	...	...	...
45-54	0.047†	0.015	0.053‡	0.025	0.038‡	0.013	0.071†	0.023
55-64	0.045†	0.009	0.069†	0.017	0.054†	0.008	0.085†	0.017

*Slopes computed by method of Cornfield et al [15]; SE signifies standard error.
†Significant at $P = 0.01$ level.
‡Significant at $P = 0.05$ level.

Table 2.—Standardized Mean Deviation of Systolic vs Diastolic Pressure Between Men and Women 38 to 69 Years of Age Developing CVAs and Those Remaining Free of CVA*

Age at Exam (yr) 2, 4, or 6	Men			Women		
	No. of Patients	Mean Deviation — Systolic	Diastolic	No. of Patients	Mean Deviation — Systolic	Diastolic
38-41	...	...	...	1	...	...
42-45	1	...	...	2	...	...
46-49	8	0.79	0.55	4	1.11	0.90
50-53	13	0.95	0.46	6	0.00	0.56
54-57	8	1.12	1.28	8	1.44	1.30
58-61	9	0.99	0.94	11	0.66	0.50
62-65	9	1.01	0.77	14	1.11	0.70
66-69	6	−0.30	−0.65	10	0.41	0.44
Average	53	0.88	0.61	53	0.81	0.70

*CVA signifies cerebrovascular accident. Standardized mean deviation is the mean pressure for cases minus the mean pressure for noncases divided by the population standard deviation. Average is obtained as follows: If n is the number of cases in an age group and $\bar{x}$ is the mean deviation for that age group, the average is $\Sigma_{ni} \cdot \bar{x_i}/\Sigma_{ni}$.

Table 3.—Average of Standardized Mean Deviations* of Systolic Blood Pressure in Men and Women 38 to 69 Years of Age Developing Disease vs Those Remaining Free of Disease†

	Coronary Heart Disease Mean Deviation			Intermittent Claudication Mean Deviation			Cardiovascular Accident Mean Deviation			Congestive Heart Failure Mean Deviation		
	No.	Systolic	Diastolic	No.	Systolic	Diastolic	No.	Systolic	Diastolic	No.	Systolic	Diastolic
Men	(252)	0.41	0.28	(58)	0.60	0.15	(53)	0.83	0.61	(44)	0.92	0.62
Women	(135)	0.68	0.39	(30)	0.23	0.03	(53)	0.81	0.70	(30)	0.93	0.65

*Standardized mean deviation = $\dfrac{\text{mean pressure of cases} - \text{mean pressure of noncases}}{\text{Population standard deviation}}$.

†This table summarizes the age specific mean deviations. The differences between disease categories is not accounted for by differences in age distribution. Mean deviations were not found to vary appreciably with age.

the whole population sample, adjusting for differences in the age composition of each quintile of the distribution of each blood pressure component, two facts became apparent: (1) there is no critical level of blood pressure evident, the risk being simply proportional to the level from the lowest to the highest

recorded; (2) gradients for systolic and diastolic pressure are quite similar with nothing to suggest a closer relationship to diastolic pressure (Fig 4).

Calculation of slopes of the regression of incidence of CVA in general and ABI in particular according to each component of the

blood pressure at each biennial examination provides a quantitative estimate of the strength of the relationship. In discrete age groups in each sex this revealed generally significant slopes with a slight tendency for diastolic pressure to predominate, when the interim pressures as well as the initial examina-

Epidemiologic Assessment—Kannel et al

192

tion pressure is taken into account. It is noteworthy that the slopes with systolic or diastolic pressure, do not flatten with advancing age (Table 1).

The absence of a demonstrable safe or critical level of blood pressure as regards risk of ABI suggests that it is more logical to examine the relative contribution of each blood pressure component throughout the range of blood pressures rather than in discrete clinical blood pressure categories (eg, "normotensives" vs "hypertensives"). Also, systolic and diastolic blood pressure are highly correlated, making an assessment of the net effect of each difficult, if not impossible, employing simple categorical cross-classification. Consequently, discriminant analysis was undertaken to assess the relative contribution of each component of the blood pressure to stroke throughout the range of pressures recorded in the population sample.

Standardized mean deviations provide an estimate of the capacity of each component of the blood pressure to discriminate those who developed CVAs from those who did not. Although in some age groups one or the other appeared dominant by this yardstick, there was nothing to suggest that overall, diastolic pressure was a better discriminator of potential strokes (Table 2). As judged by the size of the standardized mean deviations, blood pressure, systolic or diastolic, is a more powerful discriminator of potential CVAs than of any of the other major cardiovascular consequences of hypertension with the possible exception of congestive heart failure (Table 3).

It is possible that both components of the blood pressure contribute to the risk of ABI, the risk being a function of the mean arterial pressure. Consequently, the ability of the mean arterial pressure to discriminate potential ABIs was compared with that of each compo-

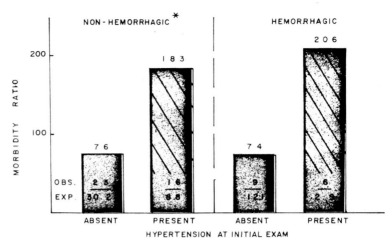

3. Risk of CVA according to blood pressure at initial exam. Men aged 30 to 62 years at entry.

4. Risk of ABI (14 years) according to systolic and diastolic blood pressure. Men and women aged 30 to 62 years at entry.

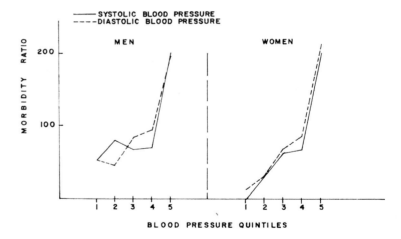

nent of the blood pressure. An examination of the standarized mean deviations for systolic, diastolic, and mean arterial pressure in men reveals, at all ages except one, a larger deviation for systolic than diastolic pressure. Also, the mean arterial pressure discriminated potential cases no better than the

systolic pressure, although it was generally better than the diastolic pressure (Table 4). In women the same generally applies although mean arterial pressure seemed to discriminate as well as systolic pressure (Table 4). This gives no indication that systolic pressure plays a minor role in ABI. That the

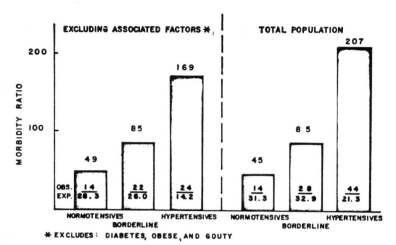

MORBIDITY RATIO

EXCLUDING ASSOCIATED FACTORS * | TOTAL POPULATION

200 — 207

169

100 — 85 85

49 45

OBS. 14 22 24 14 28 44
EXP. 28.3 26.0 14.2 31.3 32.9 21.3

NORMOTENSIVES HYPERTENSIVES NORMOTENSIVES HYPERTENSIVES
BORDERLINE BORDERLINE

* EXCLUDES : DIABETES, OBESE, AND GOUTY

5. *Risk of ABI (14 years) according to blood pressure status excluding associated factors. Men and women aged 30 to 62 at entry.*

Table 4.—Standardized Mean Deviation Systolic, Diastolic, and Mean Arterial Pressure Cases vs Those Remaining Free of ABI*

Men Age (yr)	No. of Patients	Standardized Mean Difference—Pressure		
		Systolic	Diastolic	Mean Arterial
38-41	0	...	...	...
42-45	(1)	...	...	...
46-49	3	1.716	0.973	1.386
50-53	8	1.396	1.041	1.282
54-57	6	0.384	0.858	0.682
58-61	8	0.986	0.706	0.888
62-65	6	1.482	1.088	1.356
66-69	(2)	...	...	...
Total	**31 + (3)**	**1.142**	**0.922**	**1.089**

Women Age (yr)	No. of Patients	Standardized Mean Difference—Pressure		
		Systolic	Diastolic	Mean Arterial
38-41	0	...	...	...
42-45	(1)	...	...	...
46-49	(2)	...	...	...
50-53	6	0.005	0.561	0.306
54-57	7	1.421	1.391	1.487
58-61	8	0.908	0.810	0.913
62-65	9	1.184	0.933	1.134
66-69	6	1.018	0.796	0.987
Total	**36 + (3)**	**0.945**	**0.910**	**0.991**

ABI signifies atherothrombotic brain infarction.

mean arterial pressure predicts ABIs no better than systolic pressure alone may derive from the fact that both are highly correlated and systolic pressure is more accurately measured than is diastolic. It is also consistent with the hypothesis that both components of the blood pressure are not making a greater

contribution than either alone. Once again, there was no tendency for the impact of systolic blood pressure to decrease with advancing age in either sex (Table 4).

Another way to examine the possibility that both components of the arterial pressure contribute to risk is to determine if prediction of

ABIs is better achieved employing both the systolic and diastolic blood pressure values rather than either alone. The appropriate discriminant analysis reveals that both systolic and diastolic pressure together achieved little more than systolic alone. Again, the diastolic pressure discriminated no better than the systolic and there was no decrement with advancing age (Table 5).

It is conceivable, although unlikely, owing to the strength of the relationship, that the association of elevated blood pressure with increased risk of ABI derives at least in part from factors related both to blood pressure and to risk of ABI. Categorical assessment of this possibility may be achieved by excluding from the population at risk all persons who were obese, gouty, or diabetic. When this was done it is apparent that there is still a distinct residual gradient of risk proportional to blood pressure level (Fig 5).

A more quantitative assessment of this possibility may be achieved by examining the discriminant function weights of systolic and diastolic blood pressure in relation to other related factors. It is clear that blood pressure, systolic or diastolic, is a potent discriminator of potential ABI even accounting for the effect of these variables (Table 6). Again, there is no indication that the impact of diastolic pressure is greater than that of systolic pressure or that the effect of systolic pressure decreases with age.

It is conceivable, even likely, that hypertension predisposes to strokes by virtue of its effects on the cardiovascular apparatus and on the heart in particular. Hypertension predisposes to congestive heart failure and to hypertrophy of the ventricular myocardium. Risk of strokes was distinctly increased in such persons.[4] However, even in subjects without any evidence of these cardiac features of hypertension risk of ABI was distinctly related to blood

Epidemiologic Assessment—Kannel et al

194

Table 5.—Discrimination of ABI From Patients Free According to Antecedent Systolic and Diastolic Blood Pressure Singly and Combined Men and Women*

Age at Exam (yr)	No. of Patients	Men X² Values			Discriminant Weight × 100	
		Both†	Systolic‡	Diastolic	Systolic	Diastolic
46-49	3	9.43	8.80	2.83	12.23	−5.81
50-53	8	15.47	15.44	8.58	6.90	−0.86
54-57	6	5.28	0.88	4.38	−2.59	9.93
58-61	8	7.82	7.68	3.39	4.74	−1.68
62-65	6	13.08	12.99	7.01	6.41	−1.42
Women						
50-53	6	5.28	0.00	1.87	−5.20	12.25
54-57	7	15.39	14.03	13.44	3.38	5.43
58-61	8	6.77	6.54	5.20	2.65	2.06
62-65	9	12.47	12.40	7.70	4.31	1.00
66-69	6	6.18	6.08	3.71	3.15	1.26

*There were two few patients aged 38 to 50 years to evaluate. X² signifies chisquare.

$$\dagger X^2_{2df} = \left[\frac{n_1 \cdot n_0}{n_1 + n_0}\right] (\Sigma_i \cdot L_i \cdot d_i)$$ where L_i signifies discriminant weight of ith variable, d_i signifies mean difference of ith variable, n_1 signifies number of cases, n_0 signifies number of noncases.

$$\ddagger X^2_{1df} = \left[\frac{n_1 \cdot n_0}{n_1 + n_0}\right] (d/s)^2_1$$ where s signifies standard deviation.

pressure alone (Fig 6).

Hypertension is known to accelerate lipid-induced atherogenesis in animals.[5-8] Convincing evidence that it accelerates cerebral atherosclerosis specifically is lacking however. Prospectively, cholestrol and endogenous triglyceride (as reflected by 20 to 400 sf units preβ-lipoprotein concentration) may be related to the subsequent rate of development of ABI but only when the lipid was measured prior to age 50 years.[2,4] Even in younger persons, however, hypertension was by far the more potent contributor to stroke. When associated blood pressure status is taken into account, very little additional contribution of either lipid to risk of ABI can be discerned in hypertensives. Elevated blood pressure, when present, appears to be the overriding contributor, and only in the normotensive is there possibly a residual effect of lipid (Fig 7). Small numbers, however, make even this observation speculative.

Comment

Essential hypertension is for at least two decades asymptomatic before cardiovascular sequelae appear. There is reason to believe that the heart is most vulnerable to it, the cerebral vascular apparatus being affected in comparable incidence some ten years later in life. The kidneys, often a cause of hypertension, may also be impaired by it, but appear to be relatively more resistant.

In the clinical evaluation of hypertension, a consideration of the nature of the blood pressure elevation is considered to be of paramount importance in determining its prognostic importance. The first consideration is whether or not "hypertension" is actually present. There is no bimodality in the distribution of blood pressure in the general population. The incidence of all its major cardiovascular sequelae increases in direct proportion to the blood pressure, even in the nonhypertensive range, without any identifiable critical or safe value. Consequently, any designation of some particular blood pressure value as "hypertension" must of necessity be quite arbitrary and poses a problem concerning a recommendation as to when the physician inclined to prophylaxis against

stroke should become concerned. The commonly accepted clinical criteria (ie, $\geq 160/95$) would seem a reasonable guide since this level is associated with more than tripling of risk of both CVA and coronary heart disease. The decision to treat at this level of blood pressure would seem amply justified.

The next consideration in the evaluation of hypertension is to determine the nature of the blood pressure elevation, ie, whether it is labile or fixed and predominantly systolic or diastolic. The striking relationship of causal blood pressure level to the risk of developing a stroke suggests that even labile blood pressure elevations may be important.

Despite its popularity, there is little evidence in general, and no prospective evidence at all, to support the contention that the cerebrovascular consequences of hypertension derive principally from the diastolic component of the blood pressure. Even though the pathologic physiology of essential hypertension as we understand it today suggests that it ought to be so, present prospective investigation of the incidence of ABI and of cerebrovascular disease in general, in relation to each component of the blood pressure provides little evidence of a more potent contribution of the

Epidemiologic Assessment—Kannel et al **307**

Table 6.—Standardized Discriminant Weights for Systolic and Diastolic
Blood Pressure Accounting for Other ABI Risk Factors*

	Men			Women		
Age (yr)	No. of Patients	Systolic Pressure	Diastolic Pressure	No. of Patients	Systolic Pressure	Diastolic Pressure
46-57	17	0.68	0.51	12	0.02	1.08
58-69	18	1.21	−0.54	18	0.90	0.06

*ABI signifies atherothrombotic brain infarction. From a multivariate discriminant analysis which included systolic and diastolic blood pressure, cholesterol, hemoglobin, blood sugar, cigarettes, electrocardiographic-left ventricular hypertrophy, and age.

diastolic pressure to the occurrence of stroke.

The characteristic feature of essential hypertension is alleged to be an increased peripheral resistance in the face of a normal cardiac output. If this is correct, "hypertension" should ideally be expressed in terms of the total peripheral resistance, ie, the mean arterial pressure divided by the cardiac output. Since the cardiac output is said to be normal, the mean arterial pressure, readily computed from the systolic and diastolic pressure (viz, diastolic + one third the pulse pressure), should be the best index of the severity of "hypertension." This implies that both components of the blood pressure contribute to

its severity and that each, taking into account the duration of their influence during the cardiac cycle, imposes a work load on the heart and stresses the vascular apparatus. However, the analysis presented revealed that both components of the blood pressure together, whether expressed as the mean arterial pressure or not, discriminate no better than the systolic pressure alone.

Particularly in the elderly an elevated systolic pressure is regarded as a consequence of an inelastic aorta made rigid by arteriosclerosis. As such it is usually regarded as an innocuous consequence of aging. The failure to demonstrate a declining relative contribution of systolic pressure as compared to diastolic

with advancing age suggests that this conclusion may be premature. Whether the increased risk associated with elevated systolic pressure in the elderly is merely a sign of already damaged cerebral vessels, or a direct cause, or both is uncertain. Also, evaluation of the effect of isolated systolic blood pressure elevation must await the accumulation of a larger number of such persons as the population under surveillance ages further.

The exact mechanism of hypertension in the occurrence of strokes is incompletely understood. That it accelerates atherogenesis in the cerebral arteries is not well established. That it may mechanically damage vessels seems likely. An indirect influence precipitating strokes by impaired cardiac function leading to reduced cerebral perfusion in the region of severely narrowed vessels also seems likely. The more striking relation of hypertension to stroke than to other features of atherosclerosis suggests the latter two mechanisms. Hypertension associated with evidence of cardiac involvement is clearly more ominous. Congestive failure is a potent contributor to stroke as is coronary disease and the presence of electrocardiographic abnormalities.

The evidence for a predominant role of hypertension in accelerating cerebral atherogenesis is disappointingly weak. The preponderance of evidence seems to emphasize a multifactorial causation of atherosclerosis, but if a single common denominator does in fact exist, then some aberration of the metabolism or transport of lipid must be regarded as the chief contender. Risk of all

6. *Risk of ABI (14 years) according to blood pressure status and evidence of cardiac involvement. Men and women aged 30 to 62 years at entry.*

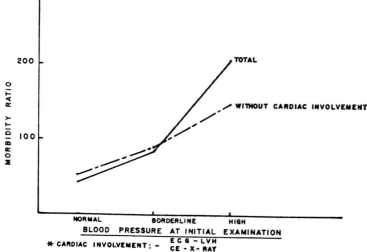

Epidemiologic Assessment—Kannel et al

Reprinted from *New England Journal of Medicine*
October 19, 1972 Volume 287
Copyright 1972 Massachusetts Medical Society

ROLE OF BLOOD PRESSURE IN THE DEVELOPMENT OF CONGESTIVE HEART FAILURE

The Framingham Study

William B. Kannel, M.D., William P. Castelli, M.D., Patricia M. McNamara,
Patrick A. McKee, M.D., and Manning Feinleib, M.D.

Abstract A representative population sample of 5192 men and women was followed for 16 years, during which overt congestive heart failure (CHF) developed in 142. In the age range from 30 to 62 years the dominant etiologic precursor was hypertension, which preceded CHF in 75 per cent of the cases. Six times more CHF developed in hypertensive than in normotensive persons.

Examination of the association of myocardial hypertrophy on x-ray or electrocardiographic study with systolic versus diastolic pressure revealed little to suggest a greater role for diastolic pressure. Systolic and diastolic pressure together, mean arterial pressure, pulse

pressure, and tension-time index discriminated potential hypertrophy and CHF no better than systolic pressure alone. Examination of the correlation of heart weight and left ventricular thickness at autopsy with premorbid systolic versus diastolic pressure revealed a better correlation with systolic than with diastolic pressure.

CHF was a lethal phenomenon, with only 50 per cent surviving for five years. Early, vigorous and sustained control of elevated blood pressure — systolic as well as diastolic — appears the chief means for preventing CHF in the general population.

STUDY of the evolution of congestive heart failure (CHF) in the general population in Framingham has revealed it to be a potent force of mortality. The dominant precursor as it occurs in the general population is hypertension, which preceded 75 per cent of the cases.[1] Despite modern management, CHF proved extremely lethal, with a 50 per cent mortality within five years of diagnosis — a death rate seven times that of the general population.[1]

In view of the dominant role of hypertension and evidence that its control can indeed delay the onset of CHF and mortality from it,[2-4] a more detailed examination of the role of hypertension in the development of CHF was undertaken.

METHODS

The Framingham study was implemented in 1949 to examine the epidemiology of cardiovascular disease in a general population sample. Since its inception 5209 men and women 30 to 62 years of age at entry have been followed biennially for the development of cardiovascular disease. Detailed descriptions of the sampling procedure, response rate, methods of examination and criteria employed have been presented else-

where.[5,6] At each biennial examination each subject received a detailed cardiovascular survey that included history and physical examination, 13-lead electrocardiogram, chest x-ray study, and vital-capacity, hemoglobin and a variety of blood chemical determinations.

Criteria

Upon completion of each biennial examination a diagnosis of CHF was entertained on clinical grounds, chest x-ray findings and total vital capacity. Persons who were suspected of having cardiac failure were seen by a second medical examiner so that two opinions could be obtained. Furthermore, the records of those suspected of having CHF on biennial heart-clinic examination, interim information from hospital records, or reports from physician's offices were reviewed by a panel of investigators using uniform criteria to provide a consistent diagnosis of known specifications. The criteria employed have previously been reported.[1] Only those classed as having definite CHF by these criteria are included in this analysis, excluding those who had CHF at entry to the study.

After persons who met criteria for CHF at the time of initial examination were excluded there were 5192 men and women at risk of a first CHF event over the ensuing 16 years. Follow-up observation was reasonably complete, with only 2 per cent completely lost. Of those who took the ninth examination, 84 per cent received every possible biennial examination; the rest were seen at less regular intervals. Admissions to the

From the Heart Disease Epidemiology Study, Framingham, Mass., the National Heart and Lung Institute, National Institutes of Health, Public Health Service, U. S. Department of Health, Education, and Welfare, Washington, D.C., Duke University Medical Center, Durham, N. C. (address reprint requests to Dr. Kannel at the Heart Disease Epidemiology Study, 25 Evergreen St., Framingham, Mass. 01701).

287:781-787 (October 19), 1972

only general hospital in the town were monitored daily.

Three blood-pressure measurements were obtained on each subject during the biennial examination — two by the examining physician, and the other by the nurse. All were casual and obtained with the subject seated. For analysis of pressure per se the first determination obtained by the examining physician — which was in general higher than the second — was used. "Hypertension" is arbitrarily defined as two systolic pressures of 160 mm of mercury or greater or two diastolic pressures of 95 mm or higher. Normotension is defined as both systolic pressures below 140, and both diastolic pressures below 90 mm of mercury.

Incidence rates for CHF were determined in the population at risk classified for systolic and diastolic pressure and "hypertensive status," as judged by the first examiner. To assess the joint effect of related variables, coefficients of a multivariate logistic risk function were estimated with the use of the discriminant-function method[7] or the maximum-likelihood method.[8]

RESULTS

In the 16 years of follow-up observation definite evidence of CHF according to the specified criteria developed in 81 men and 61 women. The 16-year incidence increased precipitously with age, with a modest male predominance.[1] However, in both young and old, risk was markedly influenced by antecedent hypertensive status. Analysis of the relation of blood-pressure status to risk of CHF at each biennial examination revealed the risk for hypertensive patients to be six times that for normotensive persons (Table 1). Hypertension not only was a potent contributor to CHF incidence but also was the most common factor in the background of victims of CHF as it occurred in the general population.[1] Fully 75 per cent of those who acquired CHF during the 16-year period had prior hypertension.

Systolic versus Diastolic Pressure

An examination of the risk of CHF in the population classified at each biennial examination according to their systolic versus their diastolic pressures reveals little to suggest a stronger relation to the diastolic component. Comparison of the smoothed curves of incidence of CHF according to antecedent systolic versus diastolic pressures (with the scales of measurement made comparable by their expression in terms of the number of standard deviations from the means of their distributions) reveals slopes that are actually steeper for systolic pressure (Fig. 1A and B). Comparison of the computed regressions of incidence of CHF on systolic (B, or regression coefficient in discriminant function, equal to 0.648) versus diastolic pressure (B equal to 0.466) in men standardized for the different range of values, and averaged over the three 10-year age groups, reveals no hint of a more pronounced relation to diastolic pressure. The same reservation applies in women (0.688 vs. 0.611). If there is any utility of one over the other, systolic would appear the better choice. Furthermore, both components of the pressure together and the mean arterial pressure discriminated potential cases of CHF no better than systolic pressure alone. This was also true for coronary heart disease and stroke, frequent concomitants of CHF that share its precursors.[9,10]

Modified Tension-Time Index

The product of the arterial pressure and heart rate has been singled out as the chief hemodynamic determinant of the myocardial oxygen uptake of the ejecting ventricle.[11,12]

In the Framingham experience the product of systolic blood pressure and pulse rate was no better a predictor of CHF than systolic pressure alone, although it was a considerable improvement over pulse rate alone (Table 2). An examination of the regressions of pulse rate, systolic blood pressure and their product on incidence of CHF reveals that taken together all are strongly related to CHF in multivariate analysis. In

Table 1. Incidence of CHF According to Hypertensive Status at Examination and According to Sex and Age.*

AGE AT EXAMINATION	PERSON-YR AT RISK AT EXAMINATION			INCIDENCE IN EXAMINATION INTERVAL			AVERAGE ANNUAL RATE/10,000			RELATIVE RISK
	TOTAL	NORMAL	HYPER-TENSION	TOTAL	NORMAL	HYPER-TENSION	TOTAL	NORMAL	HYPER-TENSION	
Men:	16,814	8,586	2,964	80	13	45	24	8	76	7.9†
35-44	4,568	2,701	522	4	0	3	4	0	29	
45-54	6,321	3,272	1,100	24	3	15	19	5	68	14.9
55-64	4,539	2,061	1,020	35	8	19	39	19	93	4.8
65-74	1,386	552	322	17	2	8	61	18	124	6.9
Women:	21,426	11,181	4,013	61	12	36	14	5	90	4.2†
35-44	5,627	4,277	331	4	3	0	4	4	0	
45-54	7,907	4,370	1,226	10	4	3	6	5	12	2.7
55-64	5,956	2,087	1,726	32	4	22	27	10	64	6.7
65-74	1,936	447	730	15	1	11	39	11	75	6.7

*Source: Table 11-18-B of Section 26 of the monograph by Shurtleff D: Some Characteristics Related to the Incidence of Cardiovascular Disease and Death: the Framingham Study: an epidemiological investigation of cardiovascular disease. Bethesda, Maryland, National Heart Institute, 1970, Section 26.

†Age-adjusted by indirect method using as standard rates the sex-age-specific incidence rates for the entire study.

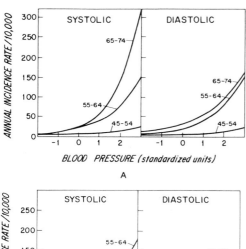

Figure 1. Smoothed Average Annual Incidence Rate for CHF According to Blood Pressure, by Age for Men (A) and for Women (B), Framingham Heart Study, at 16-Year Follow-up Examination.

Table 2. Significance of Systolic Blood Pressure (SBP), Pulse Rate (PR) and Their Product (SBP × PR) as Discriminators of CHF.

AGE AT 1ST EXAMINATION	MEN		WOMEN	
	CHI-SQUARE	DEGREES OF FREEDOM	CHI-SQUARE	DEGREES OF FREEDOM
35-44:	(n = 16)*		(n = 14)*	
SBP	36.29	1	0.49	1
PR	0.47	1	0.40	1
SBP × PR	13.18	1	0.50	1
Generalized distance†				
SBP, PR	37.46	2	0.70	2
SBP, SBP × PR	37.47	2	0.56	2
SBP, PR, SBP × PR	37.47	3	1.88	3
45-54:	(n = 33)*		(n = 28)*	
SBP	24.51	1	48.20	1
PR	2.50	1	8.25	1
SBP × PR	17.56	1	46.43	1
Generalized distance				
SBP, PR	24.55	2	50.39	2
SBP, SBP × PR	24.73	2	52.58	2
SBP, PR, SBP × PR	27.54	3	61.69	3
55-62:	(n = 28)*		(n = 19)*	
SBP	9.55	1	7.50	1
PR	7.05	1	3.10	1
SBP × PR	16.00	1	9.28	1
Generalized distance				
SBP, PR	14.25	2	8.97	2
SBP, SBP × PR	16.03	2	9.67	2
SBP, PR, SBP × PR	20.03	3	11.56	3

*CHF incidence.

†Measure of the degree of dissimilarity of the 2 populations with respect to the independent variable (or variables) described.

discriminant analysis both systolic blood pressure and the product of pulse rate and systolic pressure have a strong univariate relation to incidence of CHF, whereas pulse rate itself is significantly related in some age groups but not others (Table 2). Since the product of pulse rate and systolic pressure is strongly correlated with systolic pressure (r equal to 0.7 to 0.8) it is difficult to separate their contributions by multivariate analysis. However, a bivariate regression with systolic pressure reduces the contribution of pulse rate to incidence of CHF to near zero.

CARDIAC ENLARGEMENT

Dilatation and hypertrophy are cardinal features of CHF. Increase in cavity size and increased bulk of the myocardium can be detected clinically by chest x-ray study for cardiac enlargement and by electrocardiography for left ventricular hypertrophy. A common precursor of both dilatation and hypertrophy is hypertension. An examination of the prevalence of cardiac enlargement on the x-ray film reveals that it is indeed strikingly related to the blood-pressure level (Fig. 2). However, the prevalence of cardiac enlargement on x-ray study was no more closely related to diastolic than to systolic pressure.

Electrocardiographic evidence of left ventricular hy-

pertrophy also was strikingly related to blood pressure, systolic as much as diastolic (Fig. 2). Both these hypertensive cardiac manifestations were as strongly related

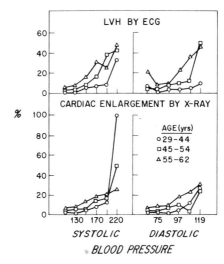

Figure 2. Prevalence of Left Ventricular Hypertrophy by Electrocardiographic or Cardiac Enlargement by X-Ray Criteria According to Initial Systolic and Diastolic Blood Pressure in Men, 30-62 Years of Age at Entry into Framingham Study.

to systolic as to diastolic pressure. The higher the pressure, the more likely was a person to have or to acquire electrocardiographic evidence of hypertrophy until at pressures of 200 mm of mercury or more, 58 per cent manifested it within 12 years.[13] However, x-ray and electrocardiographic findings of cardiac enlargement may reflect different phenomena. Only 35 per cent of men and 50 per cent of women 45 to 64 years of age with left ventricular hypertrophy apparent on electrocardiography had concurrent evidence of cardiac enlargement on x-ray examination.[13]

Analysis of autopsy specimens at Framingham reveals that some attributes measured nine years before death in the premorbid state are related to heart weight. Of these, relative body weight and blood pressure appear to be the chief determinants of myocardial thickness and cardiac weight. Again, there is little evidence that the net effect of diastolic pressure exceeds that of systolic as judged by the size of the correlation coefficients (Table 3).

Table 3. Correlation of Heart Weight and Thickness at Autopsy on 66 Men and 44 Women with Age at Death and with Blood Pressure, Relative Weight and Cholesterol Measured Nine Years before Death.

CARDIAC STATUS	CORRELATION COEFFICIENTS				
	AGE AT DEATH	FRAMINGHAM RELATIVE BODY WEIGHT	SYSTOLIC BLOOD PRESSURE	DIASTOLIC BLOOD PRESSURE	CHOLESTEROL
Men:					
Heart weight	−.073	.343*	.181	.039	.164
Left ventricular muscle thickness	−.068	.277†	.253†	.084	.264†
Women:					
Heart weight	.249	.423*	.418*	.381†	.084
Left ventricular muscle thickness	.315†	.291	.397*	.353†	.078

*Significant at 0.01 level.   †Significant at 0.05 level.

Left Ventricular Hypertrophy and CHF

Electrocardiographic evidence of left ventricular hypertrophy in the Framingham cohort was strongly associated with both hypertension and coronary disease.[13] Persons with definite evidence (including ST-segment and T-wave abnormality as well as increased voltage) were extremely vulnerable to CHF. Persons with "possible" evidence of hypertrophy (mainly voltage abnormality) had a moderately increased risk. Those with "definite" evidence had about 10 times the risk of those without any abnormality (Fig. 3A and B). The markedly increased risk of CHF associated with electrocardiographic evidence of left ventricular hypertrophy probably reflects the severity and duration of predisposing hypertension and the compensatory cardiac hypertrophy. It could also reflect ischemic myocardial involvement due to associated accelerated coronary atherosclerosis. Whatever the explanation, hypertensive heart disease with electrocardiographic manifestation of left ventricular hypertrophy is an ominous harbinger of CHF.

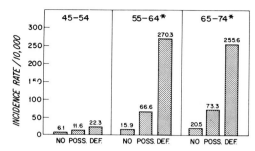

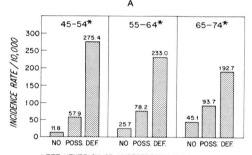

Figure 3. Smoothed Average Annual Incidence of CHF (at 16-Year Follow-up Examination) According to Electrocardiographic Evidence of Left Ventricular Hypertrophy in Women (A) and in Men (B) 45-74 Years of Age.

Heart Enlargement on X-Ray Study and CHF

Hypertension is a prominent cause of cardiac enlargement as seen on x-ray examination. Cardiac enlargement is a hallmark of CHF. Risk of CHF in persons free of overt evidence of CHF was decidedly increased, the risk increasing with the degree of enlargement (Fig. 4A and B). Since cardiac enlargement was one of the criteria for CHF, this to some extent is a self-fulfilling prophecy.

Increased blood pressure, cardiac enlargement, electrocardiographic manifestations of left ventricular hypertrophy and coronary heart disease are inter-related findings apt to coexist in adult populations. It is thus difficult to disentangle the net effect of each in the development of CHF. An examination of the regression of incidence of the disease on systolic blood pressure in multivariate analysis (standardized for the different units of measurement) allows an assessment of the net effect of systolic pressure, taking into account the other variables (Table 4). As judged by the size of the

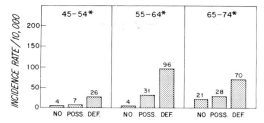

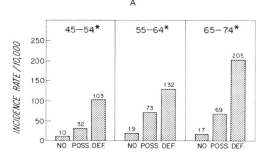

*Trend is Statistically Significant at p<0.01 Level
Source : Framingham Monograph 26

B

Figure 4. Average Annual Incidence of CHF (at 16-Year Follow-up Examination) According to Heart Enlargement on X-Ray Study in Women (A) and in Men (B) 45-74 Years of Age.

standardized regression coefficients, the net contribution of systolic pressure is as great as that of coronary heart disease, x-ray enlargement, and electrocardiographic evidence of left ventricular hypertrophy. The slightly greater coefficients for cardiac enlargement on x-ray study are no doubt accounted for in part by the use of this finding as a criterion for CHF. The multivariate regression coefficients for systolic pressure are reduced by half as compared to the univariate coefficients, suggesting that a good deal of the blood-pressure association with CHF may be explained by the coexisting enlargement of the heart, and myocardial ischemia. This is, of course, a not unreasonable pathogenetic mechanism for the action of systolic pressure in producing CHF. As might be expected risk of CHF associated with any degree of high blood pressure is enhanced when cardiac enlargement or coronary heart disease appears.

DISCUSSION

Examination of the etiologic precursors of CHF as it occurs in the general population, undistorted by the selective bias of hospital-admission practices or vary-

Table 4. Standardized Multivariate Regression Coefficients* of CHF on Systolic Blood Pressure and Heart Impairment.

AGE	INCI-DENCE OF CHF	SYSTOL-IC BLOOD PRES-SURE	HEART ENLARGE-MENT BY X-RAY STUDY	LEFT VENTRIC-ULAR HYPER-TROPHY BY ELEC-TROCAR-DIOGRAM	CORO-NARY HEART DISEASE
Men:					
45-54	24	0.5249	0.4793	0.2718	0.3074
55-64	35	0.3474	0.3584	0.2935	0.4233
65-74	17	0.0545	0.6716	0.1936	0.4587
Average (45-74)					
$\bar{b}$		0.3704	0.4497	0.2704	0.3752
SE $(\bar{b})$		0.0995	0.0898	0.0669	0.0702
Ratio: $\bar{b}$/SE $(\bar{b})$		3.72	5.01	4.04	5.35
Women:					
45-54	10	0.3765	0.4829	−0.678	0.1883
55-64	32	0.3127	0.6790	0.3735	0.1798
65-74	15	0.6086	0.1569	0.3757	0.4439
Average (45-74)					
$\bar{b}$		0.3864	0.5073	0.3088	0.2350
SE $(\bar{b})$		0.1064	0.1377	0.0807	0.0747
Ratio: $\bar{b}$/SE $(\bar{b})$		3.63	3.69	3.83	3.15

*Coefficients are obtained for multiple logistic function by the method of Duncan-Walker. Indicating the coefficient in the ith age group of a variable by b_i, & its variance by $V(b_i)$, the average of the 3 age groups & the standard error of this average are:

$$\bar{b} = \Sigma[b_i/V(b_i)]/\Sigma[1/V(b_i)]$$
$$SE\ (\bar{b}) = 1/(\Sigma[1/V(b_i)]).$$

ing criteria, reveals hypertension to be the salient feature before failure in 75 per cent of the victims of myocardial decompensation. CHF, as defined, was an extremely lethal process; 60 per cent of the men and 40 per cent of the women died within five years of onset (Table 5). This is an average annual death rate about seven times that of persons without CHF.[1] An appalling prognosis was noted for this group of predominantly hypertensive patients with CHF, even if those with established coexisting coronary heart disease are excluded. As many as 20 per cent of the men and 14 per cent of the women died within a year of diagnosis (Table 5).

It is clear that a prophylactic approach is indicated and that the key to this is the early, vigorous and sustained control of hypertension. A better understanding of the details of the relation of blood pressure to the development of CHF should contribute to more efficient prophylaxis against this lethal end stage of heart disease. Little direct evidence can be cited in support of

Table 5. Probability of Death in Interval after First Occurrence of Congestive Heart Failure.

YR AFTER EVENT	MEN		WOMEN	
	TOTAL	WITHOUT CORONARY HEART DISEASE*	TOTAL	WITHOUT CORONARY HEART DISEASE*
1	.205	.205	.140	.129
3	.452	.436	.320	.355
5	.615	.584	.433	.427
7	.707	.735	.603	.559
9	.819	.841	.691	.685

*Subjects with prior or coexisting coronary heart disease eliminated from population at risk of death.

the concept that the cardiac sequelae of essential hypertension derive principally from the diastolic component of the blood pressure and that it is meddlesome to over-react to the level of systolic blood pressure. A systematic examination of the relation of each component of the blood pressure to the occurrence of cardiac hypertrophy on x-ray study, electrocardiography or autopsy and to the development of CHF reveals nothing to suggest a more potent role for diastolic pressure. The surprising failure of diastolic pressure to predict CHF better than systolic pressure may in part be due to the greater inaccuracy in measurement of diastolic pressure and the narrower range of values for this component of the pressure.

With advancing age a widening of the pulse pressure, with a disproportionate rise in systolic pressure owing to a loss of elasticity of the large arteries, is characteristic. This is believed to be an innocuous phenomenon and not true "hypertension." Since there is no evidence of a declining influence of blood pressure in general and systolic pressure in particular on the cardiac sequelae of hypertension with advancing age this concept must be questioned.[9,10,14,15]

The evil consequences of myocardial hypertrophy induced by hypertension (which often culminates in failure) requires further explanation. Hypertensive hypertrophy appears to differ from other types, which are associated with improved cardiac performance. Perhaps the associated accelerated coronary atherosclerosis also promoted by hypertension explains the poor performance in hypertensive hypertrophy. The increased pressure load imposed on the heart is evidently well tolerated for decades. It is only when the increased muscle mass can no longer cope with the load — perhaps owing to presbycardia or more likely the progressive myocardial ischemia imposed as coronary vessels begin to shut down — that myocardial insufficiency develops.

The concept of relative ischemia was proposed by Fishberg[16] to explain hypertensive CHF as coronary flow fails to keep pace with the increased demands of the hypertrophied myocardium. That this concept is in fact valid remains to be established.[17] It has also been suggested that compression of intramural vessels by the hypertrophied myocardium may interfere with flow.[18]

Except when there is a defect in atrioventricular conduction, the tension-time index should be a better prognosticator of cardiac hypertrophy, dilatation and CHF in hypertensive patients than the level of systolic pressure alone. The failure to corroborate this hypothesis could stem from the fact that the blood pressures were casual values. Perhaps if the pressures and pulse rates were obtained under basal conditions or a standardized load the tension-time index might better reflect the pressure workload of the heart and the heart's ability to cope with its workload. It is also possible that the high correlation between tension-time index and the systolic pressure precludes the possibility of demonstrating the efficiency of one as compared to the other.

Few risk factors in coronary, hypertensive cardiovascular, and cerebrovascular disease are more easily detected and readily controlled than hypertension. Misconceptions may exist concerning the nature and consequences of hypertension that tend to impede its effective prophylactic management. Elevated blood pressure, whether predominantly systolic or diastolic, in either sex, at any age, deserves attention.[14,15] Moderately elevated diastolic pressures appear more serious when accompanied by pronounced systolic elevations than when accompanied by only modest systolic elevations. Hypertension assumes grave importance when attended by cardiac enlargement, electrocardiographic evidence of LVH (or a falling vital capacity) even though the subject may be asymptomatic at the time.

To await the onset of symptoms or evidence of target-organ involvement before treating hypertension seems imprudent. It has been convincingly demonstrated that vigorous management of moderate and severe hypertension does in fact delay failure and early mortality.[2-4] In view of the serious prognosis once failure develops it seems ill advised to await signs of it before proceeding to control the blood pressure. Consideration should also be given to the possibility that hypertensive persons with electrocardiographic evidence of left ventricular hypertrophy or x-ray enlargement of the heart may benefit from glycosides before the onset of overt failure if noninvasive procedures (e.g., systolic-time intervals, diminishing vital capacity, a rapid pulse response to moderate exertion and a rapidly enlarging heart) suggest impaired cardiac function. Proof that glycosides employed in these circumstances will delay onset of overt failure and prolong survival is lacking. Efforts to assess this hypothesis seem long overdue.

We are indebted to the biometrics research branch of the National Heart and Lung Institute for assistance in providing tabulations and consultative advice in the preparation of this manuscript.

REFERENCES

1. McKee PA, Castelli WP, McNamara PM, et al: The natural history of congestive heart failure: the Framingham study. N Engl J Med 285: 1441-1446, 1971
2. Veterans Administration Cooperative Study Group on Antihypertensive Agents: Effects of treatment on morbidity in hypertension: results in patients with diastolic blood pressures averaging 115 through 129 mm Hg. JAMA 202:1028-1034, 1967
3. Freis ED: Medical treatment of chronic hypertension. Mod Concepts Cardiovasc Dis 40:17-22, 1971
4. Veterans Administration Cooperative Study Group on Antihypertensive Agents: Effects of treatment on morbidity in hypertension. II. Results in patients with diastolic blood pressure averaging 90 through 114 mm Hg. JAMA 213:1143-1152, 1970
5. Gordon T, Kannel WB: Introduction and general background, The Framingham Study: An epidemiological investigation of cardiovascular disease. Section 1. Bethesda, National Heart Institute, 1968
6. *Idem:* The Framingham, Massachusetts, study twenty years later, The Community as an Epidemiologic Laboratory: A casebook of community studies. Edited by II Kessler, ML Levin. Baltimore, Johns Hopkins Press, 1970, pp 123-146
7. Truett J, Cornfield J, Kannel WB: A multivariate analysis of the risk of coronary heart disease in Framingham. J Chronic Dis 20:511-524, 1967
8. Walker SH, Duncan DB: Estimation of the probability of an event as a function of several independent variables. Biometrika 54:167-179, 1967
9. Kannel WB, Gordon T, Schwartz MJ: Systolic versus diastolic blood pressure and risk of coronary heart disease: the Framingham study. Am J Cardiol 27:335-346, 1971

10. Kannel WB, Wolf PA, Verter J, et al: Epidemiologic assessment of the role of blood pressure in stroke: the Framingham study. JAMA 214:301-310, 1970
11. Sarnoff SJ, Braunwald E, Welch GH Jr, et al: Hemodynamic determinants of oxygen consumption of the heart with special reference to the tension-time index. Am J Physiol 192:148-156, 1958
12. Braunwald E, Ross J Jr, Sonnenblick EH: Mechanisms of contraction of the normal and failing heart. N Engl J Med 277:962-971, 1967
13. Kannel WB, Gordon T, Offutt D: Left ventricular hypertrophy by electrocardiogram: prevalence, incidence, and mortality in the Framingham Study. Ann Intern Med 71:89-105, 1969
14. Kannel WB, Castelli WP, McNamara PM, et al: Some factors affecting morbidity and mortality in hypertension: the Framingham study. Milbank Mem Fund Q 47:116-142, Part 2, 1969
15. Kannel WB, Schwartz MJ, McNamara PM: Blood pressure and risk of coronary heart disease: the Framingham study. Dis Chest 56:43-52, 1969
16. Fishberg AM: Hypertension and Nephritis. Fifth edition. Philadelphia, Lea and Febiger, 1954
17. Mitchell JRA, Schwartz CJ: Arterial Disease. Oxford, Blackwell Scientific Publications, 1965
18. James TN: The role of small vessel disease in myocardial infarction. Circulation 40: Suppl 4:13-19, 1969

Report of Inter-Society Commission for Heart Disease Resources
*Circulation 44:A263, 1971**
Copyright 1971 American Heart Association

Guidelines for the Detection, Diagnosis and Management of Hypertensive Populations

I. Introduction

THE National Health Survey demonstrates that 15-20% of adults in the United States have hypertension as defined by casual blood pressure levels of 160 mm Hg systolic and/or 95 mm Hg diastolic or higher. More than half of these have hypertensive heart disease as determined by cardiac enlargement on x-ray or electrocardiographic evidence of left ventricular hypertrophy. It is now well established that treatment is beneficial for wide segments of the hypertensive population** and that the great majority of these patients are presently undetected, untreated or inadequately treated (Table 1).

Community control of hypertension represents a great challenge to American medicine. The large numbers affected and the relatively small percentage of hypertensive patients under adequate control suggest the magnitude of the opportunity. The scope of the problem is reflected by the lack of adequate diagnostic and therapeutic facilities to manage the case load and the relatively high prevalence of hypertension in economically underprivileged areas including overcrowded urban centers.† Solutions to the problems of detection and maintenance of effective treatment for populations of hypertensives will require long-term planning and the allocation of sufficient funds for the training of needed manpower, facilities

---

*Revised August 1972.

**Controlled clinical trials indicate that treatment is effective in reducing most of the major complications associated with hypertension. For example, the Veterans Administration Cooperative Study (JAMA 213: 1143, 1970) included male patients with fixed diastolic blood pressures of 90-114 mm Hg, many of whom exhibited evidence of cardiovascular damage. In this controlled trial, some patients were followed for as long as 5.5 years, the average follow-up being 3.3 years. Life-table analysis indicated that over a 5-year period the risk of developing a major complication was reduced from 55 to 18% by treatment with antihypertensive drugs. The benefit of treatment was related to the level of diastolic blood pressure, being highly significant in those with initial diastolic levels averaging 105 mm Hg or more, and was favorable, although not statistically significant, over the limited period of follow-up in the subset with lower diastolic

levels. Drug treatment is indicated in practically all patients exhibiting any evidence of cardiovascular disease resulting from hypertension, as well as those without such damage but whose diastolic levels are persistently 105 mm Hg or more. Controlled therapeutic trials are needed in men and women with mild and uncomplicated hypertension and with borderline hypertension to determine the effectiveness of drugs in these groups. In the meantime, it is the consensus of the Study Group that drug treatment is indicated for most patients with diastolic blood pressures consistently between 95 and 105 mm Hg. All hypertensives should have treatment for any lipid disorder and obesity and should be instructed to stop smoking cigarettes and to engage in appropriate regular exercise.

†The National Health Survey indicated a prevalence of hypertension of 21.1% in urban blacks and 13.5% in urban whites.

Table 1

Estimated Reservoir of Undetected and Untreated Individuals With Elevated Blood Pressure

Characteristics of Populations Surveyed	Baldwin Co., Georgia 1962 N = 3084	National Health Survey 1960-1962 N = 6672	Alameda Co., Calif. 1966 N = 2495
% with elev. BP ≥ 160 sys. ≥ 95 dia.	17.5%	15.2%	13.0%
% pop. on med. for hyp.	6.0%	6.5%	5.9%
% with elev. BP on med. for hyp.	18.3%	23.2%	16.9% †
Total hyp. pop.* % unknown**	630 (41.0%)	1214 (42.8%)	420 † —
% of total hyp. pop. on med.	29.7%	35.7%	35.7% †
% of total hyp. "under control"	14.0%	16.3%	22.6% †
% of those on med. "under control"	47.0%	45.6%	63.3% †

*Total hyp. pop. = those with BP ≥ 160 systolic, and/or 95 diastolic at time of survey plus those on medication for hypertension with survey pressures below those levels.

**Presence of hypertension was unknown to the individual.

†In determining proportion on medication, etc., systolic level of 165 instead of 160 was used.

Reproduced by permission from Nemat O. Borhani, M.D.

and other related costs. In the long run it should be less expensive to control hypertension than to care for those who become disabled and economically unproductive as a consequence of the disease.

Because a program to provide diagnostic and therapeutic facilities for community hypertension control must be planned with yield per dollar clearly in mind, the Study Group carefully weighed the implications of each point in the customary evaluation of the hypertensive patient. It concluded that the traditional, detailed and costly diagnostic evaluation of the hypertensive is neither pertinent nor desirable. Rather, it is feasible and medically sound to use an effective and relatively inexpensive battery of diagnostic tests that will rule out most causes of secondary hypertension and provide sufficient information to initiate and guide safe and effective medical management.

Several studies have suggested that only 15-20% of patients with hypertension are under

adequate medical management (Table 1). The reasons for this are several. Many patients are asymptomatic and unaware of their disease. Others who know they have hypertension have either not been told or do not understand the need for long-term antihypertensive therapy. Primary physicians often find it difficult to build effective patient education and follow-up into their practices. Frequently there are psychological, physical and financial barriers to continued care. If a community hypertension control program is to be successful, it must consider each of these reasons and develop techniques for continued physician and patient education, effective longitudinal patient follow-up and care and means to provide free or low-cost drugs. Some possible approaches to the solution of these problems are suggested in the section on therapy.

It should be emphasized that in most instances community hypertension control activities will be, and ideally should be, part of a comprehensive health maintenance service. Case detection for hypertension can easily be incorporated into most multiphasic screening programs. Community planners should understand that control of hypertension will yield major health and economic benefits for large numbers in our society.

II. Early Detection

Hypertension is usually an asymptomatic disease in its early phases but serious complications may occur frequently without warning. It is unrealistic, therefore, to rely on symptoms alone to prompt patients to seek medical care. There are essentially two approaches to finding hypertensives in the population: incidental screening and organized community screening. For effective hypertension control, most communities must supplement incidental screening with organized community programs for recording blood pressure in asymptomatic persons. For greater effectiveness, these should be incorporated into a plan for comprehensive cardiovascular risk factor screening.

Type of Screening

Significant numbers of cases of hypertension are detected through incidental screening procedures. Some of the sources of incidental screening are:

1. Industrial pre-employment and health maintenance physicals
2. Insurance examinations
3. Routine physician's office, emergency room, clinic or hospital visits
4. Armed Forces examinations
5. School and athletic examinations
6. Blood donor screening in Red Cross, hospitals and other programs.

At present, many patients so detected are followed up ineffectively or not at all. Efficient use of information from incidental screening should be made to assure that each patient identified receives diagnostic evaluation and, where indicated, appropriate treatment. The section on therapy suggests some approaches to this problem.

Only a small proportion of hypertensive patients are presently identified through incidental screening. Therefore, most communities will need to develop organized screening programs to identify the remaining hypertensive population.

Population to be Screened

The population between 15 and 65 years of age should be routinely screened. To reach this goal, however, most communities will have to plan long-range programs and establish priorities for screening.

The black population, irrespective of economic status, has a very high prevalence of hypertension and screening correspondingly produces a high yield of undetected, untreated or inadequately treated individuals.

Undetected and untreated hypertension is also quite common in any low income group—irrespective of geography or ethnic mix. Because of the high prevalence of all diseases and social ills in such disadvantaged areas, it is especially important that hypertension screening be incorporated as a part of comprehensive health maintenance programs for these populations. Unless adequate diagnostic and treatment resources are provided for all disorders found, screening of any kind will serve only as another source of mounting frustration.

Finally, the prognosis of hypertension in the age group 15-30 years is particularly poor and these individuals should be identified and treated as early as possible.

Criteria for Rescreening

Criteria for rescreening and referral of different population segments based on age and blood pressure levels are outlined in Figure 1.

Location of Screening

There are several successful models of screening programs. They may be part of an employer and/or labor sponsored health program or of a multiphasic screening program; they may be carried out in community centers to which people are urged to come annually, in mobile multiphasic units, or as

Figure 1

Blood Pressure Criteria for Rescreening and Referral.

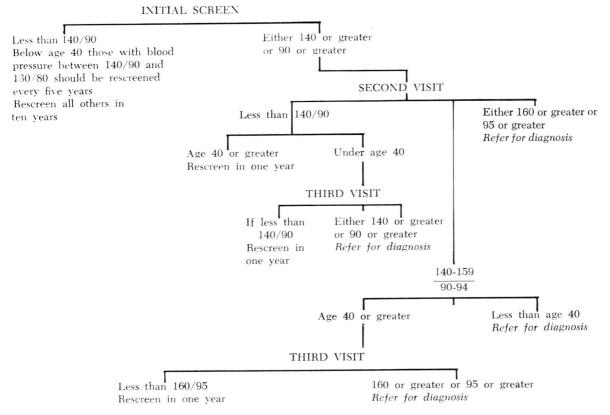

door-to-door community surveys.

Mobile screening units are used primarily for initial case finding, whereas secondary screening and diagnostic evaluation which usually require more than one visit, are best conducted in a fixed unit. The exact location and organization of this unit will vary depending on local circumstances and practice patterns.

Training of Screening Personnel

Allied health workers such as licensed practical nurses and nurses aides, if properly trained and supervised, may be used to conduct the screening. If these are not available, it has been shown that it is possible to train nonprofessional community personnel to carry out satisfactory screening. An average of two weeks of training has been necessary to assure accuracy. Periodic retraining and continuous supervision by a professional (nurse or physician) are required to maintain a high level of performance.

If nurses are available, they can contribute in a vital manner by virtue of their knowledge and technical competence and their ability to provide professional guidance as head of the screening team. They can also give greater in-depth interpretation of findings to the patient and their interest in and understanding of the need for patient education and long-term care is conducive to adherence to protocol. In these matters in particular, the nurse carries an authority that has been difficult to transfer to the nonprofessional.

Equipment

Equipment and methods outlined in the American Heart Association's publication, "Recommendations for Human Blood Pressure Determination by Sphygmomanometers," should be followed with the exception that to expedite screening the blood pressure may be taken in only one arm.

There is a great need for an inexpensive, portable instrument that will accurately record blood pressure automatically. If such an instrument were available it would greatly increase the efficiency of large scale screening programs.

Space and Personnel Requirement

These requirements will vary according to the screening procedure used and the size of the population to be screened; thus, they should be determined locally.

Expected Yield of Positive Cases of Hypertension

Yield will vary with the age, sex and race of the population being studied, but a yield of more than 15% can be expected in most unselected population groups between the ages of 15 and 65. In some black populations the yield may exceed 20%.

Method of Follow-Up

It is extremely important that better use be made of the information regarding patients with hypertension identified by various types of incidental screening programs. This effort requires more comprehensive professional education concerning the necessity for following and treating these patients, and more effective patient education regarding the importance of early diagnosis and adequate long-term management. Various methods to assure maximum follow-up of those patients identified through incidental screening should be developed and evaluated in each community.

Hypertensives identified in community screening programs should be referred according to the criteria outlined in Figure 1. Since there is a tendency for many patients to ignore screening findings, repeated follow-up is usually required, and intensive educational programs for patients and their families may be necessary to assure cooperation.

Professional and Public Education

To be successful, any community program for the early recognition of hypertension must be accompanied by intensive professional and public education. Professionals should be alerted to the significance of hypertension as a serious disease and the importance of long-term follow-up for the labile hypertensive. They should be made aware of the recent evidence that therapy both decreases the rate of damage to the vascular system and prevents complications and they should know that even patients with moderate hypertension may benefit from effective treatment. It should be emphasized that hypertension is not a curable disease in most instances and must be evaluated periodically for the duration of the patient's life. Hypertension carries a familial relationship and its presence in one member of the family should alert physicians to screen relatives for unsuspected or untreated disease. If teenagers are screened, special instructions should be sent to physicians outlining the importance of borderline blood pressure levels and guidelines for therapy in this population. If the screening program is to succeed, it is essential that the professional education program precede that of the public. However, an intensive public information program will be necessary before and during the community screening.

III. Diagnostic Evaluation

Case finding and diagnostic evaluation are separate functions of the program but must be coordinated in order to provide for an orderly progression of patients from detection through diagnosis to therapy. The guiding principles in the diagnostic evaluation of those identified in the screening program are:

1. Identify the cause of the hypertension
2. Assess the effects of the hypertension and the extent of the associated cardiovascular disease
3. Make predictions concerning prognosis
4. Obtain information that will guide the course of medical management

5. Wherever possible identify other risk factors in the development of atherosclerotic disease* and discover other unrelated diseases.

Diagnostic programs must strike a balance between the information gained from a given procedure and the cost of that procedure. Certain procedures such as the intravenous pyelogram, while yielding positive diagnostic information in a small percentage of patients, need not be applied to all identified as hypertensive. To do so would overtax existing facilities and personnel. Further, many patients with renovascular hypertension can be effectively treated medically. Therefore, such procedures should not be considered a part of the routine diagnostic evaluation and should be reserved for selected cases (see below) when medically indicated.

Identifying Data and History

It is recommended that a standard questionnaire be used for the collection of essential historical data. This should be designed so that it may be administered by allied health personnel. The data should be adaptable to computerization and coding.

Physical and laboratory findings should also be reported and coded in a uniform manner. Information gathered in this way will facilitate transfer of records from one health unit to another and will be most useful in long-term follow up of patients and in administrative and epidemiological research. Care must be taken to assure personal privacy in handling this data.

Physical Examination

Most of the physical examination essential for management of the hypertensive patient can be performed by properly trained and supervised allied health personnel. Two stations in an evaluation center might include:

1. A point where height, weight and sitting blood pressure are recorded, and gait and limb motion are noted for evidence of gross neurological deficits.

2. A point where a trained assistant would examine the heart for murmurs and gallop rhythm, the neck for bruits and thrills, the abdomen for masses and bruits, the lower extremities for the presence of femoral, dorsalis pedis and posterior tibial pulses and edema. Heart size should be evaluated separately by chest x-ray, and rate and rhythm by an electrocardiogram.

Laboratory Evaluation

Certain basic laboratory studies should be performed on all persons referred from the screening program as described in Figure 1. These include a serum creatinine or BUN, potassium, cholesterol, uric acid, hematocrit and random blood sugar.* The urine should be examined for protein, sugar and blood. Other necessary laboratory tests include the electrocardiogram and chest x-ray. In addition to these routine tests, microscopic examination of the urinary sediment is indicated in special circumstances such as the following: history suggesting urinary tract disease, diastolic blood pressure of 115 mm Hg or higher, or the presence of proteinuria or hematuria.

Many laboratory determinations can be automated and processed in regional laboratories. To be most economical, automated programs require high volume and a continuous flow of samples. Several community screening programs may be coordinated to maintain a stable, high volume input into a regionalized automated laboratory.

Physician's Recommendation

The physician should evaluate the patient at the first visit. He should confirm and elaborate on positive historical or physical findings, and examine the eye grounds. He will make recommendations concerning the need for further diagnostic procedures, therapy and management and will establish an appropriate

---

*Report of Inter-Society Commission for Heart Disease Resources: The Primary Prevention of the Atherosclerotic Diseases.

*A random blood sugar was chosen because experience has taught that obtaining fasting blood sugar, postprandial blood sugar or postglucose meal blood sugar represent scheduling problems that greatly reduce the efficiency of the program.

Figure 2

A Stratified Organization of Medical Resources for Hypertension Control

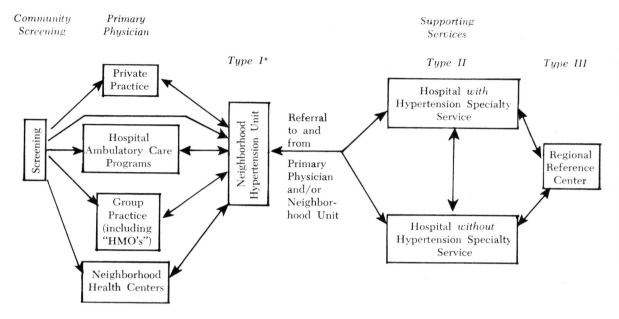

Community   Primary   Supporting
Screening   Physician   Services

The Neighborhood Hypertension Unit is a community service which assists the primary physician with long term follow-up and management of his hypertensive patients. Since many patients with hypertension have combinations of cardiovascular risk factors, it is preferable that this service be incorporated as part of a comprehensive risk factor intervention program, e.g., diet and cigarette smoking control, exercise programs, diabetes control. Depending on local needs, these services can stand alone in their own facility or, what is more likely, they can be incorporated into other facilities and programs such as comprehensive neighborhood health centers, hospital ambulatory care programs, group practices (including HMO's), health department programs, community health educations centers, etc.

follow-up schedule. Patients who do not show appropriate responses to therapy should be evaluated more completely for correctable causes of hypertension.

In addition to appropriate evaluation of abnormal findings as listed in this basic examination, the physician who reviews the data may wish certain patients to have further diagnostic studies, e.g., intravenous pyelograms, measurement of urinary catecholamines and their metabolites, and renal angiograms. Examples of such patients include: (a) those with hypertensive emergencies who should be immediately hospitalized, (b) the relatively young and moderately severe hypertensive (e.g., below age 25 with diastolic blood pressures greater than 110 mm Hg), (c) older hypertensives with severe blood pressure elevation (e.g., over age 25 with diastolic blood pressure greater than 130 mm Hg), and (d) pheochromocytoma suspects.

IV. Resources for Therapy

Since two-thirds of the patients identified as hypertensive are either not aware of their disease or have discontinued therapy, screening programs may triple the case load requiring treatment. Long-range local planning will be required to manage effectively this patient population without seriously overloading existing medical facilities.

The stratified system of care suggested here represents one approach to the problem (Figure 2). Stratified care means that a community's medical facilities are organized into a layered system in which each plays a separate but essential role. One level is composed of various facilities for ambulatory care including physicians' offices, hospital outpatient clinics and neighborhood health centers. These are supplemented by specialized neighborhood hypertension units. At another level is a regional reference center for hypertension. Between are specialty hypertension services located in community hospitals of various sizes which provide both inpatient and outpatient facilities for management problems that cannot be handled effectively by the primary physician at the neighborhood level. Other community hospitals are incorporated into the system as described below.

Organizing medical resources into a stratified system for hypertension control should help reduce duplication and overlap of function among facilities, provide additional supportive services for primary physicians and, thereby, enhance access to more comprehensive care for larger segments of the hypertensive population.

Neighborhood Hypertension Unit

The neighborhood hypertension unit is designed to relieve community physicians of as much of the load of routine follow-up as is consistent with good medical care. According to local needs these units could be separate from or part of existing medical facilities. In either case, nurses and allied health personnel trained in the management of patients with chronic hypertension would assume a major role in the routine follow-up of the patient. Facilities for advanced diagnostic procedures and hospitalization should be available and integrated with these units.

The unit should be under the medical supervision of a physician who would visit it at appropriate intervals, be responsible for the quality of its medical surveillance and provide consultation for patient management problems. In addition, he would provide or arrange for medical care for those patients

referred to the unit who do not have a private physician.

After a patient is regulated on a therapeutic regimen, care would be provided by nurses or by specially trained allied health personnel. They would make appointments, record symptoms, heart rate and blood pressure, keep records, dispense prepackaged medications and recognize adverse drug reactions. They would also provide patient education relating to hypertension and the modification of other cardiovascular risk factors* and would perform other activities such as teaching patients or members of the family to take blood pressure readings. Patients developing other than routine medical problems or complications would be seen by the unit physician or referred to their private physician, the hospital specialty service or some other appropriate facility.

Allied health personnel would be supervised by a registered nurse who might be responsible for the operation of several units. They would receive training at the regional hospital or hospitals with hypertension specialty services and, in addition to routine skills, would be given background knowledge in physiology, pathology, medicine, pharmacology and nutrition as they apply to hypertension. They would receive periodic refresher courses and examinations.

The services of a social worker as well as a dietician and/or nutritionist would also be available. Funds for public transportation of patients to the unit would be provided as needed. Home visits by a trained health worker would be scheduled for patients unable to travel to the unit or who do not keep appointments.

Medical management must always remain under the direction of a physician and there would be no assumption of responsibility for patient care in competition with him. Special services from the neighborhood unit such as

---

*Report of Inter-Society Commission for Heart Disease Resources: The Primary Prevention of the Atherosclerotic Diseases.

periodic recording of blood pressure and patient education programs would be provided at the request of the physician. Major diagnostic or therapeutic procedures would be carried out with his cooperation and permission with referral back to him upon completion of the requested procedures. The purpose of the neighborhood treatment unit is to support and extend the services of the primary physician and thereby increase his ability to manage effectively larger numbers of hypertensive patients.

Hospitals with Hypertension Specialty Service

Depending upon local needs, one or more hospitals would provide a service specializing in the care of hypertensive patients. Under the direction of physicians with special competence in hypertension these would provide services for primary physicians and neighborhood health units. They would include both inpatient and outpatient facilities for the diagnosis of curable or other unusual forms of hypertension, for the treatment of complicated cases and for the management of acute hypertensive emergencies.* In addition, the physician director would serve as a community or regional consultant on therapeutic problems. In cooperation with primary physicians he would assist in making decisions regarding referral of patients to the regional center. The specialty service could also assist with the staffing and supervision of the neighborhood units and provide other services such as delivery of prepackaged medications from a central pharmacy.

This hospital service would not be a long-term care center except for patients with unusual complications such as renal failure. It would be equipped for peritoneal dialysis and angiography and have an intensive care unit which need not be limited to the treatment of hypertension.

Following initial evaluation at the service, the director would recommend that the patient be referred back to the primary physician with suitable instructions; that treatment be readjusted and regulated over a period of weeks or months followed by referral back to the primary physician; or that the patient be referred to the regional center. All major decisions will be made in cooperation with the referring physician.

Hospitals without Hypertension Specialty Service

Certain complications of chronic hypertension, while benefited by hospitalization, do not require the facilities of a specialized hypertension service and can be managed in a general community hospital. Examples of such complications include:

1. Myocardial infarction that can be managed in any hospital with a coronary care unit*
2. Congestive heart failure
3. Immediate treatment of acute hypertensive states,† when it is not feasible to admit the patient promptly to the specialized hypertension service
4. Strokes, many of which can be managed in the community hospital while others may require special facilities.

Regional Referral Center

The regional referral center should be located in a large medical center and directed by a physician specially qualified in the diagnosis and treatment of all forms of hypertension. It would be the referral point for patients who cannot be managed successfully by the specialty service of a community hospital and would provide highly specialized resources such as those required for renal transplantation. In cooperation with local hospitals, neighborhood units and primary physicians, it would develop:

1. Physician education programs tailored to meet local and regional needs

---

*Report of the Inter-Society Commission for Heart Disease Resources: Resources for the Management of Emergencies in Hypertension.

---

*Report of the Inter-Society Commission for Heart Disease Resources: Resources for the Optimal Care of Patients with Acute Myocardial Infarction.

†Ibid: Resources for the Management of Emergencies in Hypertension.

2. Programs for the training of specialized nurses and allied health personnel for neighborhood units

3. Continuing communication and consultation with neighborhood units and directors of hospital specialty services.

It is recognized that there are great advantages in having regional hypertension referral centers associated with general hospitals or teaching centers. Patients referred to this service are likely to have a wide variety of medical complications requiring ready access to facilities and experts representing a broad range of biomedical disciplines. Equally important is that training of physician and nurse specialists in hypertension be based upon and continually related to the broader field of diagnosis and therapy in internal medicine. It is for these reasons that we recommend that the referral center for hypertension be located within the confines of a large medical complex which includes an organized continuing postgraduate educational program.

Conclusion

Existing medical services often fail to provide satisfactory long-term care for patients with hypertension as evidenced by the large number who either leave therapy or receive inadequate treatment (Table 1). In particular, economically underprivileged urban residents require more individualized management than can presently be provided in the depersonalized and overcrowded outpatient clinics of many large municipal and community hospitals. The development and evaluation of new and more effective techniques for delivering long-term care to all hypertensive patients is urgently needed. The proposed stratified system for organizing community resources for hypertension control, incorporating the concept of the neighborhood hypertension unit, represents one possible solution. Since this approach is relatively new, initial testing in the form of pilot studies will be necessary to evaluate effectiveness and feasibility and to make necessary modifications to meet local needs. Implementation of the system and the neighborhood unit concept and tailoring it to meet local needs necessarily involves a long-range organized approach to community and regional planning.

V. Planning and Evaluation

Each community and region should assume responsibility for developing hypertension control programs. The Study Group believes that the stratified program described herein with appropriate modifications to meet local needs can be adapted to many areas and should be studied and considered for application by all communities. To accomplish this, we recommend that an interdisciplinary committee with broad professional and lay representation be established in each region or community to study existing community resources and to guide the development, review and evaluation of a comprehensive hypertension control program.

Acknowledgments

We gratefully acknowledge the helpful criticisms and suggestions offered by Drs. Frederick C. Bartter, Nemat O. Borhani, Morton C. Creditor, Harriet P. Dustan, Roger B. Hickler, Norman M. Kaplan, John H. Laragh, and Robert W. Wilkins.

A Guide for Obtaining Resource Materials on Hypertension

This section contains information about available material on hypertension. It is arranged as follows:

Major Sources of Hypertension Materials

American Heart Association

One of the best sources for hypertension materials of all kinds. (See pages 225 and 227 for abbreviated listing.) Catalogs of currently available materials are accessible through your local Heart Association. National and international organizations may apply for materials directly to:

American Heart Association
44 East 23rd Street
New York, N.Y. 10010

American Medical Association

Patient literature available. (See page 225 for example.)

American Medical Association
535 N. Dearborn Street
Chicago, Ill. 60610

Department of Health, Education and Welfare

Information
Variety of hypertension materials available. In addition, the High Blood Pressure Information Center of the National Heart and Lung Institute serves as a focal point for the collection and dissemination of both public and professional information related to hypertension.

High Blood Pressure Information Center
120/80 National Institutes of Health
Bethesda, Md. 20014

Speakers Bureau
The Speakers Bureau of the High Blood Pressure Information Center provides speakers on various aspects of hypertension for professional and general audiences at national, regional, and state meetings.

Speakers Bureau
High Blood Pressure Information Center
120/80 National Institutes of Health
Bethesda, Md. 20014

Inter-Society Commission for Heart Disease Resources

Develops professional materials on hypertension.
    Inter-Society Commission for Heart Disease Resources
    Suite 204
    44 East 23rd Street
    New York, N.Y. 10010

World Health Organization

Issues reports on hypertension.
    World Health Organization
    c/o Columbia University Press
    2960 Broadway
    New York, N.Y. 10027

Miscellaneous Sources of Information

Continuing Education
Postgraduate courses provided by many organizations (e.g., American College of Chest Physicians, 112 E. Chestnut St., Chicago, Ill. 60611). Up-to-date listings often published in the Journal of the American Medical Association and other professional publications.

Professional and Lay Materials
Pharmaceutical companies with interests in the field of hypertension supply materials for physicians and patients. See Physicians' Desk Reference for company addresses.

Citizens for the Treatment of High Blood Pressure, Inc.
Planning to issue professional material on hypertension.
    Citizens for the Treatment of High Blood Pressure, Inc.
    5530 Wisconsin Ave., N.W. (Suite 1630)
    Washington, D.C. 20015

Lay Materials on Hypertension

Book
"The Silent Disease: Hypertension"
by Lawrence Galton
New York: Crown Pubs., Inc., 1973
(Introduction by Frank A. Finnerty, Jr., M.D.)

Pamphlets
The pamphlets listed are available from the sources shown and are often revised to reflect current knowledge.

American Heart Association

"High Blood Pressure (Hypertension)"
For the patient with hypertension and for members of his family. Explains what hypertension is and how the patient can cooperate with his physician. 16 pages. (AHA Publ. #EM 32)

"Your Blood Pressure"
Brief discussion on blood pressure and hypertension. Small folder. (AHA Publ. #EM 33)

"1973 Heart Facts"
General discussion of cardiovascular disease and its implications, treatment, etc. Useful general lay reference source. 16 pages. (AHA Publ. #EM 509A)

SOURCE: American Heart Association publications are available from your local Heart Association. National and international organizations may apply for materials directly to:
American Heart Association
44 East 23rd Street
New York, N.Y. 10010

Department of Health, Education and Welfare

"Hypertension (High Blood Pressure)"
Detailed discussion for laymen on all aspects of hypertension. Includes glossary. 48 pages. (National Institutes of Health Publ. #1714)

SOURCE: Available from Superintendent of Documents, U.S. Government Printing Office, Washington, D.C. 20402.

American Medical Association
"Your Blood Pressure"
Brief discussion on blood pressure and hypertension. Small folder. (AMA Publ. #OP-44)

SOURCE: Available from
American Medical Association
535 N. Dearborn Street
Chicago, Ill. 60610

Reader's Digest
"Join the Campaign to Conquer High Blood Pressure"
By Lawrence Galton, 4 pages.
Reprinted from February 1973 issue of *Reader's Digest*.

SOURCE: Available as reprint from
　　Reprint Editor
　　Reader's Digest
　　Pleasantville, N.Y. 10570

Visual Presentation
"Hypertension" by M. B. Bentz et al.
This is a 54-page, easel-backed presentation used to familiarize patients with all aspects of hypertension. (Used by the Hypertension Clinic, Georgetown University Hospital. See chapter 6.)

SOURCE:
　　Robert J. Brady Company
　　130 Que St., N.E.
　　Washington, D.C. 20002

Movies
"High Blood Pressure" (1957)
16 mm, 7 min., color/sound, rent/sale
"What Goes Up" (1970)
16 mm, 11½ min., color/sound, rent/sale, English or Spanish
SOURCE:
　　Film Library
　　American Heart Association
　　267 West 25th Street
　　New York, N.Y. 10001

Radio/TV
For up-to-date list, contact source below.
SOURCE:
　　American Heart Association
　　44 East 23rd Street
　　New York, N.Y. 10010

Speakers

Speakers on various aspects of hypertension for national, regional, and state meetings.

SOURCE:

Speakers Bureau
High Blood Pressure Information Center
120/80 National Institutes of Health
Bethesda, Md. 20014

Miscellaneous

Pharmaceutical companies with interests in the field of hypertension supply various patient materials. See Physicians' Desk Reference for addresses.

The Citizens for the Treatment of High Blood Pressure, Inc. is planning to issue lay information on high blood pressure.

SOURCE:

Citizens for the Treatment of High Blood Pressure, Inc.
5530 Wisconsin Ave., N.W. (Suite 1630)
Washington, D.C. 20015

Professional Materials on Hypertension

One of the best sources for professional materials on hypertension is the American Heart Association. Following is a partial listing of resources and services available through local chapters or the national headquarters:

Journals (General)

CIRCULATION—A monthly devoted to clinical research and advances in the cardiovascular field. It presents original articles, symposia, editorials, clinical progress, and abstracts of current literature. Approximately six supplements a year are included in the subscription. Written for the physician, investigator, and student.

CIRCULATION RESEARCH—A monthly concerned with basic research in the cardiovascular field. It publishes original articles and editorials for clinicians interested in basic science and for research workers in anatomy, biology, biochemistry, biophysics, microbiology, physiology, pharmacology, and pathology, as well as experimental medicine. Approximately three supplements annually are included in the subscription.

STROKE–A JOURNAL OF CEREBRAL CIRCULATION–
A bimonthly. The first scientific journal concerned with stroke, it
is of interest to the practicing physician—especially the internist,
cardiologist, and neurologist—as well as the teacher, clinical investigator, laboratory scientist, and student. Articles include clinical
conferences and deal with prevention, diagnosis, treatment, and
rehabilitation.

RECURRING BIBLIOGRAPHY OF HYPERTENSION–A
bimonthly published by AHA in cooperation with the National
Library of Medicine. Provides a rapid survey of current published
developments in the field.

MODERN CONCEPTS OF CARDIOVASCULAR DISEASE
—A concise monthly review of one cardiovascular subject written
by an authority. (Physicians outside the United States may order
from the American Heart Association.)

CARDIO-VASCULAR NURSING–A bimonthly designed to
bring new developments in care for patients with heart disease to
the attention of the nursing profession.(Order from local Heart
Association.)

CURRENT CONCEPTS OF CEREBROVASCULAR DIS-
EASE-STROKE–A quarterly offering practical information to
the practicing physician in an area of increasing medical interest.
(Order from local Heart Association.)

Pamphlets
"Hypertension: Drug Treatment" (EM 422). Booklet.
Irvine H. Page, M.D. and Harriet P. Dustan, M.D.
Discusses drugs commonly used, with table and summary for con-
venient reference of physician. 16 pages. Revised 1969.

"Hypertension: Office Evaluation" (EM 375). Booklet.
Edward D. Freis, M.D.
For the practicing physician, a discussion of hypertension and
treatment. Selected references. 22 pages. 1972.

"Medical Treatment of Chronic Hypertension" (AM 532).
Reprinted from *Modern Concepts of Cardiovascular Disease*, Vol.
XI, No. 4, April 1971.
Edward D. Freis, M.D.
The results of a study by the Veterans Administration Coopera-

tive Study Group. Major antihypertensive agents and recommended regimens of treatment are discussed. 6 pages.

"The Minnesota Symposium on Prevention in Cardiology: Reducing the Risk of Coronary and Hypertensive Disease" (EM 498). Book. Reprinted from *Minnesota Medicine*, Vol. 52, No. 8, August 1969. Symposium sponsored by the Minnesota Heart Association in cooperation with the Mayo Clinic, the Mayo Foundation, the University of Minnesota, and the Council on Clinical Cardiology of the American Heart Association, May 1968.
Twenty-five articles of interest to practicing physicians, internists, and cardiologists. Practical suggestions for reducing risk by controlling hypertension, diet, obesity, cigarette smoking, and physical inactivity. 140 pages.

"New York Heart Association Conference on Coronary Heart Disease: Preventive and Therapeutic Aspects" (EM 481). Book. Reprinted from *Bulletin of the New York Academy of Medicine*, Vol. 44, No. 8, August 1968.
Ten papers discuss the course of coronary heart disease and the multiple risk factors relating to prognosis. 148 pages.

"Cardiac Clinic Record Forms" (EM 244).
Standard forms for clinics revised by the New York Heart Association. Single sheets (8½" x 11") printed on one side of sheet only.

> *Hypertension and Renal Disease*
> Initial History 1A H-R
> Initial History 1B H-R
> Narrative History 1C H-R
> Initial Examination 1D H-R
> Subsequent Record 2 H-R

"Inter-Society Commission for Heart Disease Resources Report" (EM 504 series).
This comprehensive report, being published in installments in CIRCULATION, establishes guidelines for the prevention of cardiovascular diseases and the treatment and rehabilitation of patients. Reprints are available as the reports are issued. The following titles are currently available:
> "Primary Prevention of Hypertension"
> "Resources for the Management of Emergencies in Hypertension." Reprinted from February 1971 CIRCULATION (EM 504F).

"Recommendations for Human Blood Pressure Determination by Sphygmomanometers" (EM 34). Booklet.
Reprinted from CIRCULATION, Vol. XXI, No. 6, December 1967. Authorized by the Central Committee for Medical and Community Program of the AHA and prepared by a special AHA committee. 24 pages.

Audio/Visual Aids
"Diagnostic Testing Units"
Prepared by the American Heart Association Committee on Medical Education for use at medical meetings, these units enable physicians to test themselves on various diagnostic problems. Query local Heart Association for complete details. Unit now available:
    "Diagnostic Testing Unit on Hypertensive Diseases"
    (EM 493). 1969.

"The Eye-Grounds in Hypertension" (EM 293).
Cassette available.

"Hypertension: The Challenge of Diagnosis" (EM 450).
Film. 16 mm, 20 min., color/sound. 1968.
This film was produced by the American Heart Association. More information about this and other cardiovascular films will be found in the catalog, Professional and Public Education Films (EM 26).

SOURCES: Local Heart Associations have many films available on loan or will arrange for their rental from the American Heart Association Film Library, 267 West 25th Street, New York, N.Y. 10001.

Books
"Hypertension Volume XX—1972 Blood Pressure—Regulation and Control" (EM 335 N).
Edited by James C. Hunt, M.D.
18 papers from the 1971 session of the Council for High Blood Pressure Research. Reprinted from CIRCULATION RESEARCH, Sept. 1972. Paper cover. 220 pages.
    (NOTE: This is one volume of the American Heart Association's "Hypertension Series" based on the annual two-day scientific sessions of their Council for High Blood Pressure Research. Published annually. Contact American Heart Association for list of other available volumes.)

Miscellaneous Resources

Speakers
Speakers on various aspects of hypertension for national, regional, and state meetings.
SOURCE:
> Speakers Bureau
> High Blood Pressure Information Center
> 120/80 National Institutes of Health
> Bethesda, Md. 20014

Miscellaneous

Department of Health, Education and Welfare

Variety of hypertension materials available. In addition, the High Blood Pressure Information Center of the National Heart and Lung Institute serves as a focal point for the collection and dissemination of both public and professional information related to hypertension.
> High Blood Pressure Information Center
> 120/80 National Institutes of Health
> Bethesda, Md. 20014

Continuing Education

Postgraduate courses provided by many organizations (e.g., American College of Chest Physicians, 112 E. Chestnut St., Chicago, Ill. 60611). Up-to-date listings often published in the Journal of the American Medical Association and other professional publications.

Professional and Lay Materials

Pharmaceutical companies with interests in the field of hypertension supply materials for physicians and patients. See Physicians' Desk Reference for company addresses.

Veterans Administration

Included among material available is:
"The Modern Management of Hypertension"
By Edward D. Freis, M.D.
A 21-page pamphlet covering these subjects: epidemiology, pathology, and pathogenesis of lesions, "curable" hypertension, indications for medical treatment of hypertension, patients who should

be treated, clinical pharmacology of the principal antihypertensive agents, programs of treatment and practical details of management, the problems of compliance, and recommended criteria for treatment.

Write: Superintendent of Documents, U.S. Government Printing Office, Washington, D.C. 20402.

Stock number 5100-00067, January 1973.

Subject Index

Notes

Notes